Workbook to Accompany
Political Economics:
Explaining Economic Policy

by Torsten Persson and Guido Tabellini

Workbook to Accompany
Political Economics:
Explaining Economic Policy

by Torsten Persson and Guido Tabellini

Isabelle Brocas
Micael Castanheira
Ronny Razin
David Strömberg

The MIT Press
Cambridge, Massachusetts
London, England

ISBN 0-262-52291-8

Contents

Preface

This book accompanies the textbook "Political Economics: Explaining Economic Policy" by Torsten Persson and Guido Tabellini and suggests solutions to the problems contained in each chapter of the textbook. The construction and the resolution of the problems have allowed us to become more familiar with the concepts developed in the textbook and have been an extremely useful exercise to understand them in more detail. We are grateful to Torsten Persson and Guido Tabellini for giving us the opportunity to be part of their project.

Each problem is meant either to extend a model developed in the main text, or to present a simplified version of a related work. The aim of the book is to help the reader to become acquainted with the techniques and the economic intuitions presented in the textbook. Moreover, it provides an overview of the main developments made in the literature so far. Naturally, we take on the responsibility for any remaining error and invite the reader to indicate us any mistake he/she may find and to give us his/her comments. For greater convenience, please contact the corresponding author:

Isabelle Brocas, `brocas@ulb.ac.be`: Chapters 2, 3, 11 and 12, as well as problems 5.3 and 13.5;

Micael Castanheira, `mcasta@ulb.ac.be`: Chapters 15, 16, 17 and 18, as well as problems 13.1-13.4;

Ronny Razin, `rrazin@phoenix.princeton.edu`: Chapters 8, 9, 10 and 14, as well as problems 4.3-4.5;

David Strömberg, `stromberg@iies.su.se`: Chapters 6 and 7, as well as problems 4.1-4.2, 5.1-5.2, 5.4-5.6 and 10.6.

Part I

Tools of political economics

Chapter 2

Preferences and institutions

2.1 Existence and non existence of a Condorcet winner under simple majority rule

Consider three voters indexed by $i \in \{1, 2, 3\}$, each of them characterized by an intrinsic parameter α^i, where $\alpha^1 < \alpha^2 < \alpha^3$. Agent i derives a utility $W(q_j; \alpha^i)$ over policy q_j. Three possible policies $q_j \in \{q_1, q_2, q_3\}$ can be implemented. A policy is selected by simple majority rule.

a. The preferences of agent $i \in \{1, 2, 3\}$ are such that

$$W(q_1; \alpha^1) > W(q_3; \alpha^1) > W(q_2; \alpha^1)$$

$$W(q_2; \alpha^2) > W(q_1; \alpha^2) > W(q_3; \alpha^2)$$

$$W(q_3; \alpha^3) > W(q_2; \alpha^3) > W(q_1; \alpha^3).$$

Moreover, the agenda is open and agents vote sincerely. Prove that no Condorcet winner exists under majority rule. Discuss.

b. Suppose that agents have the same preferences as in question (a) but agent 1 is the agenda setter. He selects two rounds in which all agents vote sincerely. What is the optimal agenda from the perspective of agent 1? Suppose now that agent 1 sets the agenda and agents 2 and 3 vote sincerely. Can agent 3 improve his welfare by voting strategically? Discuss.

c. Suppose that the agents have the following preferences:

$$W(q_1; \alpha^1) > W(q_2; \alpha^1) > W(q_3; \alpha^1)$$

$$W(q_2; \alpha^2) > W(q_1; \alpha^2) > W(q_3; \alpha^2)$$

$$W(q_3; \alpha^3) > W(q_2; \alpha^3) > W(q_1; \alpha^3)$$

with $q_1 < q_2 < q_3$. Is there a Condorcet winner? Explain.

3

d. Suppose that the preferences of agent 2 are such that

$$W(q_2; \alpha^2) > W(q_1; \alpha^2) > W(q_3; \alpha^2)$$

with $q_1 < q_2 < q_3$. Construct the preferences (ordering) of agents 1 and 3 so that they verify the single-crossing property. Then, show that the median voter is a Condorcet winner.

Answer

a. Consider a pairwise vote. Suppose that a vote is first taken over q_1 versus q_2. Both agents 2 and 3 prefer q_2 and therefore q_2 beats q_1. If q_2 is posed against q_3 in the next round, then q_3 beats q_2 since agents 1 and 3 prefer q_3. Now, if a vote is taken over q_3 versus q_1, q_1 is selected by agents 1 and 2. Pairwise voting does not lead to a clear-cut winner since pitching q_2 against q_1 makes the previous cycle start again. In other words, simple majority rule does not lead to a transitive binary relation between the alternatives q_1, q_2 and q_3. This has been first evidenced by Le Marquis de Condorcet in 1785 in the case of simple majority rule. This result has been generalized by Arrow 1951 to any constitution.

b. According to the previous question, an open agenda does not lead to a Condorcet winner. Then, the only way to reach an outcome is to restrict the agenda. Agent 1 prefers policy q_1. If agent 1 can decide over the agenda and if agents 2 and 3 vote sincerely, agent 1 can manipulate the agenda in order to reach his best outcome. If a first vote is taken over q_2 versus q_3, then q_3 is selected by agents 1 and 3. If the winner, i.e. q_3, is posed against q_1 in the second round, then q_1 is elected. Therefore, setting an agenda that poses q_2 against q_3 first and then q_1 against the winner of the first round is the optimal procedure in two rounds from the perspective of agent 1. Since agent 3 prefers q_3 to q_2 and q_2 to q_1, voting sincerely when other agents vote also sincerely leads him to the worst outcome. However, if he votes for q_2 in the first round, q_2 is posed against q_1 in the second round, where q_2 beats q_1. In other words, agent 3 can improve his situation by voting strategically. The reason for this is that agent 3 is pivotal in the first round. Indeed, agent 1 prefers q_3 and agent 2 prefers q_2. Then, the vote of agent 3 determines the winning policy at the first round.

c. Given these new preferences, suppose that a vote is taken over q_2 against q_1. Then q_2 is selected by agents 2 and 3. Now if q_2 is pitched against q_3, then q_2 is again elected since agents 1 and 2 vote for it. In that case, there is a Condorcet winner which is q_2. There is a Condorcet winner because the preferences of the agents are single peaked: the bliss point of agent 1 is q_1 and his preferences are such that $W(q_2; \alpha^1) > W(q_3; \alpha^1)$ for $q_3 > q_2 > q_1$, which satisfies the Definition of single-peakedness. The same applies to agents 2 and 3. Therefore, q_2 is a Condorcet winner because (i) preferences are single peaked and (ii) it is the median ranked bliss point. Indeed, if a vote is taken over q_2 against q_1, then agent 3 prefers q_2 and q_2 is elected. By the same reasoning, if a vote is taken over q_2 against q_3, then agent 1 prefers q_2 and q_2 is elected.

d. By definition, the voters' preferences satisfy the single crossing property if:

$$\text{if } q_2 < q_3 \text{ and } \alpha_1 < \alpha_2$$
$$\text{then } W(q_2; \alpha^2) \geq W(q_3; \alpha^2) \Rightarrow W(q_2; \alpha^1) \geq W(q_3; \alpha^1)$$

or

$$\text{if } q_1 < q_2 \text{ and } \alpha_3 < \alpha_2$$
$$\text{then } W(q_2; \alpha^2) \geq W(q_1; \alpha^2) \Rightarrow W(q_2; \alpha^3) \geq W(q_1; \alpha^3)$$

In that example, α^2 is the median value. If the previous conditions are satisfied, then voters 2 and 3 prefer q_2 to q_1 where q_2 is the bliss point associated to the median value α^2. Similarly, voters 1 and 2 prefer q_2 to q_3. Then q_2 wins in a pairwise vote against any other alternative.

2.2 Simple majority rule and uni-dimensional public consumption

Consider a society inhabited by a continuum of citizens and normalize the size of the population to 1. Suppose that the preferences of agent i over a publicly provided good y and a privately provided good c^i are

$$w^i = c^i + \alpha^i V(y)$$

where $V(\cdot)$ is a concave, well behaved function and α^i is an intrinsic parameter of agent i distributed according to $F(\cdot)$ with mean α. Assume, in addition, that all individuals have initial resources in private good $e^i = 1$ for all i. Suppose also that one unit of private good is required to produce one unit of public good. Last, to finance the production of the public good, the government raises a tax q on each individual so that agent i's budget constraint is $c^i \leq 1 - q$.

a. What is the (utilitarian) social optimum in this economy?

b. Compute each individual's policy preferences. What is the preferred policy $q(\alpha^i)$ of agent i?

c. Under majority rule, what is the selected policy? Compare this to the social optimum. When does the social optimum coincide with the equilibrium policy?

d. Suppose now that each agent's preferences are given by

$$w^i = c^i + (\alpha^i - \hat{\alpha})^2 V(y)$$

where $\hat{\alpha}$ is a given value of α^i. Again, compute the social optimum as well as the policy preferences of individuals. Do we reach the same conclusions as in question (c)?

Answer

a. Using the utilitarian criterion, the social optimum is given by the following program:

$$\max_y \int_i c^i + \alpha^i V(y) dF$$

$$\text{st} \int_i 1 - c^i - y dF \geq 0$$

The first order condition is then $-1 + \alpha V_y(y) = 0$ where V_y denotes the derivative. Then, the optimal provision of public goods in this economy is $y^* = V_y^{-1}(\frac{1}{\alpha})$.

b. Given q, the budget constraint of each agent is $c^i \leq 1 - q$. Naturally, he chooses $c^i = 1 - q$. Besides, the quantity of public good is equal to the total amount of taxes paid, i.e. $y = \int_i q dF = q$. Therefore, his policy preferences can be written as:

$$W(q; \alpha^i) = 1 - q + \alpha^i V(q)$$

Then, the preferred policy of agent i is such that $-1 + \alpha^i V_y(q) = 0$. In other words, $q(\alpha^i) = V_y^{-1}(\frac{1}{\alpha^i})$ which is increasing in α^i.

c. The preferences are single peaked, so there is a Condorcet winner under simple majority rule and this winner is the median ranked bliss point. Since $q(\alpha^i)$ is increasing in α^i, the median bliss point corresponds to the bliss point of the median value of α^i. Let us call this value α^m. The provision of publicly provided good is then $y^m = V_y^{-1}(\frac{1}{\alpha^m})$. This quantity coincides with the social optimum if and only if $\alpha^m = \alpha$.

d. The social optimum of this economy is given by:

$$\max_y \int_i c^i + (\alpha^i - \hat{\alpha})^2 V(y) dF$$

$$\text{st} \int_i 1 - c^i - y dF \geq 0$$

The first order condition is then $-1 + V_y(y) \int_i (\alpha^i - \hat{\alpha})^2 dF = 0$. Then, the optimal provision of public good in this economy is $y^* = V_y^{-1}(\frac{1}{E[(\alpha_i - \hat{\alpha})^2]})$ where $E[\cdot]$ denotes the expected value. By the same reasoning as before, the policy preferences of agent i are given by:

$$W(q; \alpha^i) = 1 - q + (\alpha^i - \hat{\alpha})^2 V(q)$$

and the preferred policy of agent i is then $q(\alpha^i) = V_y^{-1}(\frac{1}{(\alpha^i - \hat{\alpha})^2})$. The preferences are again single peaked. There is a Condorcet winner which corresponds to the median ranked bliss point but not to the bliss point of the median value of α^i. Let us call it q^m and call the intrinsic parameter associated to it $\tilde{\alpha}^m$. Then, the provision of public good selected under majority rule is $\tilde{y} = V_y^{-1}(\frac{1}{(\tilde{\alpha}^m - \hat{\alpha})^2})$.

Note that $E[(\alpha_i - \hat{\alpha})^2] = \sigma^2 + (\alpha - \hat{\alpha})^2$ where σ^2 denotes the variance of the distribution. In that case, having the mean of the distribution coinciding with the median is not a sufficient condition to obtain the social optimum under majority rule.

2.3 Labor and consumption taxation

Consider an economy in which the preferences of individual i are quasi-linear, namely,

$$w^i = c^i + V(x^i)$$

where c^i represents his consumption and x^i his leisure. Moreover, $V(\cdot)$ is increasing and concave in x^i. The private budget constraint of each agent is given by

$$(1 + q_C)c^i \leq (1 - q_L)l^i + f,$$

where q_L is the income tax rate, q_C the consumption tax rate and f a fixed subsidy from the government. The real wage of each agent is exogenous and normalized to unity. Furthermore, each agent has a private productivity parameter α^i so that agents have different amounts of effective time available. More precisely, they face the following time constraint:

$$1 + \alpha^i \geq x^i + l^i$$

Assume that α^i is drawn from a distribution with mean α and median α^m.

a. Compute the optimal labor supply for each individual. What are the effects of an increase in q_L (respectively, q_C) on the individual labor supply? Discuss the result.

b. Write the government budget constraint and derive the level of the subsidy as a function of $\mathbf{q} = (q_L, q_C)$. Compute the policy preferences $W(\mathbf{q}; \alpha^i)$ of individual i.

c. Does a Condorcet winner exist in that case? If yes, who is the Condorcet winner?

d. Compute the utilitarian welfare and determine the socially optimal policy. What is the winning policy $\mathbf{q}$ when $\alpha^i = \alpha$ for all i? What happens if agents are heterogeneous?

Answer

a. In equilibrium, each agent selects consumption and leisure such that $c^i(1 + q_C) = (1 - q_L)l^i + f$ and $1 + \alpha^i = x^i + l^i$. Then, his maximization program turns to:

$$\max_{l^i} \frac{(1 - q_L)l^i + f}{1 + q_C} + V(1 + \alpha^i - l^i)$$

The first order condition for labor supply is:

$$V_x(1 + \alpha^i - l^i) = \frac{1 - q_L}{1 + q_C}$$

and can be rewritten as:

$$l^i = L(q_L, q_C) + (\alpha^i - \alpha)$$

where $L(q_L, q_C) = 1 + \alpha - V_x^{-1}(\frac{1-q_L}{1+q_C})$ is decreasing in both q_L and q_C. Then, in equilibrium, consumption is given by:

$$c^i = \frac{1-q_L}{1+q_C} L(q_L, q_C) + \frac{1-q_L}{1+q_C}(\alpha^i - \alpha) + \frac{f}{1+q_C}$$

The labor supply is decreasing in the tax levels. The higher the tax on labor, the smaller the incentives to work. Besides, if consumption is also taxed, the willingness to work in order to increase the consumption level diminishes with the tax rate. Last, the labor supply increases in the productivity parameter α^i.

b. Let l denote the average labor supply. By definition of the distribution:

$$l = \int_{\alpha^i} L(q_L, q_C) + (\alpha^i - \alpha)dF(\alpha^i) = L(q_L, q_C)$$

Let c be the average consumption. By the same argument,

$$c = \frac{1-q_L}{1+q_C} L(q_L, q_C) + \frac{f}{1+q_C}$$

The government budget constraint is $f \leq q_L l + q_C c$. In equilibrium, this constraint is binding and can be rewritten as:

$$f = q_L L(q_L, q_C) + q_C \left[\frac{1-q_L}{1+q_C} L(q_L, q_C) + \frac{f}{1+q_C} \right]$$

Therefore, the subsidy f given by the government satisfies:

$$f = L(q_L, q_C)[q_L + q_C]$$

Substituting labor supply, consumption and the subsidy into the utility function of agent i, we get that his policy preferences are:

$$W(q_L, q_C; \alpha^i) = (\alpha^i - \alpha)\frac{1-q_L}{1+q_C} + L(q_L, q_C) + V(1 + \alpha - L(q_L, q_C))$$

c. Let $K(\alpha^i) = \alpha^i - \alpha$, $H(q_L, q_C) = \frac{1-q_L}{1+q_C}$ and $J(q_L, q_C) = L(q_L, q_C) + V(1 + \alpha - L(q_L, q_C))$. The policy preferences of agent i can be rewritten as:

$$J(q_L, q_C) + K(\alpha^i)H(q_L, q_C)$$

and $K(\alpha^i)$ is monotonic in α^i. Therefore, agents have intermediate preferences. As a consequence, a Condorcet winner exists and is given by the bliss point of the median value of the intrinsic parameter, i.e. by α^m.

d. The utilitarian social welfare in this economy is:

$$\int_{\alpha^i} W(q_L, q_C; \alpha^i)dF(\alpha^i) = J(q_L, q_C)$$

Then, the social optimal policy corresponds to the preferred policy of the average citizen. Therefore, if $\alpha^i = \alpha$ for all i, then $\alpha^m = \alpha$ and the median voter equilibrium corresponds to the social optimum. If not, the social optimum is generally not decentralized through majority rule.

2.4   Multidimensional public consumption in the presence of a Condorcet winner

Suppose that all individuals in the economy have the same exogenous income $y > 4$ and are subject to the same income tax τ. Government revenue per capita τy is spent on two types of publicly provided goods 1 and 2, in per capita amounts of q_1 and q_2. Individuals also consume a privately provided good, denoted by c. Agents have heterogeneous preferences for public goods and their utility function is summarized by

$$w^i = U(c) + \alpha^i G(q_1) + (1 - \alpha^i)F(q_2)$$

where α^i is an intrinsic parameter of agent i. The functions $U(\cdot)$, $G(\cdot)$ and $F(\cdot)$ are continuous, twice continuously differentiable, strictly increasing and strictly concave.

a. Write each individual's budget constraint as well as that of the government. Derive the policy preferences of agent i and verify that they satisfy the intermediate preferences property. What does this imply? Determine the optimal quantity $q_1(q_2, \alpha^i)$ (respectively, $q_2(q_1, \alpha^i)$) from agent i's perspective for a given level q_2 (respectively, q_1). When q_2 (respectively, q_1) increases, what is the effect on the optimal provision of q_1 (respectively, q_2) for agent i? How does α^i affect these quantities?

b. To simplify the analysis, suppose that $U(x) = G(x) = F(x) = \ln(x)$. Compute agent i's bliss point $(q_1(\alpha^i), q_2(\alpha^i))$. Suppose the economy consists of three agents (or three groups of agents) $i = \{1, 2, 3\}$ with different intrinsic parameters. More precisely, $\alpha^1 = 0$, $\alpha^2 = 1/2$ and $\alpha^3 = 1$. Determine the optimal provision of public goods for each agent. Which policy is implemented under majority rule?

c. Suppose now that the preferences of agent i are summarized by

$$w^i = U(c) + \alpha^i G(q_1) + (1 - \alpha^i)F(q_2) + h(\alpha^i)H(q_1, q_2),$$

where $U(x) = G(x) = F(x) = \ln(x)$ and $H(q_1, q_2) = ln(q_1 q_2)$. Derive the individual's policy preferences. Discuss. Suppose that $h(\alpha^i) = (\alpha^i)^2$. Determine the optimal quantity $q_1(q_2, \alpha^i)$ (respectively, $q_2(q_1, \alpha^i)$) from agent i's perspective for a given level q_2 (respectively, q_1). When q_2 (respectively, q_1) increases, what is the effect on the optimal provision of q_1 (respectively, q_2) for agent i? Compute the equilibrium public consumptions. How does α^i affect these quantities?

d. Suppose that the economy consists of three agents $i = \{1, 2, 3\}$ for which $\alpha^1 = 0$, $\alpha^2 = 1/2$ and $\alpha^3 = 1$. Determine the optimal provision of public goods for each agent. Is there a Condorcet winner?

e. Suppose now that voters' preferences are given by

$$w^i = U(c) + K(\alpha^i)[G(q_1) + F(q_2)],$$

with $U(x) = G(x) = F(x) = \ln(x)$. Compute public consumption levels in equilibrium. Suppose that $K(\alpha^i) = (\alpha^i - \frac{1}{2})^2$ and that the economy consists of agents with type $\alpha^1 = \frac{1}{4}$, $\alpha^2 = \frac{1}{3}$ and $\alpha^3 = 1$. Is there a Condorcet winner in this economy?

Answer

a. The budget constraint of an individual is $c \leq y(1 - \tau)$, which is binding in equilibrium. The budget constraint of the government is $q_1 + q_2 \geq \tau y$, which is also binding in equilibrium. According to this, the policy preferences of individual i are:

$$W(q_1, q_2; \alpha^i) = U(y - q_1 - q_2) + F(q_2) + \alpha^i(G(q_1) - F(q_2))$$

Let $K(\alpha^i) = \alpha^i$, $H(q_1, q_2) = G(q_1) - F(q_2)$ and $J(q_1, q_2) = U(y - q_1 - q_2) + F(q_2)$. The policy preferences of agent i can be rewritten as:

$$J(q_1, q_2) + K(\alpha^i)H(q_1, q_2)$$

$K(\alpha^i)$ is monotonic in α^i, then agents have intermediate preferences. This implies that a Condorcet winner exists and is given by the bliss point of the median value of α^i.

The optimal public consumption levels from the perspective of agent i are given by:

$$\max_{q_1, q_2} W(q_1, q_2; \alpha^i)$$

Then, the optimal quantity $q_1(q_2, \alpha^i)$ satisfies the first order condition related to q_1:

$$U_c(y - q_1(q_2, \alpha^i) - q_2) = \alpha_i G_{q_1}(q_1(q_2, \alpha^i))$$

and the optimal quantity $q_2(q_1, \alpha^i)$ is given by the first order condition associated to q_2:

$$U_c(y - q_1 - q_2(q_1, \alpha^i)) = (1 - \alpha_i)F_{q_2}(q_2(q_1, \alpha^i))$$

Differentiating the first (respectively, second) expression with respect to q_2 (respectively, q_1) leads to:

$$-U_{cc}(y - q_1(q_2, \alpha^i) - q_2)\left[1 + \frac{\partial q_1(q_2, \alpha^i)}{\partial q_2}\right] = \alpha_i G_{q_1 q_1}(q_1(q_2, \alpha^i))\frac{\partial q_1(q_2, \alpha^i)}{\partial q_2}$$

$$-U_{cc}(y - q_1 - q_2(q_1, \alpha^i))\left[1 + \frac{\partial q_2(q_1, \alpha^i)}{\partial q_1}\right] = (1 - \alpha_i)F_{q_2 q_2}(q_2(q_1, \alpha^i))\frac{\partial q_2(q_1, \alpha^i)}{\partial q_1}$$

We have immediately that $\frac{\partial q_1(q_2, \alpha^i)}{\partial q_2} < 0$ and $\frac{\partial q_2(q_1, \alpha^i)}{\partial q_1} < 0$. The higher the provision of public good 1 (respectively, 2), the lower the willingness to pay for public good 2 (respectively, 1). In other words, publicly provided goods are substitutes. Besides, differentiating the two first order conditions with respect to α yields:

$$-U_{cc}(y - q_1(q_2, \alpha^i) - q_2)\frac{\partial q_1(q_2, \alpha^i)}{\partial \alpha^i} = \alpha_i G_{q_1 q_1}(q_1(q_2, \alpha^i))\frac{\partial q_1(q_2, \alpha^i)}{\partial \alpha^i}$$
$$+ G_{q_1}(q_1(q_2, \alpha^i))$$

$$-U_{cc}(y - q_1 - q_2(q_1, \alpha^i))\frac{\partial q_2(q_1, \alpha^i)}{\partial \alpha^i} = (1 - \alpha_i)F_{q_2 q_2}(q_2(q_1, \alpha^i))\frac{\partial q_2(q_1, \alpha^i)}{\partial \alpha^i}$$
$$- F_{q_2}(q_2(q_1, \alpha^i))$$

As a consequence, $q_1(q_2, \alpha^i)$ is increasing in α^i and $q_2(q_1, \alpha^i)$ is decreasing in α^i. The higher α^i, the higher (respectively, smaller) the willingness to benefit from the first (respectively, second) public consumption.

b. According to the derivations in question (a), we have:

$$q_1(q_2, \alpha^i) = \frac{\alpha^i}{1 + \alpha^i}(y - q_2)$$

$$q_2(q_1, \alpha^i) = \frac{1 - \alpha^i}{2 - \alpha^i}(y - q_1)$$

Replacing the equilibrium expression of $q_2(q_1, \alpha^i)$ into $q_1(q_2, \alpha^i)$, gives:

$$q_1(\alpha^i) = \frac{\alpha^i}{2}y \qquad q_2(\alpha^i) = \frac{1 - \alpha^i}{2}y$$

As a consequence, $q_1(\alpha^i) + q_2(\alpha^i) = \frac{1}{2}y$ which means that $\tau = 1/2$. This gives us immediately:

$$q_1(0) = 0 \qquad q_2(0) = \frac{y}{2}$$

$$q_1\left(\frac{1}{2}\right) = \frac{y}{4} \qquad q_2\left(\frac{1}{2}\right) = \frac{y}{4}$$

$$q_1(1) = \frac{y}{2} \qquad q_2(1) = 0$$

Group 2 is median and his choice his selected under majority rule.

c. Following the same reasoning as in the previous question, the policy preferences of agent i are given by:

$$W(q_1, q_2; \alpha^i) = \ln(y - q_1 - q_2) + \alpha^i \ln q_1 + (1 - \alpha^i) \ln q_2 + h(\alpha^i) \ln q_1 q_2$$

Voters do not have intermediate preferences which suggests that a Condorcet winner may not exist in this economy.

The first order conditions related to q_1 and q_2 are respectively :

$$\frac{1}{y - q_1 - q_2} = \frac{\alpha^i + h(\alpha^i)}{q_1}$$

$$\frac{1}{y - q_1 - q_2} = (1 - \alpha_i + h(\alpha^i))\frac{1}{q_2}$$

We can derive the optimal public consumption levels:

$$q_1(q_2, \alpha^i) = f(\alpha^i)[y - q_2] \quad \text{where} \quad f(\alpha^i) = \frac{\alpha^i + h(\alpha^i)}{1 + \alpha^i + h(\alpha^i)}$$

$$q_2(q_1, \alpha^i) = g(\alpha^i)[y - q_1] \quad \text{where} \quad g(\alpha^i) = \frac{1 - \alpha^i + h(\alpha^i)}{2 - \alpha^i + h(\alpha^i)}$$

and the bliss points of agent i:

$$q_1(\alpha^i) = \frac{f(\alpha^i)[1 - g(\alpha^i)]}{1 - f(\alpha^i)g(\alpha^i)} y$$

$$q_2(\alpha^i) = \frac{g(\alpha^i)[1 - f(\alpha^i)]}{1 - f(\alpha^i)g(\alpha^i)} y$$

Therefore, $\frac{\partial q_1(\alpha^i)}{\partial \alpha^i} \propto 1 + h(\alpha^i) - \alpha^i h_{\alpha^i}(\alpha^i) + h_{\alpha^i}$ and $\frac{\partial q_2(\alpha^i)}{\partial \alpha^i} \propto \alpha^i h_{\alpha^i}(\alpha^i) - 1 - h(\alpha^i)$.
Suppose now that $h(\alpha^i) = (\alpha^i)^2$. The optimal public consumption levels can be rewritten as:

$$q_1(q_2, \alpha^i) = f(\alpha^i)[y - q_2] \quad \text{where} \quad f(\alpha^i) = \frac{\alpha^i(1 - \alpha^i)}{1 + \alpha^i(1 + \alpha^i)}$$

$$q_2(q_1, \alpha^i) = g(\alpha^i)[y - q_1] \quad \text{where} \quad g(\alpha^i) = \frac{1 - \alpha^i + (\alpha^i)^2}{2 - \alpha^i + (\alpha^i)^2}$$

$q_1(q_2, \alpha^i)$ (respectively, $q_2(q_1, \alpha^i)$) is decreasing in q_2 (respectively, in q_1). Public goods are substitutes. Moreover, $f(\alpha^i)$ is increasing in α^i, then $q_1(q_2, \alpha^i)$ is increasing in α^i. Last, $g(\alpha^i)$ is convex in α^i with a minimum in $\alpha^i = \frac{1}{2}$. As a consequence, $q_2(q_1, \alpha^i)$ is also convex in α^i with the same minimum value. Using the previous results, we have that $\frac{\partial q_1(\alpha^i)}{\partial \alpha^i} \propto -(\alpha^i)^2 + 2\alpha^i + 1 > 0$ and $\frac{\partial q_2(\alpha^i)}{\partial \alpha^i} \propto (\alpha^i)^2 - 1 < 0$.

d. From the previous question, we obtain:

$$q_1(0) = 0 \qquad q_2(0) = \frac{y}{2}$$

$$q_1\left(\frac{1}{2}\right) = \frac{3y}{10} \qquad q_2\left(\frac{1}{2}\right) = \frac{3y}{10}$$

$$q_1(1) = \frac{y}{2} \qquad q_2(1) = \frac{y}{4}$$

Suppose that a vote is taken over $(q_1(0), q_2(0))$ versus $(q_1(\frac{1}{2}), q_2(\frac{1}{2}))$. In that case the third group of voters prefer the policy of group 2, which is elected. If a vote is then taken over $(q_1(\frac{1}{2}), q_2(\frac{1}{2}))$ versus $(q_1(1), q_2(1))$, the voters in group 1 prefer $(q_1(\frac{1}{2}), q_2(\frac{1}{2}))$ since $2 \ln \frac{y}{4} < \ln \frac{4y}{10} + \ln \frac{3y}{10}$ for $y \geq 4$. Therefore, group 2 is a Condorcet winner. In that case, the agent with the median value of α^i is elected.

e. In this case, the bliss points are:

$$q_1(\alpha^i) = q_2(\alpha^i) = q(\alpha^i) = \frac{K(\alpha^i)y}{1 + 2K(\alpha^i)}$$

If $K(\alpha^i) = (\alpha^i - \frac{1}{2})^2$, then $q(\alpha^i)$ is convex in α^i with a minimum in $\alpha^i = \frac{1}{2}$. Note that the equilibrium quantities belongs to $[0, \frac{1}{6}y]$. In equilibrium, the utility of agent i when the bliss point of agent j is implemented is:

$$W(q(\alpha^j), q(\alpha^j), \alpha^i) = \ln(y - 2q(\alpha^j)) + 2K(\alpha^i) \ln(q(\alpha^j))$$

which is concave in $q(\alpha^j)$ with a maximum in $q(\alpha^j) = q(\alpha^i)$. In addition, we have $q(1) = q(0) > q(\frac{1}{4}) > q(\frac{1}{3})$ and $W(q, q; 1) < W(q, q; 1/4) < W(q, q; 1/3)$. Therefore, if a vote is taken over $q(1)$ versus $q(\frac{1}{4})$, $q(\frac{1}{4})$ is elected. If a vote is then taken over $q(\frac{1}{4})$ versus $q(\frac{1}{3})$, $q(\frac{1}{4})$ is elected again. Then $q(\frac{1}{4})$ is a Condorcet winner. In the two cases analyzed in questions (c)-(e), the preferences of individuals do not satisfy the intermediate preferences property. However, there exists a Condorcet winner (which may not be the agent with the median value of α^i). This means that the intermediate preferences property is a sufficient condition to have a Condorcet winner but it is not necessary.

2.5   Structure induced equilibrium and multidimensional public consumption

Consider the same model as in problem 4 but suppose now that the economy consists of three types of agents. The preferences w^i of type i are

$$w^1 = \ln(c) + \ln(q_1 + 1)$$

$$w^2 = \ln(c) + a \ln(q_2 + 1)$$

$$w^3 = \ln(c) + \ln(q_1 + 1) + b \ln(q_2 + 1)$$

a. Compute the bliss points of each type of agents. Is there a Condorcet winner if $y = 3$, $a = 3$ and $b = 1$?

b.   Find the conditions for a Condorcet winner not to exist.[Hint: it could be convenient to derive such conditions by first considering a vote over 1 versus 2 and by assuming that 1 wins in this round.] Verify that there is no Condorcet winner when $y = b = \frac{1}{a}$ with $y = \frac{11}{10}$.

c. Suppose that decisions related to the provision of public goods are taken by an open agenda process where agents vote separately, sincerely and sequentially over each good. First, decisions are made over q_1 and then over q_2. Describe the vote in the last stage (where q_1 is taken as given). What is the selected quantity of q_2? Determine the policy selected at stage 1 anticipating the decision at stage 2. What happens if the agenda is reversed?

Answer

a. The preferences over policies of type 1 are:

$$W(q_1, q_2; 1) = \ln(y - q_1 - q_2) + \ln(q_1 + 1)$$

and his bliss points are:

$$q_2(1) = 0 \qquad q_1(1) = \frac{y - 1}{2}$$

For type 2, we have:

$$W(q_1, q_2; 2) = \ln(y - q_1 - q_2) + a \ln(q_2 + 1)$$

and:

$$q_1(2) = 0 \qquad q_2(2) = \frac{ay - 1}{1 + a}$$

Last, type 3's preferences are:

$$W(q_1, q_2; 3) = \ln(y - q_1 - q_2) + \ln(q_1 + 1) + b \ln(q_2 + 1)$$

and the bliss points are:

$$q_1(3) = \frac{y - b}{2 + b} \qquad q_2(3) = \frac{b(y + 1) - 2}{2 + b}$$

Suppose $y = 3$, $a = 3$ $b = 1$, then $q_1(1) = 1$, $q_2(1) = 0$, $q_1(2) = 0$, $q_2(2) = 2$ and $q_1(3) = q_2(3) = \frac{2}{3}$. If a vote is first taken over type 1 versus type 2, we have $W(1, 0; 2) > W(0, 2; 2)$ and type 1 is elected. If a vote is then taken over type 1 versus type 3, we have $W(\frac{2}{3}, \frac{2}{3}; 2) > W(1, 0; 2)$ and type 3 is elected. Last, $W(\frac{2}{3}, \frac{2}{3}; 1) > W(0, 2; 1)$ and type 3 is elected again. As a consequence, type 3 is a Condorcet winner.

b. Consider a vote over type 1 versus type 2. Type 1 wins if:

$$W(q_1(1), q_2(1); 3) > W(q_1(2), q_2(2); 3)$$

A necessary condition for 1 not to be a Condorcet winner is that in the next round, he is not elected. In other words, we must have:

$$W(q_1(1), q_2(1); 2) < W(q_1(3), q_2(3); 2)$$

in which case type 3 is elected. For the cycle start again, we need last:

$$W(q_1(2), q_2(2); 1) > W(q_1(3), q_2(3); 1)$$

and type 2 wins. These conditions can be rewritten respectively as:

$$2 \ln \frac{y + 1}{2} > \ln \frac{y + 1}{1 + a} + b \ln \frac{a(y + 1)}{1 + a}$$

$$\ln\frac{y+1}{2} < \ln\frac{y+2}{2+b} + a\ln\frac{b(y+2)}{2+b}$$

$$\ln\frac{y+1}{1+a} > 2\ln\frac{y+2}{2+b}$$

Suppose that $a = \frac{1}{y}$ and $b = y$, then the last condition is satisfied if $y > 1$. If $y = \frac{11}{10}$, then both the first and the second conditions are satisfied. Therefore, there is no Condorcet winner in that case.

c. If agent 1 has to decide over one policy variable, he will choose $q_1(1) = \frac{1}{20}$ if he is asked to choose the provision of the first good and $q_2(1) = 0$ if he has to select the provision of the second. Similarly, agent 2 will select $q_1(2) = 0$ and $q_2(2) = 0$. Last, agent 3 picks up quantities such that $q_1 = \frac{1}{20} - \frac{1}{2}q_2$ and $q_2 = \frac{11}{21}(\frac{11}{10} - q_1) - \frac{10}{21}$. Ideally, he would like to have $q_1(3) = 0$ and $q_2(3) = \frac{1}{10}$. Consider the last stage where a vote is taken over q_2 for a given q_1. Agents 1 and 2 agree on $q_2 = 0$ which is selected. In the first stage, anticipating that q_2 will be zero, both agents 1 and 3 agree on selecting $q_1 = \frac{1}{20}$. If the vote is reversed, then at the last stage, agent 3 is pivotal and picks $q_1 = \frac{1}{20} - \frac{1}{2}q_2$. At the first stage, agent 1 wants $q_2 = 0$ and agent 3 finds optimal to set $q_2 = \frac{1}{10}$. If agent 1 makes the decision, then $q_2 = 0$ and $q_1 = \frac{1}{20}$. By contrast, if agent 3 has to decide, then he selects $q_2 = \frac{1}{10}$ and therefore $q_1 = 0$ in the next round. According to the previous question, agent 2 prefers the last solution. To sum up, the outcome is different when the timing is reversed.

Chapter 3

Electoral competition

3.1 Non credible commitments and probabilistic voting

Suppose that agents' preferences over policies (q_1, q_2) are given by

$$\ln(y - q_1 - q_2) + \alpha^i \ln(q_1) + (1 - \alpha^i) \ln(q_2)$$

with $y > 4$, $\alpha^i \in (0, 1)$ and $q_1 + q_2 < y$. The timing is the following. First, two politicians $P = A, B$ select platforms (q_1^P, q_2^P). They can commit to implement policy q_1^P but not policy q_2^P. Second, the election is held. Last, the winner implements q_1^P and selects q_2^P according to his preferences, that is, he maximizes

$$\max_{q_2} \ln(y - q_1^P - q_2) + \alpha^P \ln(q_1^P) + (1 - \alpha^P) \ln(q_2)$$

We assume that the intrinsic parameters of voters α^i are drawn from a common knowledge distribution $F(\cdot)$. At the date the platforms are offered, voters have beliefs about the politicians' preference parameters, α^P. They are represented by the probability distributions $F^P(\cdot)$.

a. Determine the policy q_2^P that is selected by the winner. Characterize the expected utility of voter i when politician P announces q_1^P. Show that the voters' preferences over politician P 's policy depend on their beliefs.

b. Characterize the voter who is indifferent between voting for politician A and voting for politician B when q_1^A and q_1^B are announced. Characterize the vote share of politician A for all (q_1^A, q_1^B).

c. Suppose that agents have the same beliefs about politicians, i.e. $F^A = F^B$. Which platforms guarantee half of the electorate for each politician? What happens if beliefs differ?

Answer

a. After the election, politician P selects the policy that maximizes his utility, i.e.:

$$q_2^P(q_1^P, \alpha^P) = \frac{1 - \alpha^P}{2 - \alpha^P}(y - q_1^P)$$

Then, the expected utility of voter i when q_1^P is announced can be written as:

$$W(q_1^P; \alpha^i) = \int_{\alpha^P} \left[\ln \frac{1}{2 - \alpha^P}(y - q_1^P) + \alpha^i \ln q_1^P + (1 - \alpha^i) \ln \frac{1 - \alpha^P}{2 - \alpha^P}(y - q_1^P) \right] dF^P(\alpha^P)$$

The expected utility depends on the beliefs that agents have over politicians.

b. The agent who is indifferent between voting for politician A and politician B has preferences such that $W(q_1^A; \alpha^i) = W(q_1^B; \alpha^i)$. Note that:

$$\frac{\partial}{\partial \alpha^i}[W(q_1^A; \alpha^i) - W(q_1^B; \alpha^i)] = h(q_1^A, q_1^B, F^A, F^B)$$

where:

$$h(q_1^A, q_1^B, F^A, F^B) = \ln q_1^A - \ln q_1^B - \int_{\alpha^A} \ln \left[\frac{1 - \alpha^A}{2 - \alpha^A}(y - q_1^A) \right] dF^A(\alpha^A)$$

$$+ \int_{\alpha^B} \ln \left[\frac{1 - \alpha^B}{2 - \alpha^B}(y - q_1^B) \right] dF^B(\alpha^B)$$

Fix q_1^B, then $\frac{\partial h}{\partial q_1^A} = \frac{1}{q_1^A} + \frac{1}{y - q_1^A} > 0$. Therefore, there exists $q_1^A(q_1^B)$ such that for all $q_1^A < q_1^A(q_1^B)$, $h(q_1^A, q_1^B, F^A, F^B) < 0$ and for all $q_1^A > q_1^A(q_1^B)$, $h(q_1^A, q_1^B, F^A, F^B) > 0$. Note that in $(q_1^A(q_1^B), q_1^B)$, $W(q_1^A, \alpha^i) - W(q_1^B, \alpha^i) = d$ where d is a constant. Note that if $d = 0$, then all agents are indifferent between politician A and B and vote for each with probability $\frac{1}{2}$. More generally, we have for all q_1^B:

- for all $q_1^A < q_1^A(q_1^B)$, there exists $\alpha_1(q_1^A, q_1^B, F^A, F^B)$ such that for all $\alpha^i < \alpha_1(q_1^A, q_1^B, F^A, F^B)$, i vote for A. Therefore, the vote share of politician A is given by:

$$\pi_A = F(\alpha_1(q_1^A, q_1^B, F^A, F^B))$$

and is increasing in α_1.

- for all $q_1^A > q_1^A(q_1^B)$, there exists $\alpha_2(q_1^A, q_1^B, F^A, F^B)$ such that for all $\alpha^i > \alpha_1(q_1^A, q_1^B, F^A, F^B)$, i vote for A. Therefore, the vote share of politician A is given by:

$$\pi_A = 1 - F(\alpha_2(q_1^A, q_1^B, F^A, F^B))$$

which is decreasing in α_2.

c. Suppose that agents have the same beliefs over politicians, then $q_1^A(q_1^B) = q_1^B$. In (q_1^A, q_1^B), $W(q_1^A, \alpha^i) - W(q_1^B, \alpha^i) = 0$. If politician A selects q_1^A such that $\pi_A > \frac{1}{2}$, then politician B can select $q^B = q^A$ and get half of the electorate. If beliefs differ, politician are expected to pick different policies to get half of the electorate.

3.2   Downsian competition in a simple public good model

Consider the economy described in problem 2 of chapter 2. More precisely, agent i's preferences over a publicly provided good y and a privately provided good c^i is expressed by

$$w^i = c^i + \alpha^i V(y)$$

where $V(\cdot)$ is a concave well-behaved function and α^i is the intrinsic parameter of agent i that is drawn from distribution $F(\cdot)$ with mean α. Again, all individuals have initial resources only in the private good, $e^i = 1$ for all i, and one unit of private good is required to produce one unit of public good. To finance the public good production, the government raises a tax q on each individual so that agent i's budget constraint is $c^i \leq 1 - q$.

a. Derive the policy preferences of each agent $W(q; \alpha^i)$ as well as the social optimum in this economy.

Suppose that two politicians $P = A, B$ select platforms q^A and q^B. Assume that each of them maximizes the expected value of some exogenous rent R. Call π_P, the vote share for politician P, then P's probability of winning the election is $p_P = \text{Prob}(\pi_P \geq 1/2)$ and his expected utility is then $p_P R$. First, the two candidates announce their platforms simultaneously and non cooperatively. Then, elections are held. Last, the elected politician implements his announced policy.

b. Assume that $\alpha^i = \alpha$. Determine the candidates' probability of winning. What are the announced platforms and which one is implemented? Discuss.

c. Suppose that agents are heterogeneous. Determine the probability of winning for each candidate. What are the selected platforms in that case? Which one is implemented?

d. What are the economic predictions of the model? Discuss.

Answer

a. The policy preferences of individual i are given by:

$$W(q; \alpha^i) = 1 - q + \alpha^i V(q)$$

The social optimum is obtained by maximizing $\int_{\alpha^i} W(q; \alpha^i) dF(\alpha^i)$ under the constraint $\int_{\alpha^i} 1 - c^i - y dF(\alpha^i) \geq 0$. This results in $q^* = V_q^{-1}(\frac{1}{\alpha})$. The optimal provision of public good is then $y^* = q^*$.

b. Voters vote for the politician whose platform provide them the highest utility. In case of indifference, they vote for A with probability $\frac{1}{2}$. Therefore, the probability of winning for politician A is:

$$p_A = \begin{cases} 0 & \text{if} \quad W(q^A; \alpha) < W(q^B; \alpha) \\ \frac{1}{2} & \text{if} \quad W(q^A; \alpha) = W(q^B; \alpha) \\ 1 & \text{if} \quad W(q^A; \alpha) > W(q^B; \alpha) \end{cases}$$

Naturally, the probability that politician B win is $p_B = 1 - p_A$. Since $\alpha^i = \alpha$, all voters prefer y^*. Then, each candidate increases his probability of winning by getting closer to y^*. As a consequence, there is a unique equilibrium in which politicians converge to the same platform:

$$q^A = q^B = q^*$$

c. If agents are heterogeneous, then only agents with type $\alpha^i = \alpha$ prefer unambiguously y^*. Then, the social optimum is expected not to be implemented. Formally, the probability that agent i vote for politician A is:

$$\begin{cases} 0 & \text{if} \quad W(q^A; \alpha^i) < W(q^B; \alpha^i) \\ \frac{1}{2} & \text{if} \quad W(q^A; \alpha^i) = W(q^B; \alpha^i) \\ 1 & \text{if} \quad W(q^A; \alpha^i) > W(q^B; \alpha^i) \end{cases}$$

Recall that the preferences of agents are single peaked so that, if voters make a pairwise vote, the preferred policy of the agents with median value of α^i would be selected. As a consequence, each politician finds in his interest to select the platform corresponding to the policy preferred by α^m since it guarantees victory. As this reasoning is the same for both politicians, the unique equilibrium is:

$$q^A = q^B = q^m$$

d. The social optimum is achieved only under restrictive conditions on the distribution of the population. This implies that, absent these conditions, the majority rule generates under-production or over-production of public good.

3.3 A simple model of probabilistic voting

Consider the same model as in problem 2, but assume that the voting strategy of voter i is affected by three components: (i) the economic policy implemented q, (ii) his individual ideological bias σ^i towards candidate B, and (iii) the popularity δ of politician B. We assume that σ^i is uniformly distributed on $[-\frac{1}{2\phi}, \frac{1}{2\phi}]$. Moreover, δ is the same for all voters and is drawn from the uniform distribution on $[-\frac{1}{2\psi}, \frac{1}{2\psi}]$. The distributions are common knowledge but only agent i observes his parameter σ^i. Then, i's preferences over the policy implemented by A are summarized by $W(q^A; \alpha^i)$, while the preferences over the policy implemented by politician B take the final form

$$W(q^B; \alpha^i) + \sigma^i + \delta$$

The timing is as follows: first, each voter observes σ^i and politicians simultaneously and non-cooperatively announce platforms q^A and q^B. Second, δ is realized. Third, elections take place and last, the announced policy is implemented.

a. Give an interpretation of σ^i. Characterize the agent who is indifferent between voting for politician A and B for given policies q^A and q^B. Suppose that $\alpha^i = \alpha$. Deduce the vote share of candidate A as well as his probability of winning.

b. Which platforms are selected by politicians? Which one is implemented? Discuss.

c. Suppose that agents are heterogeneous. What does this imply for the equilibrium?

d. Discuss your results and compare them with the results obtained in problem 2.

Answer

a. The parameter σ^i can be interpreted as a measure of the ideological "bias" (or preference) of agent i. The agent who is indifferent between voting for politician A and B for given platforms q^A and q^B is characterized by:

$$W(q^A; \alpha^i) = W(q^B; \alpha^i) + \sigma^i + \delta$$

Suppose that $\alpha^i = \alpha$ for all i. Then, for all q^A and q^B, there exists an agent with intrinsic parameter $\tilde{\sigma}(q^A, q^B, \delta)$ who is indifferent between the two platforms and:

$$\tilde{\sigma}(q^A, q^B; \delta) = W(q^A; \alpha) - W(q^B; \alpha) - \delta$$

The vote share of politician A is simply:

$$\pi_A = \text{Prob}(\sigma \leq \tilde{\sigma}) = \left[\tilde{\sigma} + \frac{1}{2\phi}\right]\phi$$

The probability of winning of politician A is $p_A = \text{Prob}(\pi_A \geq \frac{1}{2})$, and given the distributional assumptions of the model:

$$p_A = \psi\left[W(q^A, \alpha) - W(q^B, \alpha)\right] + \frac{1}{2}$$

b. Each politician maximizes his probability of winning. Then, politician A's selected platform when B announces q^B is:

$$q^A = V_y^{-1}[\frac{1}{\alpha}]$$

Naturally, the problem is symmetric for politician B, then both politicians converge to $q^A = q^B = q^*$. In this case, the social optimum is achieved.

c. Suppose now that agents are heterogeneous. Then, for all α^i, there exists $\tilde{\sigma}(\alpha^i, q^A, q^B, \delta)$ such that an agent with intrinsic parameters α^i and $\tilde{\sigma}(\alpha^i, q^A, q^B, \delta)$ is indifferent between platforms A and B. Formally,

$$\tilde{\sigma}(\alpha^i, q^A, q^B, \delta) = W(q^A; \alpha^i) - W(q^B; \alpha^i) - \delta$$

The vote share for politician A is $\pi_A = \int_{\alpha^i} \text{Prob}[\sigma < \tilde{\sigma}(\alpha^i, q^A, q^B, \delta)] dF(\alpha^i)$, which can be rewritten as:

$$\pi_A = \int_{\alpha^i}\left[\tilde{\sigma}(\alpha^i, q^A, q^B, \delta) + \frac{1}{2\phi}\right]\phi dF(\alpha^i) = [W(q^A; \alpha) - W(q^B; \alpha) + \delta]\phi + \frac{1}{2}$$

Therefore, the probability of winning of politician A is:

$$p_A = \psi[W(q^A; \alpha) - W(q^B; \alpha)] + \frac{1}{2}$$

As before, each politician maximizes his probability of winning. The selected platforms are again $q^A = q^B = q^*$. So, heterogeneity does not affect the equilibrium.

d. We have seen in Problem 2 that majority rule does not lead in general to the social optimum when agents are heterogeneous. For any policies q^A and q^B, there exists a unique agent with type $\alpha^i(q^A, q^B)$ who is indifferent between policy A and policy B. Therefore, the vote share of politician A is simply $F(\alpha^i(q^A, q^B))$. Then politicians optimally select policies such that the vote share is $\frac{1}{2}$. This is the case if and only if $\alpha^i(q^A, q^B) = \alpha^m$. In other words, politicians have no other choice than offering the preferred policy of the median voter to get half of the electorate. Naturally, it would be socially optimal to offer the preferred policy of the voter whose type is the mean of the distribution of types. Consider now the model in Problem 3. Given the uncertainty parameter δ, there is uncertainty on the agent who is indifferent between the two announced policies. As a consequence, the median voter is not the Condorcet winner anymore. To sum up, platforms will always converge to the platform preferred by the "mean" voter and not to that of the median voter.

3.4   Probabilistic voting in the presence of groups of voters

Consider a modified version of the previous model. More precisely, we assume that the population consists of three kinds of voters $J = \{R, M, P\}$ with intrinsic parameters α^J. The proportion of agents in group J is denoted by λ^J and $\sum_{J=1}^{3} \lambda^J = 1$. Besides, $\sum_{J=1}^{3} \alpha^J \lambda^J = \alpha$. Once more, the voting strategy of voter i in group J is affected by (i) the economic policy that is implemented q, (ii) his individual ideological bias σ^{iJ} towards candidate B and (iii) the popularity δ of politician B. We assume that σ^{iJ} is uniformly distributed on $[-\frac{1}{2\phi^J}, \frac{1}{2\phi^J}]$, where ϕ^J is group specific and that δ is drawn from the uniform distribution on $[-\frac{1}{2\psi}, \frac{1}{2\psi}]$. As in the previous problem, the distributions are common knowledge but only agent i observes his parameter σ^i. The preferences of i over the policy implemented by A are summarized by $W(q_A; \alpha^J)$, whereas his preferences over the policy implemented by politician B are given by

$$W(q^B; \alpha^J) + \sigma^{iJ} + \delta$$

The timing is the same as in problem 3.

a. Which voter is indifferent between voting for A or B in each group? Deduce the vote share for candidate A and compute his probability of winning for given platforms.

b. Characterize the optimal platform for each politician. Is the selected policy the socially optimal one? Provide an economic intuition of the result.

c. Suppose now that σ^{iJ} is drawn from a general common knowledge distribution $G^J(\cdot)$ with density $g^J(\cdot)$. Show that the results are not qualitatively affected by restricting oneself to a uniform distribution.

d. Suppose that δ is drawn from the distribution $L(\cdot)$ with density $l(\cdot)$ and that σ^{iJ} remains uniformly distributed. Again, show that the results are not qualitatively affected by restricting oneself to a uniform distribution.

Answer

a. The voter who is indifferent between voting for politician A and politician B for given platforms q^A and q^B is the voter with ideology $\sigma^J(q^A, q^B, \delta)$ such that:

$$W(q^A; \alpha^J) = W(q^B; \alpha^J) + \sigma^J(q^A, q^B, \delta) + \delta$$

In the remaining of the question, we omit the arguments q^A, q^B and δ in the cutoff $\sigma^J(q^A, q^B, \delta)$ to simplify the notations. Following the same reasoning as in the previous exercise, the vote share of candidate A is:

$$\pi_A = \sum_J \lambda^J \phi^J \left[\sigma^J + \frac{1}{2\phi^J} \right]$$

and his probability of winning is:

$$p_A = \frac{\psi}{\phi} \sum_J \lambda^J \phi^J [W(q^A; \alpha^J) - W(q^B; \alpha^J)] + \frac{1}{2}$$

where $\phi = \sum_J \lambda^J \phi^J$.

b. Each politician maximizes his probability of winning. Consider politician A. The optimal platform given the platform q^B announced by his competitor satisfies:

$$\frac{\psi}{\phi} \sum_J \lambda^J \phi^J W_{q^A}(q^A; \alpha^J) = 0$$

Let $\tilde{\alpha} = \frac{1}{\phi} \sum_J \lambda^J \phi^J \alpha^J$, then $q^A = V_y^{-1}(\frac{1}{\tilde{\alpha}})$. Naturally, politician B selects the same platform, and the equilibrium is then:

$$q^A = q^B = V_y^{-1}(\frac{1}{\tilde{\alpha}})$$

The equilibrium does not correspond anymore to the preferred policy of the mean voter.

c. If σ^i is drawn from a distribution $G(\cdot)$, the definition of σ^J is not affected. However, in that case, the vote share of candidate A is:

$$\pi_A = \sum_J \lambda^J G^J(\sigma^J(q^A, q^B))$$

The probability of winning is then:

$$p_A = \text{Prob}[\sum_J \lambda^J G^J(W(q^A; \alpha^J) - W(q^B; \alpha^J) - \delta) \geq \frac{1}{2}]$$

Let $H(W(q^A; \alpha^J), W(q^B; \alpha^J), \delta) = \sum_J \lambda^J G^J(W(q^A; \alpha^J) - W(q^B; \alpha^J) - \delta)$. Clearly, this function is decreasing in δ and such that $\frac{\partial H}{\partial W(q^A; \alpha^J)} = \lambda^J g^J(\sigma^J)$ as well as $\frac{\partial H}{\partial W(q^B; \alpha^J)} = -\lambda^J g^J(\sigma^J)$. There exists $\hat{\delta}$ such that $H(W(q^A; \alpha^J), W(q^B; \alpha^J), \hat{\delta}) = \frac{1}{2}$. More precisely,

$$\hat{\delta} = H^{-1}(W(q^A; \alpha^J), W(q^B; \alpha^J), \frac{1}{2})$$

and the probability of winning is then:

$$\text{Prob}[\delta \leq \hat{\delta}] = \psi\hat{\delta} + \frac{1}{2}$$

Therefore, the optimal platform from the perspective of politician A satisfies:

$$\psi[\sum_J \frac{\partial H^{-1}}{\partial W(q^A; \alpha^J)} W_{q^A}(q^A; \alpha^J)] = 0$$

As a consequence, the solution obtained in the previous question is not modified qualitatively.

d. If δ is drawn from a distribution $L(\cdot)$ then, the probability of winning of politician A is:

$$p_A = L\left(\frac{1}{\phi} \sum_J \lambda^J \phi^J[W(q^A; \alpha^J) - W(q^B; \alpha^J)]\right)$$

Politician A maximizes his probability of being elected. His platform satisfies:

$$l\left(\frac{1}{\phi} \sum_J \lambda^J \phi^J[W(q^A; \alpha^J) - W(q^B; \alpha^J)]\right) \frac{1}{\phi} \sum_J \lambda^J \phi^J[-1 + \alpha^J V_y(q^A)] = 0$$

Both politicians converge to the same platform and offer $q^A = q^B = V_y^{-1}(\frac{1}{\alpha})$. Here again, the distributional assumption is not restrictive.

3.5 Lobbying

Consider the same model as in problem 4 but now assume that each group can decide to contribute to the campaign of politician P. Let O^J be the indicator variable that takes the value of 1 if group J wants to finance a party and the value of 0 if group J does not contribute to any campaign. Suppose that the willingness to contribute is exogenous. Let C_P^J denote the contribution per member in group J to politician P. The total contribution of each member in group J is thus $C_A^J + C_B^J$. For any agent in group J, the cost of contributing to the campaign is $D(C_A^J + C_B^J) = 1/2(C_A^J + C_B^J)^2$. Whenever a candidate receives a contribution, he spends the money and his popularity is affected. For simplicity, the popularity of party B is given by

$$\delta = \tilde{\delta} + h \cdot (C_B - C_A),$$

where C_P represents the sum of the contributions received by party P, namely $C_P = \sum_J O^J \alpha^J C_P^J$ and h a parameter measuring the effectiveness of the campaign. Assume that $\tilde{\delta}$ is uniformly distributed with density on $[-\frac{1}{2\psi}, \frac{1}{2\psi}]$. The timing is as follows. First, each voter observes σ^i and politicians announce their platforms. Second, groups fix their contributions simultaneously. Third, the popularity parameter is realized and the election takes place. Last, the platform of the winner is implemented.

a. In each group, characterize the agent who is indifferent between voting for politician A and B for given levels of contributions. Determine the vote share of politician A as well as his probability of winning the election.

b. From an ex ante perspective, what is the objective function of each member in the group if the latter wants to finance politicians? Determine the optimal contribution per member in each group. Discuss.

c. Determine the platforms that are selected by politicians if all groups are willing to contribute (i.e. $O^J = 1$ for all J) or no group contributes (i.e. $O^J = 0$ for all J). What are the contributions in equilibrium? What happens if σ^i has the same distribution in all groups, namely $\phi^J = \phi$ for all J. Discuss.

d. Suppose now that some groups prefer not to finance politicians (i.e. there exists J such that $O^J = 0$). What are the platforms and which policy is finally implemented? Discuss. Which groups have the highest incentives to become organized?

Answer

a. In each group, the agent indifferent between voting for politician A and B has an ideological bias towards politician B such that:

$$\sigma^J = W(q^A; \alpha^J) - W(q^B; \alpha^J) + h(C_A - C_B) - \tilde{\delta}$$

Therefore, the probability of winning of politician A is:

$$p_A = \frac{\psi}{\phi} \sum_J \lambda^J \phi^J [W(q^A; \alpha^J) - W(q^B; \alpha^J) + h(C_A - C_B)] + \frac{1}{2}$$

b. The objective of each agent in group J is to maximize:

$$p_A W(q^A; \alpha^J) + (1 - p_A)W(q^B; \alpha^J) - D(C_A^J + C_B^J)$$

Taking the derivatives of this expression with respect to C_A^J and C_B^J , we get respectively:

$$\frac{h\psi}{\phi}[W(q^A, \alpha^J) - W(q^B, \alpha^J)] - C_A^J - C_B^J \leq 0$$

$$-\frac{h\psi}{\phi}[W(q^A, \alpha^J) - W(q^B, \alpha^J)] - C_B^J - C_A^J \leq 0$$

Note that if $W(q^A, \alpha^J) < W(q^B, \alpha^J)$, the first derivative is negative. Therefore the optimal contribution of group J to politician P is such that:

$$C_P^J = \max\{0, \frac{h\psi}{\phi}[W(q_P, \alpha^J) - W(q_{P'}, \alpha^J)]\}$$

where P' represents the rival of politician P. It is never optimal to finance both politicians. Besides, the group rewards the politician who gives it the highest welfare.

c. Consider the decisions of politicians. Given the symmetry of the problem, they will both converge to the same platforms. Replacing the expression of the contributions into p_A, politician A maximizes:

$$\frac{1}{2} + \frac{1}{\phi}\sum_J \lambda^J \phi^J [\psi + O^J (h\psi)^2][W(q^A; \alpha^J) - W(q^B; \alpha^J)]$$

If no group contribute or all groups contribute, then $q^A = q^B = V_y^{-1}(\frac{1}{\alpha})$ and we are back to the result obtained in the previous problem. The intuition of the result is immediate when no group is organized: this case is formally equivalent to the case studied in the previous problem. When a group is organized, its contribution reflects the marginal benefit and cost of the public good for its members. Therefore, when receiving a political contribution, the politician internalizes the interests of his voters. If all groups are organized, then the benefits and costs of all the agents are internalized by politicians. In equilibrium, the provision of public good is not distorted with respect to the case in which no group is organized. Only the sizes of the groups matter. Note that, when $\phi^J = \phi$, the equilibrium coincides with the social optimum.

d. If some groups do not contribute, then $q^A = q^B = V_y^{-1}(\frac{1}{\hat\alpha})$ where:

$$\hat\alpha = \frac{\sum_J \lambda^J \phi^J \alpha^J [\psi + O^J (h\psi)^2]}{\sum_J \lambda^J \phi^J [\psi + O^J (h\psi)^2]}$$

The equilibrium is tilted in favor of the organized groups. With respect to the social optimum, lobbying induces underprovision or overprovision of public goods.

Chapter 4

Agency

4.1 Political rents in lop-sided elections

This question deals with issues analyzed in Polo (1999). There are two political candidates (A and B) each proposing a level of taxes τ and a level of spending on public goods g. The public good g is financed through proportional income taxes. The candidates can, however, also use public funds for private consumption. The amount diverted to private consumption is denoted r. A continuum of citizens of measure one, indexed by i, all have the same income 1. The governments budget constraint is thus $\tau = g + r$. Their preferences over private consumption, c, and a public good, g, are described by

$$u^i = c^i + H(g),$$

$c^i = (1 - \tau)$. Citizen i will vote for candidate A if

$$(1 - g_A - r_A) + H(g_A) > (1 - g_B - r_B) + H(g_B) + \sigma^i + \delta.$$

The parameters σ^i and δ describe the individuals preference in favor of party B and are distributed uniformly on

$$\left[-\frac{1}{2\phi}, \frac{1}{2\phi}\right] \quad \text{and} \quad \left[-\frac{1}{2\varphi}, \frac{1}{2\varphi}\right]$$

respectively. The political candidates care only about their private consumption, r, and their utilities are r if they win the election and zero otherwise.

a. First consider the case in which the candidates know that the value of δ is 0. Solve for the equilibrium levels of taxes and rents.

b. Now consider the case in which the candidates know that the value of δ is greater than 0. Solve for the equilibrium levels of taxes and rents.

c. Now consider the case in which the candidates do not know the value of δ, but they know that its expected value is zero. Solve for the equilibrium levels of taxes and rents.

27

d. Finally consider the case in which the candidates do no know the value of δ, and where δ is uniformly distributed on

$$\left[\alpha - \frac{1}{2\varphi}, \alpha + \frac{1}{2\varphi}\right],$$

that is one candidate may have a competitive advantage. Solve for the equilibrium levels of taxes and rents as well as equilibrium probabilities of winning the election. Are expected rents higher in this equilibrium than in the equilibrium without advantage for either candidate. It is not necessary to specify the conditions for existence of equilibrium.

Answer

a. A share

$$s^A = \frac{1}{2} + \phi \left[\left(1 - g^A - r^A\right) + H\left(g^A\right) - \left(1 - g^B - r^B\right) - H\left(g^B\right)\right]$$

will vote for party A. The probability that candidate A will win the election is therefore1

$$p^A = \begin{array}{ll} 1 & \text{if } s^A > \frac{1}{2} \\ \frac{1}{2} & \text{if } s^A = \frac{1}{2} \\ 0 & \text{if } s^A > \frac{1}{2} \end{array}$$

The candidates maximize expected utility $p^A r$. The platform which satisfies $g = g^* = H'^{-1}(1)$ and $r = 0$ is the Condorcet winner and can not be beaten by any other platform. To see that this platform can not be beaten, assume that one party has this platform. Since this platform maximizes $1 - g - r + H(g)$ it cannot be beaten by any other platform. To see that this is the only equilibrium, assume that some other platform g^A, r^A is chosen by party A. The best reply for party B is to set a platform such that $g^B = g^*$ and r^B is determined by

$$\left(1 - g^A - r^A\right) + H\left(g^A\right) + \varepsilon = \left(1 - g^* - r^B\right) + H\left(g^*\right),$$

where ε is a very small number. Candidate B will then win the election for sure and get rents r^B. However, given that this is the platform of party B, then the best reply of party A is to set $g^A = g^*$, and r^A just below r^B. In a similar fashion as in Bertrand price competition, this drives down equilibrium rents to zero.

b. Now candidate B has a competitive advantage over party A. In equilibrium, party B will maximize its rents, given that the utility of the median citizen is high enough so that party A can never win the election, even if promising $g^A = g^*$, $r^A = 0$. The problem is thus

$$\max r^B$$

subject to

$$(1 - g^*) + H(g^*) \leq \left(1 - g^B - r^B\right) + H\left(g^B\right) + \delta.$$

The solution to this problem is $g^B = g^*, r^B = \delta$. Candidate B can use his popularity to win for sure and extract positive rents. Candidate B's behavior is similar to a limit pricing strategy. By setting his rents (price) low enough, he prices the opponent out of the market.

c. The probability that candidate A will win the election is now

$$
\begin{aligned}
p^A &= \Pr\left[\delta < \left(1 - g^A - r^A\right) + H\left(g^A\right) - \left(1 - g^B - r^B\right) - H\left(g^B\right)\right] \\
&= \frac{1}{2} + \varphi\left[\left(1 - g^A - r^A\right) + H\left(g^A\right) - \left(1 - g^B - r^B\right) - H\left(g^B\right)\right].
\end{aligned}
$$

Given that candidate B has chosen the platform g^B, r^B, the best reply for candidate A maximizes $p^A r^A$. The first order conditions characterizing A:s best reply are

$$p^A - \varphi r^A = 0,$$

$$-1 + H'\left(g^A\right) = 0.$$

Similarly, the best reply condition for candidate B is characterized by

$$p^B - \varphi r^B = 0,$$

$$-1 + H'\left(g^B\right) = 0.$$

The second condition implies that both candidates set the level of public good at the efficient level $g^B = g^A = g^*$. Inserting this in the first order conditions for the rents yields:

$$\frac{1}{2} + \varphi\left[r^B - r^A\right] - \varphi r^A = 0,$$

$$\frac{1}{2} + \varphi\left[r^A - r^B\right] - \varphi r^B = 0.$$

Subtracting the second equation from the first yields

$$2\varphi\left[r^B - r^A\right] - \varphi r^A + \varphi r^B = 0,$$

or

$$r^A = r^B.$$

This implies that $p^A = p^B = \frac{1}{2}$, and $r^A = r^B = \frac{1}{2\varphi}$. Rents are increasing in the level of uncertainty about the election outcome, $\frac{1}{\varphi}$. When the uncertainty approaches zero, rents approach zero.

d. The probability that candidate A will win the election is now

$$
\begin{aligned}
p^A &= \Pr\left[\delta < \left(1 - g^A - r^A\right) + H\left(g^A\right) - \left(1 - g^B - r^B\right) - H\left(g^B\right)\right] \\
&= \frac{1}{2} - \alpha\varphi + \varphi\left(\left(1 - g^A - r^A\right) + H\left(g^A\right) - \left(1 - g^B - r^B\right) - H\left(g^B\right)\right).
\end{aligned}
$$

Given that candidate B has chosen the platform g^B, r^B, the best reply for candidate A maximizes $p^A r^A$. The first order conditions characterizing A's best reply are

$$p^A - \varphi r^A = 0,$$

$$-1 + H'\left(g^A\right) = 0.$$

Similarly, the best reply condition for candidate B is characterized by

$$p^B - \varphi r^B = 0,$$

$$-1 + H'\left(g^B\right) = 0.$$

The second condition implies that both candidates set the level of public good at the efficient level $g^B = g^A = g^*$. Inserting this in the first order conditions for the rents yields:

$$\frac{1}{2} - \alpha\varphi + \varphi\left[r^B - r^A\right] - \varphi r^A = 0,$$

$$\frac{1}{2} + \alpha\varphi - \varphi\left[r^B - r^A\right] - \varphi r^B = 0,$$

or equivalently

$$r^A = \frac{1}{2}\left(r^B + \frac{1}{2\varphi} - \alpha\right)$$

$$r^B = \frac{1}{2}\left(r^A + \frac{1}{2\varphi} + \alpha\right).$$

Combining the two equations yields.

$$r^A = \frac{1}{2\varphi} - \frac{1}{3}\alpha,$$

$$r^B = \frac{1}{2\varphi} + \frac{1}{3}\alpha.$$

The party that is ahead will extract more rents in equilibrium. The equilibrium probabilities of winning the election are

$$p^A = \frac{1}{2} - \frac{1}{3}\alpha\varphi,$$

$$p^B = \frac{1}{2} + \frac{1}{3}\alpha\varphi.$$

So candidate B is more likely to win the election. Therefore, expected rents are

$$p^A r^A + p^B r^B = \frac{1}{2\varphi} + \frac{2}{9}\alpha^2\varphi.$$

This is larger than in the case with no competitive advantage for either candidate. The reason is that the candidate that is more likely to win the election is the one that has higher rents. Note that if elections are lop-sided, then an increase in the number of marginal voters, φ has an ambiguous effect on expected rents. On one hand it makes political competition more fierce which lowers $\frac{1}{2\varphi}$ on the other hand, it increases the probability that the candidate with lower rents will win the election.

4.2 Political rents with term limits

Consider the model in subsection 4.4. An incumbent politician proposes a level of spending on public goods, g, and a level of private rents for himself, r. The public good g is financed through proportional income taxes. A continuum of citizens of measure one, indexed by i, all have the same income y. The government's budget constraint is $\tau y = \theta g + r$, where θ is a parameter which measures the cost of providing public goods. Citizen i's preferences over private consumption c^i and a public good g as described by

$$u^i = c^i + H(g),$$

where $c^i = y(1-\tau)$. The incumbent's utility consists only of consumption of the rents, $u = \gamma r$. The following game is repeated infinitely many periods. (1) θ_t is realized and observed by everybody. (2) Voters set a reservation utility for re-electing the incumbent. (3) The incumbent sets the policy variables, r_t and g_t. (4) Elections are held in which the voters choose between the incumbent and an opponent which has the same characteristics as the incumbent. A politician maximizes

$$\sum_{t=0}^{\infty} \beta^t p_t \gamma r_t,$$

where β^t is the subjective discount factor and p_t is the probability that the incumbent is in office at period t. Assume that a politician who is voted out of office cannot be reelected.

The incumbent at period 0 maximizes

$$\gamma r_0 + \delta p_1 R_{I,1}$$

where $R_{I,1}$ is the value of being an incumbent in period 1. The voters coordinate on the same retrospective voting strategy, voting for the incumbent if their utility is higher than or equal to $\varpi_t(\theta_t)$.

a. Solve for the optimal voting strategy $\varpi_t(\theta_t)$.

b. Suppose term limits are imposed that do not allow the incumbent to stay in office more than three periods. How will this affect the voters' ability to discipline the incumbent?

c. Now suppose that there are two parties to which the candidates may belong, as before there are term limits after three terms. Assume that the voters use the rule to vote for a candidate belonging to the same party as the incumbent if and only if rents are below some specific level. Suppose further that a new party candidate may bribe the incumbent not to keep rents too high in his third term. What is the new equilibrium level of rents?

Answer

a. In case the incumbent wishes to be re-elected, he must keep rents below

$$r\left(\theta_t\right) = y - w_t(\theta_t) + H\left(g^*(\theta_t)\right) - \theta_t g^*(\theta_t).$$

If the incumbent prefers not to be re-elected, the best policy is to set rents as high as possible, i.e. $r_t = y$. The incumbent in period t prefers to be re-elected if

$$\gamma r_t + \delta V_{I,t+1} \geq \gamma y.$$

Given this strategy, the voters' optimal strategy is to allow the incumbent to extract rents so that the above constraint binds.

$$r_t^* = \max\left[0, y - \frac{\delta}{\gamma} V_{I,t+1}\right].$$

Since r_{t+1}^* will be set in the same way, the value of being an incumbent at period $t+1$ is

$$V_{I,t+1} = \gamma r_{t+1}^* + \delta V_{I,t+2} = \gamma y,$$

and equilibrium rents are $r_t^* = r_t = (1 - \delta)\, y$.

b. During his third term, the incumbent will extract as much rents as possible, setting $r_3 = y$. In the second period the voters must offer

$$\gamma r_2 + \delta \gamma y \geq \gamma y$$

$$r_2 = (1 - \delta)\, y$$

in the second period, and

$$\gamma r_1 + \delta\left(1 - \delta\right)\gamma y \geq \gamma y$$

$$r_1 = \left(1 - \delta + \delta^2\right) y$$

in the first period. However, re-electing the incumbent in the third period is not a subgame-perfect strategy for the voters, given that the incumbents follow the above strategies. The voters could do better by electing a new incumbent after the second period and requiring rents at $r_1 = \left(1 - \delta + \delta^2\right) y$ instead of being stuck with a third term incumbent extracting $r_3 = y$. Realizing that they will never be re-elected for a third term, incumbents extract all rents in their second period, $r_2 = y$. With a similar logic, it is not subgame perfect for voters to ever re-elect an incumbent for a second term if the equilibrium is that the incumbents extract less rents in their first term. Thus the only equilibrium is that all incumbents extract all rents when term limits are imposed.

c. Let the level of the bribe be b. The third period incumbent will keep the level r_3 if

$$\gamma r_3 + b \geq \gamma y.$$

Therefore, the voters will demand

$$r_3 = y - \frac{1}{\gamma} b.$$

In period two the incumbent will keep the level r_2 if

$$\gamma r_2 + \delta \gamma y \geq \gamma y.$$

Therefore, the voters will demand

$$r_2 = (1 - \delta) y.$$

Similarly, in the first incumbency period the voters will demand

$$r_1 = (1 - \delta) y.$$

The value of being a first period incumbent is therefore

$$(1 - \delta) \gamma y + \delta (1 - \delta) \gamma y + \delta^2 \gamma y = \gamma y.$$

Therefore the new candidate is willing to pay $\delta \gamma y$ to the old candidate. In order for the equilibrium to be subgame perfect, the voters must prefer to re-elect the incumbent for the third term to electing a new incumbent. This will be the case if

$$r_3 \leq r_1 = r_2 = (1 - \delta) y,$$

or, equivalently,

$$\gamma \delta y \leq b.$$

The rents in this equilibrium are thus $r_1 = r_2 = r_3 = (1 - \delta) y$, $b = \gamma \delta y$. The incumbents are always elected for three periods, and the value of being a politician is zero except for the very first politician.

4.3   Electoral cycles with seignorage

Assume the following model of electoral cycles with seignorage. Let us write the government budget constraint as:

$$g_t = \eta_t (\bar{\tau} y + s_t),$$

where $\bar{\tau}$ denotes fixed taxes, there are no endogenous rents r, and the variable s_t denotes "seignorage", or more generally a hidden and distorting tax observed and paid by the voters only after the elections. Therefore, voters' welfare is:

$$w_t = y(1 - \bar{\tau}) - s_t - V(s_t) + \alpha g_t,$$

where $V(\cdot)$ is a convex function capturing the distortions of seignorage. As is common in these models, the politician's competency is determined by

$$\eta_t = \mu_t + \mu_{t-1},$$

where μ_t is distributed uniformly with mean 1 and density ξ, and it is serially uncorrelated. Politicians maximize

$$E(w_t \mid \mu_{t-1}) + p_t R,$$

where p_t is the probability of re-election.

The stage game at time t is given by: The politician chooses s_t given μ_{t-1} and without observing μ_t. Nature determines μ_t. Voters observe only g_t. If t is an election period voters vote to re-elect the incumbent or to elect a new contender, drawn from the same distribution. If t is an off-election period we move to the election period. The stage game is infinitely repeated.

a. Show that in off-election periods the incumbent sets s_t optimally.

b. Find the equilibrium seignorage in on-election periods. Show that they are larger than off-election seignorage (the social optimum level).

c. Perform comparative statics with respect to the effects of the exogenous spoils of office (R), the sensitivity of reelection probability (ξ) and the total taxes available ($\bar{\tau}$).

Answer

First note that in off–election periods, the incumbent's actions do not affect the probability of winning, and thus he maximizes social welfare:

$$\max E(w_t \mid \mu_{t-1}).$$

This yields a socially optimal solution with the first order condition:

$$V_s(s) = \alpha - 1.$$

We now characterize the equilibrium strategy for an on–election period, which we denote by $t + 1$. Observing g_{t+1} and knowing the equilibrium strategy $\tilde{s}_{t+1}$ and μ_t, voters can guess μ_{t+1}:

$$g_{t+1} = (\tilde{\mu}_{t+1} + \mu_t)(\bar{\tau}y + \tilde{s}_t) \Leftrightarrow \tilde{\mu}_{t+1} = \frac{g_{t+1}}{\bar{\tau}y + \tilde{s}_{t+1}} - \mu_t.$$

Hence, they re-elect the incumbent if and only if $\tilde{\mu}_{t+1} \geq 1$. How does the politician choose s_{t+1}? The smaller is public good provision, the more incompetent he is perceived to be. By the budget constraint, we can derive an expression for g_{t+1}:

$$g_{t+1} = (\mu_t + \mu_{t+1})(\bar{\tau}y + s_{t+1}) \Rightarrow \tilde{\mu}_{t+1} = \frac{(\bar{\tau}y + s_{t+1})}{\bar{\tau}y + \tilde{s}_{t+1}}(\mu_t + \mu_{t+1}) - \mu_t.$$

Therefore, the incumbent maximizes

$$\max_{s_{t+1} \geq 0} E(w_{t+1} \mid \mu_t) + p_{t+1} R$$

where

$$
\begin{aligned}
p_{t+1} &= \Pr(\tilde{\mu}_{t+1} \geq 1) = \Pr\left(\frac{\bar{\tau}y + s_{t+1}}{\bar{\tau}y + \tilde{s}_{t+1}}(\mu_t + \mu_{t+1}) - \mu_t \geq 1\right) \\
&= \Pr\left(\mu_{t+1} \geq \frac{\bar{\tau}y + \tilde{s}_{t+1})}{\bar{\tau}y + s_{t+1}} - \mu_t \frac{s_{t+1} - \tilde{s}_{t+1}}{\bar{\tau}y + s_{t+1}}\right) \\
&= \frac{1}{2} + \xi \cdot \left(\frac{\bar{\tau}y + \tilde{s}_{t+1}}{\bar{\tau}y + s_{t+1}} - \mu_t \frac{\tilde{s}_{t+1} - s_{t+1}}{\bar{\tau}y + s_{t+1}}\right),
\end{aligned}
$$

and

$$
\begin{aligned}
E(w_{t+1}|\mu_t) &= E(y - \bar{\tau} - s_{t+1} - V(s_{t+1}) + \alpha g_{t+1} \mid \mu_t) \\
&= y - \bar{\tau} - s_{t+1} - V(s_{t+1}) + \alpha(\mu_t + 1)(\bar{\tau}y + s_{t+1})
\end{aligned}
$$

Thus, the politician maximizes

$$
\max_{s_{t+1}} \left(y - \bar{\tau} - s_{t+1} - V(s_{t+1}) + \alpha(\mu_t + 1)(\bar{\tau}y + s_{t+1})\right)
$$

$$
+R \cdot \left[\frac{1}{2} + \xi \cdot \left(\frac{\bar{\tau}y + \tilde{s}_{t+1}}{\bar{\tau}y + s_{t+1}} - \mu_t \frac{\tilde{s}_{t+1} - s_{t+1}}{\bar{\tau}y + s_{t+1}}\right)\right]
$$

$$
\text{s.t. } s_{t+1} \geq 0
$$

The first order condition (and imposing $s_{t+1} = \tilde{s}_{t+1}$) yield then:

$$
1 + V_s(\tilde{s}_{t+1}) = \alpha + \xi \cdot R \cdot \frac{\mu_t - 1}{\bar{\tau} + \tilde{s}_{t+1}}
$$

For large enough R we have a solution $\tilde{s}_{t+1} > 0$.

Note that if $\alpha + \xi R \frac{(\mu_t - 1)}{\bar{\tau} + \tilde{s}_{t+1}} > \alpha$, the solution entails

$$
\tilde{s}_{t+1} > \tilde{s}^{social\ optimum}.
$$

Furthermore, from this condition it is obvious that, for $\mu_t > 1$:
1) If $R \uparrow$ then $\tilde{s}_{t+1} \uparrow$.
2) If $\xi \uparrow$ then $\tilde{s}_{t+1} \uparrow$.
3) If $\bar{\tau} \uparrow$ then $\tilde{s}_{t+1} \downarrow$.

4.4   Equilibrium selection in the adverse selection model

Assume the following two–period model with adverse selection. In this model, a politician knows his competence level when deciding on the rents he extracts. Suppose taxes are fixed at $\bar{\tau}$ and the government budget must be balanced in both periods. Preferences of the voters in period $t = 1, 2$ are:

$$w_t = y(1 - \bar{\tau}) + \alpha g_t,$$

where $\alpha \geq 1$ is an exogenous parameter and $y = 1$ denotes income. Politicians' only choice is whether to use the given tax revenues to provide public goods, pleasing the voters, or to appropriate rents for themselves. The government budget constraint is

$$g_t = \eta(\bar{\tau} y - r_t)$$

where η is a variable reflecting the politician's competence in providing the public good. The variable η can take on one of two values, $1/\theta$ and $1/\lambda\theta$, with equal probability, where $\lambda < 1$. A politician with competence η in period 1 retains that level of competence in period 2 as well. If the politician is not re-elected a contender is chosen with competence η^c, where $1/\theta < \eta^c < 1/\lambda\theta$. Rents are constrained to be non negative. Assume rents' upper bound is binding at a level below the available tax revenue: $r_t \leq \bar{r} < \bar{\tau} y$. The objective of the period–1 incumbent politician is

$$r_1 + p_I \delta(r_2 + R),$$

where $0 < \delta < 1$ is a discount factor and p_I is the probability that the incumbent is re-elected. The quantity r_t denotes rents grabbed in period t, and R denotes the exogenous rents from winning the elections.

Policy commitments are not possible ahead of the elections. Specifically, the timing of events is as follows: (i) An incumbent politician is in office in period 1 and chooses rents for that period, r_1, knowing his own competence η. (ii) The value of the public good provision g_1 is determined residually. Voters observe their own utility, but neither η nor r_1. (iii) Elections are held. If the incumbent wins, his competence remains η. If he loses, an opponent is appointed with competence η^c. (iv) Period 2 rents r_2 are set, and the game ends.

a. Assume that if the politician's strategies do not reveal the politician's competency level, voters are not willing to re-elect him. Show that a pooling equilibrium does not exist in this case.

b. Assume now that even if the politician's strategy does not reveal his competency level, voters are willing to re-elect him. Show that pooling equilibria exist, and that they survive the intuitive criterion.

Answer

a. The incumbent sets r knowing η, and voters know the equilibrium strategies. Voters observe g_t and update their beliefs. A pooling equilibrium has the same strategy for both types, i.e., $\tilde{r}_t(\theta)$ and $\tilde{r}_t(\lambda\theta)$ such that

$$\frac{\bar{\tau} - \tilde{r}_t(\theta)}{\theta} = \frac{\bar{\tau} - \tilde{r}_t(\lambda\theta)}{\lambda\theta} = \tilde{g}_t.$$

In this case the politician is not re-elected along the equilibrium path. Thus, he must set rents at $\bar{r}$. But this is not a pooling equilibrium as now voters can learn his actual type.

b. Now voters are willing to reelect the incumbent even if they are not sure that he is competent. Suppose beliefs are such that if $g_t \neq \tilde{g}_t$, then it is believed that the politician is incompetent, and thus not re-elected.

Let g' and g'' satisfy

$$\bar{\tau} - \theta g' + \delta(R + \bar{r}) = \bar{r},$$

$$\bar{\tau} - \theta g'' + \delta(R + \bar{r}) = \bar{r}.$$

Incentive constraints are now given by

$$\bar{\tau} - \theta \tilde{g}_t + \delta(R + \bar{r}) \geq \bar{r}$$

$$\bar{\tau} - \lambda\theta \tilde{g}_t + \delta(R + \bar{r}) \geq \bar{r}$$

which are satisfied if $\bar{\tau} - \theta \tilde{g}_t + \delta(R + \bar{r}) \geq \bar{r}$ and thus for all $g < g'$.

In order to find a pooling equilibrium that survives the intuitive criterion we need to modify beliefs. First note that beliefs on (g', g'') must be modified to probability one on the competent type. Thus the incentive constraint for the competent type is now changed to

$$\bar{\tau} - \lambda\theta \tilde{g}_t + \delta(R + \bar{r}) \geq \bar{\tau} - \lambda\theta g' + \delta(R + \bar{r})$$

as he can always ensure this payoff by deviating to g'. But now we can show that with these modified beliefs there is a pooling equilibrium at any $g \leq g'$ that survives the intuitive criterion. Assume such an equilibrium at $g^* \leq g'$. Any deviation to (g^*, g') is unreasonable for both types as at most they get less than equilibrium payoffs. Thus any belief can be sustained in this region. Any deviation to $(0, g^*)$ is reasonable for both types and thus any belief can be sustained in this region. Thus this equilibrium survives the intuitive criterion.

4.5   Challenger selection procedure

In the same model as problem 4.4, now assume that at the election stage the contender's competency η^c is drawn from a distribution of competency levels $\theta - \varepsilon$ and $\lambda\theta + \varepsilon$ with equal probability (ε small). Voters then compare the contender's competency to the incumbent's expected competency and choose the candidate with the higher competency level. In case of a tie, the new candidate is chosen. The prior belief about the contender is that he has competency levels θ and $\lambda\theta$ with equal probability.

a. Write the expression for the incumbent's probability of winning.

b. Find a separating equilibrium in this model.

c. Show that pooling equilibria exist, but that they do not survive the intuitive criterion.

Answer

a. First let us compute the incumbent's probability of winning the election

$$
p = \Pr(E[\eta|g] < \eta^c) = \begin{cases} 0 & \text{if } E[\eta|g] \geq \theta - \varepsilon \\ \frac{1}{2} & \text{if } \lambda\theta + \varepsilon \leq E[\eta|g] < \theta - \varepsilon \\ 1 & \text{if } E[\eta|g] < \lambda\theta + \varepsilon \end{cases}
$$

where $E[\eta|g]$ is the expected competency level of the politician as perceived by voters who observed g.

b. In a separating equilibrium voters are able to discern the type of the politician. So we have that $\tilde{r}(\theta)$ and $\tilde{r}(\lambda\theta)$ are such that

$$
\tilde{g}^\theta = \frac{\bar{\tau} - \tilde{r}(\theta)}{\theta} \neq \frac{\bar{\tau} - \tilde{r}(\lambda\theta)}{\lambda\theta} = \tilde{g}^{\lambda\theta}.
$$

Beliefs that support this equilibrium put probability one on the incompetent type if $g \neq \tilde{g}^\theta, \tilde{g}^{\lambda\theta}$. Thus incentive constraints become

$$
\bar{\tau} - \theta\tilde{g}^{\lambda\theta} + \delta(R + \bar{r}) \geq \bar{r}
$$

$$
\bar{r} \geq \bar{r}
$$

and hence $\tilde{g}^\theta = \frac{\bar{\tau} - \bar{r}}{\theta}$ and $\tilde{g}^{\lambda\theta} > g''$.

c. Now $\tilde{g}^\theta = \tilde{g}^{\lambda\theta} = \tilde{g}$. Now voters set $E[\eta|\tilde{g}] = \theta/2 + \lambda\theta/2$, and thus the probability of reelection is $1/2$. Suppose beliefs are such that if $g \neq \tilde{g}$, then it is believed that the politician is incompetent and thus not reelected.

Incentive constraints are now given by

$$\bar{\tau} - \theta\tilde{g}_t + \frac{1}{2}\delta(R + \bar{r}) \geq \bar{r}$$

$$\bar{\tau} - \lambda\theta\tilde{g}_t + \frac{1}{2}\delta(R + \bar{r}) \geq \bar{r}$$

which are satisfied if $\bar{\tau} - \theta\tilde{g}_t + \delta(R + \bar{r}) \geq \bar{r}$ and thus for all $g < \hat{g}'$, where $\hat{g}'$ and $\hat{g}''$ are given by

$$\bar{\tau} - \theta\hat{g}' + \frac{1}{2}\delta(R + \bar{r}) = \bar{r}$$

$$\bar{\tau} - \lambda\theta\hat{g}'' + \frac{1}{2}\delta(R + \bar{r}) \geq \bar{r}.$$

We now show that these pooling equilibria do not survive the intuitive criterion. Let $g^* < \hat{g}'$ represent a pooling equilibrium. The payoff of the incompetent politician in this equilibrium is $\bar{\tau} - \theta g^* + \frac{1}{2}\delta(R + \bar{r})$. Define $g^{*\prime}$ and $g^{*\prime\prime}$ to satisfy

$$\bar{\tau} - \theta g^{*\prime} + \delta(R + \bar{r}) = \bar{\tau} - \theta g^* + \frac{1}{2}\delta(R + \bar{r})$$

$$\bar{\tau} - \lambda\theta g^{*\prime\prime} + \delta(R + \bar{r}) = \bar{\tau} - \lambda\theta g^* + \frac{1}{2}\delta(R + \bar{r})$$

Thus at $g^{*\prime}$ (respectively $g^{*\prime\prime}$), the most the incompetent (resp. competent) politician can hope for his equilibrium payoff. Simplifying, we get

$$g^{*\prime} = g^* + \frac{1}{2\theta}\delta(R + \bar{r})$$

$$g^{*\prime\prime} = g^* + \frac{1}{2\lambda\theta}\delta(R + \bar{r}) > g^{*\prime}.$$

Now consider a deviation to $(g^{*\prime}, g^{*\prime\prime})$. Obviously the incompetent politician has nothing to gain from this deviation. At most he obtains a payoff that is smaller than his equilibrium payoff. On the other hand, competent politicians can potentially obtain a payoff that is strictly higher than this equilibrium payoff. Thus, any reasonable beliefs will put probability one on the competent politician after observing $g \in (g^{*\prime}, g^{*\prime\prime})$. The competent politician will therefore deviate. Thus, pooling equilibria do not survive the intuitive criterion.

Chapter 5

Partisan politicians

5.1 Probabilistic voting with outcome-seeking politicians

Assume that the indirect utility function of tax policy is described by

$$w^i = -\left(\tau - \tau^i\right)^2.$$

There are two political parties, one with preferred tax rate 0, the other with preferred tax rate 1. The parties can commit to a party platform that will be implemented should the party win the election. The political parties are uncertain about the most preferred tax rate τ^m of the median voter and assign a uniform probability distribution between $(\frac{1}{2} - a)$ and $(\frac{1}{2} + a)$ to τ^m. The parameter $a \in (0, 1)$. The parties are exclusively policy motivated. Let τ_0 and τ_1 be the policies proposed by parties 0 and 1 respectively.

a. Show that the parties will never choose their bliss points and will never converge completely.

b. Solve for the equilibrium policies given that the equilibrium is symmetric, that is $\tau_0 = 1 - \tau_1$. Discuss how the equilibrium policies depend on the level of uncertainty as described by a.

c. Show that the equilibrium must be of the form $\tau_0 = 1 - \tau_1$.

Answer

a. Let p_0 be the probability that party 0 wins the election. Party 0 maximizes

$$\max_{\tau_0} -p_o\tau_0^2 - (1 - p_o)\,\tau_1^2.$$

The first order condition to this problem is

$$-\frac{dp_o}{d\tau_0}\left(\tau_0^2 - \tau_1^2\right) - 2p_o\tau_0 = 0.$$

By raising the tax level above its most preferred level 0, party 0 increases the probability that it will win the election and implements its platform. On the other hand by raising its proposed tax level, party 0 gets to implement a less preferred policy if it wins the election. If the parties had converged completely, then there would be no incentive for the party to increase its probability of winning the election but the incentive to move closer to its ideal point would still be present. Therefore, total convergence can not be an equilibrium. If the parties choose their most preferred points, then they would have no incentives to move closer to their ideal points, while they would have an incentive to increase their probability of winning the election. Therefore this could not be an equilibrium.

b. The probability that party 0 will win the election is

$$p_0 = \Pr\left(\tau_m < \frac{\tau_0 + \tau_1}{2}\right) = \frac{1}{2a}\left(\frac{\tau_0 + \tau_1}{2} - 1/2 + a\right) = \frac{1}{2} + \frac{\tau_0 - (1 - \tau_1)}{4a}$$

for

$$\frac{1}{2} - a < \frac{\tau_0 + \tau_1}{2} < \frac{1}{2} + a.$$

Inserting the expression for p_0 in the first order condition of party 0 yields

$$\tau_0 = \frac{1}{2 + 4a},$$

and similarly for party 1

$$\tau_1 = 1 - \frac{1}{2 + 4a}.$$

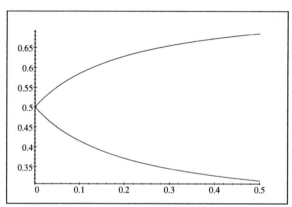

Tax platforms and uncertainty

As uncertainty grows, the competition to win the election becomes less sharp and the parties move away from the expected median voter position and closer to their own ideal points.

c. Party 1 solves

$$\max_{\tau_1} -p_o \left(\tau_0 - 1\right)^2 - \left(1 - p_o\right)\left(\tau_1 - 1\right)^2$$

The first order condition to this problem is

$$-\frac{dp_o}{d\tau_1}\left(\left(\tau_0 - 1\right)^2 - \left(\tau_1 - 1\right)^2\right) - 2\left(1 - p_o\right)\left(\tau_1 - 1\right).$$

Let $x = \tau_0$ and $y = 1 - \tau_1$. The first order conditions for party 0 is then

$$-\frac{1}{4a}\left(x^2 - \left(1 - y\right)^2\right) - 2\left(\frac{1}{2} + \frac{x - y}{4a}\right)x = 0.$$

This equation implicitly defines x as a function of y. Call this function $x = f(y)$. The first order condition for party 1 is

$$-\frac{1}{4a}\left(y^2 - \left(1 - x\right)^2\right) - 2\left(\frac{1}{2} + \frac{y - x}{4a}\right)y = 0.$$

This equation has the same form as that above and therefore implicitly defines y as the same function $y = f(x)$. Therefore $x = f(f(x))$ or $f^{-1}(x) = f(x)$. The only function f which is equal to its inverse is the identity function, $f(x) = x$. Therefore $x = y$.

5.2 The citizen-candidate model

Consider a society inhabited by a continuum of citizens with incomes distributed uniformly between 0 and 2. Each citizen i has preferences over private consumption c and a publicly provided private good g that are given by

$$w^i = \sqrt{c^i} + \sqrt{g}.$$

The public good g is financed through a proportional income tax τ, and the government budget constraint is $\tau y = g$ where y is average income. Private consumption is $c^i = (1 - \tau)y^i$.

Consider the following timing: (1) Any citizen may enter as a political candidate at a cost ε. (2) An election is held among the candidates; the candidate who gets plurality wins the election, and a tie is resolved by the toss of a coin. (3) The winning candidate selects a tax rate; if there are no candidates, then a default tax rate $\bar{\tau}$ is implemented.

a. What policy would a winning candidate with income y^i implement?

b. Suppose that $\varepsilon = \sqrt{2} - \sqrt{\frac{3}{4}} - \sqrt{\frac{1}{4}}$. In what region must the status quo policy, $\bar{\tau}$, lie in order for the equilibrium with only the citizen with median income as candidate to exist. Do there exist other one-candidate equilibria?

c. Characterize the two-candidate equilibria.

d. Describe what would happen in a two-candidate equilibrium if the median candidate would enter. How would the set of possible equilibria change if voters voted sincerely, that is voted for the candidate that gave them highest utility.

Answer

a. The most preferred tax rate of candidate with income y^i is the solution to

$$\max_\tau \sqrt{(1 - \tau)y^i} + \sqrt{\tau y}.$$

This is solved by

$$\tau^i = \frac{y}{y^i + y},$$

which is the policies that a candidate with income y^i would implement.

b. The median and mean incomes both equal 1, and the most preferred tax rate of the median income citizen is thus $1/2$. For the citizen with median income to stand candidate, it must be the case that $w^m(\tau^m) - w^m(\bar{\tau}) \geqslant \varepsilon$, or equivalently

$$\sqrt{\frac{1}{2}} + \sqrt{\frac{1}{2}} - \left(\sqrt{(1 - \bar{\tau})} + \sqrt{\bar{\tau}}\right) \geqslant \sqrt{2} - \sqrt{\frac{3}{4}} - \sqrt{\frac{1}{4}}.$$

This holds for $\bar{\tau} \leq 0.25$ and $\bar{\tau} \geq 0.75$.

Yes, there exist other one-candidate equilibria. Suppose another candidate runs. If the candidate is sufficiently close to the median, then all of the other candidates that would beat him are so close to his own position that they do not find it worthwhile to run.

c. To run for office, both candidates must have some chance of winning the election. Thus the median voter must be indifferent between the two, that is $\tau^1 = (1 - \tau^2)$. Both candidates must also prefer to stay in the race rather than to drop out and let the other candidate win, thus $w^1(\tau^1) - w^1(\tau^2) \geqslant \varepsilon$ and $w^2(\tau^2) - w^2(\tau^1) \geqslant \varepsilon$. In terms of incomes this implies $y^1 = \frac{1 - \tau^1}{\tau^1}$, $y^2 = \frac{\tau^1}{1 - \tau^1} = \frac{1}{y^1}$. We know that $\tau^1 = \frac{1}{1 + y^1}$, and $\tau^2 = (1 - \tau^1) = \frac{y^1}{1 + y^1}$. Inserting these tax rates into the utility function of citizen 1 yields:

$$\sqrt{\left(1 - \frac{1}{1 + y^1}\right)y^1} + \sqrt{\frac{1}{1 + y^1}} - \sqrt{\left(1 - \frac{y^1}{1 + y^1}\right)y^1} - \sqrt{\frac{y^1}{1 + y^1}} = \varepsilon$$

The solution is found numerically : $y^1 = 1.64$, $y^2 = 0.61$. All pairs (y^1, y^2) such that $y^2 = \frac{1}{y^1}$ in the interval $y^1 \in (1.64, 2)$, $y^2 \in (0.5, 0.61)$, are equilibria.

d. If the median candidate enters the race, then although many voters would prefer the median voter, they would still vote for their preferred candidate among 1 and 2. The reason is that if they changed their vote in favor of the median voter, then they would cause their least preferred candidate to win.

If voters were sincere, then the most polarized platform pairs would no longer be equilibria. The reason is that with extreme platforms, a third candidate could enter in the middle and win the election.

5.3 Lobbying in a representative democracy

This problem is based on Besley and Coate 1997 and 1999. Consider a model with N citizens $i \in \{1, ..., N\}$. They derive a utility from consuming a private and a public good. Each citizen is endowed with $y^i = 1$ unit of private good. The public good can be produced at any level g. One unit of private good is required to produce one unit of public good. Let c^i be the quantity of private good consumed by agent i, his utility being

$$w^i = c^i + \theta^i \ln(g),$$

where θ^i represents the preference of agent i for the public good. Assume that $\theta^i \in \{\theta^1, ..., \theta^T\}$ where $\theta^{k+1} = \theta^k + 1$ for all $k \in \{1, ..., T-1\}$. Let η^k be the number of citizens with type θ^k. Naturally, $\sum_{k=1}^{T} \eta^k = N$. There exists a median type denoted by θ^m. The timing of the game is as follows. First, each citizen decides whether to become candidate and pays a cost δ if he does. Second, the voting stage takes place and at most one candidate is elected. Denote the elected candidate by e. Assume that citizens vote sincerely and abstain when indifferent. Moreover, when n candidates receive the same vote share, each is elected with probability $\frac{1}{n}$. If nobody is elected, the game ends. Last, there exists a single lobby of type $\theta^l > \theta^m$ composed by $n^l \leq \eta^l$ citizens. The lobby maximizes the sum of its members' utilities of its members and chooses a contribution to e of $B_{le}(g) \geq 0$ to e. Then e chooses the amount of public good to produce, financed through a per-citizen tax $t = \frac{g}{N}$.

a. Determine the policy preferences of citizens as well as the optimal provision of public good for each agent of type θ^i, denoted by $\hat{g}(\theta^i)$.

b. Consider the last stage of the game. Characterize the lobby's optimization problem. Determine the provision of the public good $g^*(\theta^e, \theta^l)$ as well as the lobby's contribution, when the elected citizen is of type $\theta^e \neq \theta^l$ and $\theta^e = \theta^l$. Compare $g^*(\theta^e, \theta^l)$ with $\hat{g}(\theta^e)$. What is the utility of citizen e and what are the utilities of all citizens $j \neq e$. Discuss.

c. Show that an ordinary citizen is indifferent between electing a member of the lobby and electing a citizen of the same type as the lobby members. Demonstrate that for each citizen j, there exists a unique type $\theta^*(\theta^j)$ that he prefers as candidate. Verify that both ordinary citizens and lobby group members have single peaked preferences over candidates.

d. Consider an equilibrium with identical candidates. Demonstrate that if δ (the cost of candidacy) is sufficiently small, $\theta^*(\theta^m)$ has an interest in becoming a candidate against any other candidates of types θ^l and $\theta^k \neq \{\theta^l, \theta^*(\theta^m)\}$. What is the maximum number $s^{\max}$ of candidates of type $\theta^*(\theta^m)$? Show that when $\delta \in (0, \frac{B_{l\theta^*(\theta^m)}}{2})$, then $s^{\max} > 0$ and the equilibrium exists.

e. Consider a vote over q versus r with $\theta^q < \theta^r < \theta^l$. Moreover, suppose that the median group divides the electorate exactly into two (i.e. $\sum_{k=1}^{m-1} \eta^k = \sum_{k=m+1}^{T} \eta^k$) and that citizens in the median group are indifferent between $g^*(\theta^q, \theta^l)$ and $g^*(\theta^r, \theta^l)$. Assume that $g^*(\theta^q, \theta^l) \neq \hat{g}(\theta^r)$. Show that the number of citizens preferring r to q is equal to the number of citizens preferring q to r. Demonstrate that any entrant s will lose the election if $\eta^m < \frac{N}{3} - 1$. Last, prove that both r and q have an interest in becoming candidates when δ is sufficiently small.

Answer

a. Consumption is $c^i = 1 - \frac{g}{N}$, and therefore the policy preferences of agent i are:

$$W(g, \theta^i) = 1 - \frac{g}{N} + \theta^i V(g)$$

The optimal provision of public good for an agent with type θ^i is then $\hat{g}(\theta^i) = V_g^{-1}(\frac{1}{N\theta^i}) = N\theta^i$. Note that it is increasing in θ^i.

b. Suppose first that the elected citizen does not belong to the lobby, i.e. $\theta^e \neq \theta^i$. The lobby chooses B_{le} and the corresponding provision of public good that solves the following program:

$$\max_{B_{le}, g} \quad n_l W(g, \theta^l) - B_{le}$$

$$\text{s.t.} \quad W(g, \theta^e) + B_{le} \geq \max_x \ W(x, \theta^e) = W(\hat{g}(\theta^e), \theta^e)$$

where the constraint reflects the fact that the elected citizen must be better off when offered a contribution. Naturally, this constraint is binding in equilibrium: the contribution from the lobby is just sufficient to bring e to the utility level that he would obtain without lobbying. Therefore, the provision of public good as well as the contribution are defined by:

$$g^*(\theta^e, \theta^l) = \operatorname{argmax}_g \ n_l W(g, \theta^l) - W(\hat{g}(\theta^e), \theta^e) + W(g, \theta^e)$$

$$B_{le}^* = W(\hat{g}(\theta^e), \theta^e) - W(g^*(\theta^e, \theta^l), \theta^e) \geq 0$$

In terms of our model, the provision of public good is simply:

$$g^*(\theta^e, \theta^l) = (n_l \theta^l + \theta^e) \frac{N}{1 + n_l}$$

which is increasing in both θ^e and θ^l. Note that if $\theta^l < \theta^e$, then $\hat{g}(\theta^e) < g^*(\theta^e, \theta^l) < \hat{g}(\theta^l)$, and if $\theta^l > \theta^e$, then $\hat{g}(\theta^e) > g^*(\theta^e, \theta^l) > \hat{g}(\theta^l)$. This is due to the fact that the lobby maximizes the combined surplus of the lobby members and the policy-maker. The lobby group extracts all the surplus from dealings between itself and the policymaker. Indeed, the policymaker's utility is $W(\hat{g}(\theta^e), \theta^e)$ in equilibrium. But the incumbent e earns a rent compared to ordinary citizens since his utility remains the same as if he had implemented its preferred policy. Indeed, for all $j \neq e$, $W(g^*(\theta^e, \theta^l), \theta^j) < W(\hat{g}(\theta^j), \theta^j)$. Suppose now that the elected citizen is of type θ^l, then $B_{ll} = 0$ and $g^*(\theta^l, \theta^l) = \hat{g}(\theta^l)$.

c. For an ordinary citizen with type θ^j, the payoff from having e elected is $W(g^*(\theta^e, \theta^l), \theta^j)$. Then, ordinary citizens are indifferent between a policymaker of type θ^l who does not belong to the lobby and a policymaker who is member of the lobby. From the perspective of a citizen with type θ^j, the optimal policymaker is:

$$\theta^*(\theta^j) = \text{argmax}_{\theta^e} \quad W(g^*(\theta^e, \theta^l), \theta^j)$$

Therefore, we have:

$$\theta^*(\theta^j) = \theta^j(1 + n_l) - n_l \theta^l$$

Naturally, $g^*(\theta^*(\theta^j), \theta^l) = \hat{g}(\theta^j)$. Note that $\theta^*(\theta^j)$ is unique for all θ^j. Moreover, if $\theta^j < \theta^l$ (respectively, $\theta^j > \theta^l$), then $\theta^*(\theta^j) < \theta^j$ (respectively, $\theta^*(\theta^j) > \theta^j$). Besides, $\theta^*(\theta^1) < .. < \theta^*(\theta^T)$.

Consider two candidates with types $\theta^q < \theta^r$. If $\theta^r < \theta^*(\theta^j)$, then j votes for r. Similarly, if $\theta^q > \theta^*(\theta^j)$, then j votes for q. Moreover, if $\theta^r < \theta^l$, the lobby prefers r, and it prefers q if $\theta^q > \theta^l$. Therefore, both ordinary citizens and lobby group members have single peaked preferences over candidates.

d. Consider an equilibrium with identical candidates. There are two cases: (i) candidates have type θ^l or (ii) candidates do not belong to the lobby.

(i) Suppose first that citizens with type θ^l have entered. If another candidate with type $\theta^*(\theta^m)$ enters, he will be elected for sure, as he is preferred by the median voter (single peakedness property). Indeed, for all $\theta^j \in \{\theta^1, ..., \theta^{m-1}\}$, $\theta^*(\theta^j) < \theta^*(\theta^m) < \theta^l$. In this case, he gets:

$$W(g^*(\theta^*(\theta^m), \theta^l), \theta^*(\theta^m)) + B_{l\theta^*(\theta^m)} - \delta = W(\hat{g}(\theta^*(\theta^m)), \theta^*(\theta^m)) - \delta$$

Instead, if he does not run against the first candidates, his utility is:

$$W(g^*(\theta^l, \theta^l), \theta^*(\theta^m))$$

Therefore, for δ sufficiently small, citizens with type $\theta^*(\theta^m)$ always run against θ^l. Anticipating this, θ^l does not enter in the first place.

(ii) Suppose now that citizens with type $\theta^k \neq \{\theta^l, \theta^*(\theta^m)\}$ have entered. If a citizen of type $\theta^*(\theta^m)$ does not enter, his utility is:

$$W(g^*(\theta^k, \theta^l), \theta^*(\theta^m))$$

If he enters, then he gets:

$$W(\hat{g}(\theta^*(\theta^m)), \theta^*(\theta^m)) - \delta$$

and again, if δ is sufficiently small, citizens with type $\theta^*(\theta^m)$ run against θ^k. Anticipating this, θ^k does not enter in the first place.

Let s be the number of candidates with type $\theta^*(\theta^m)$. Consider another citizen with the same type but who has not entered. His utility is:

$$W(g^*(\theta^*(\theta^m), \theta^l), \theta^*(\theta^m))$$

If he enters, all agents with type $\theta^j \neq \theta^*(\theta^m)$ are indifferent between the two candidates and abstain. Each candidate votes for himself and therefore wins with probability $\frac{1}{s+1}$, in which case he receives $B_{l\theta^*(\theta^m)}$. The expected payoff when entering is then:

$$W(g^*(\theta^*(\theta^m), \theta^l), \theta^*(\theta^m)) + \frac{B_{l\theta^*(\theta^m)}}{s+1} - \delta$$

Therefore, as long as $s + 1 < \frac{B_{l\theta^*(\theta^m)}}{\delta}$, new citizens enter. In addition, the equilibrium number of candidates is smaller than $s^{\max} = \frac{B_{l\theta^*(\theta^m)}}{\delta}$. Moreover, for $\delta \in (0, \frac{B_{l\theta^*(\theta^m)}}{2})$, then $s^{\max} > 2$. To conclude an equilibrium with identical candidates with type $\theta^*(\theta^m)$ exists.

e. All citizens in the median group are indifferent between θ^r and θ^q and they abstain. Let:

$$H(\theta^j) = W(g^*(\theta^q, \theta^l), \theta^j) - W(g^*(\theta^r, \theta^q), \theta^j)$$

We have $H_{\theta^j} = \ln g^*(\theta^q, \theta^l) - \ln g^*(\theta^r, \theta^l) < 0$. Moreover, $H(\theta^m) = 0$ and therefore, for all $\theta^j < \theta^{m-1}$ (respectively, $\theta^j > \theta^{m+1}$), j votes for q (respectively, r). Since $\sum_{k=1}^{m-1} \eta^k = \sum_{m+1}^{T} \eta^k = a$, the number of citizens preferring r to q is equal to the number of citizens preferring q to r. Let $\eta^m = b$, in which case $2a + b = N$.

Suppose that a third candidate with type $\theta^s < \theta^q$ enters. Citizens with median type are still indifferent between θ^q and θ^r but do not want θ^s to be elected. Moreover, all $\theta^j > \theta^{m+1}$ vote for r, and there exist citizens with types $\theta^j \leq \theta^{m-1}$ who prefer s. If those citizens vote for θ^s and if their candidate is likely to be elected, then median type voters are not indifferent anymore, and vote for r. Therefore, r collects $b + a$ votes and is elected. The same reasoning applies when $\theta^s > \theta^r$.

Suppose now that $\theta^q < \theta^s < \theta^r$. Then, median type voters prefer s. Consider $\theta^j \neq \theta^m$ who prefers s to q and votes for s. In this case, q collects $a - 1$ votes, r gets a votes and s receives $b + 1$ votes. If $b + 1 > a$, s wins. If $b + 1 < a$ then r wins but, anticipating this, j prefers voting for q. Therefore, s is not elected. In other words, if $b + 1 < a$, all agents continue to vote for q and r as before, and the new entrant, s, cannot win. Combining the conditions $2a + b = N$ and $b + 1 < a$, we find that an equilibrium with two different candidates may exist if $b < \frac{N}{3} - 1$.

Last, to run against each other, the payoffs of r and q must satisfy the following two constraints:

$$\frac{1}{2}W(\hat{g}(\theta^q), \theta^q) - \delta > \frac{1}{2}W(g^*(\theta^r, \theta^l), \theta^q)$$

$$\frac{1}{2}W(\hat{g}(\theta^r), \theta^r) - \delta > \frac{1}{2}W(g^*(\theta^q, \theta^l), \theta^r)$$

This is satisfied if and only if $g^*(\theta^q, \theta^l) \neq \theta^r$, and for δ sufficiently small.

5.4   Equilibria when the single-crossing condition is violated

The problem is based on Besley and Coate (1997). Each citizen i has preferences over private consumption c and a publicly provided private good g that are given by $c + H(g)$. Assume that the individuals have themselves provided the service g to a certain level g_i and that the utility from the government-provided good is described by $H(g) = \frac{3}{2}\sqrt{g - g_i}$ for $g \geq g_i$ and 0 otherwise. There are five groups with $g_i = \{0, 0.4, 0.5, 0.7, 1\}$, and these groups have sizes $\{35, 10, 20, 20, 10\}$ respectively. The public good g is financed through a proportional income tax τ, and the government budget constraint is $\tau y = g$ where y is average income. Private consumption is $c^i = (1 - \tau)y^i$. All groups have the same income of 1.

Consider the following timing: (1) Any citizen may enter as a political candidate at a cost $\varepsilon = 1$. (2) An election is held among the candidates; a candidate that gets plurality wins the election, and a tie is resolved by the toss of a coin. (3) The winning candidate selects a tax rate; if there are no candidates, then a default tax rate $\overline{\tau}$ is implemented.

a. Show that this utility function does not satisfy the Gans-Smart condition.

b. What policy would a winning candidate from each group advocate, and how would members of the different groups rank the policies put forward by the candidates.

c. What would be the equilibrium outcomes in pairwise elections between the bliss points.

d. Show that there exists a three-candidate equilibrium in which three citizens, with $g_i = 1$, $g_j = 0.4$, and $g_k = 0$, are candidates. Discuss the reasons why the different candidates stay in the race and why the policy that would loose in a pairwise election against either of the other alternatives nevertheless wins the three-candidate election.

Answer

a. Let the policy variable τ correspond to the policy variable q and the preference variable g_i correspond to the preference variable α^i in equation 2.4. Now $\tau = 1 > \tau' = 0$ and $g_i' = 0.4, 0.5, 0.7, 1 > g_i = 0$. This implies that if $w(1; 0) \geq w(0; 0)$, which is true, then $w(1; g_i') \geq w(0; g_i')$ for all the above values of g_i'. However, the latter is not true for $g_i' = 0.7, 1$. Therefore the Gans-Smart condition is violated.

b. Study the following figure of the utility of each group as a function of the tax level

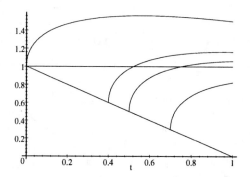

The tax levels most preferred by the groups are $\{0.56, 1, 1, 0, 0\}$. Name the different levels of the public good – 0, 0.56, 1 – 0, g_l and g_h respectively. The ranking of the different possible policy choices are:

group	1	2	3	size
0	g_l	g_h	0	35
0.4	g_h	g_l	0	10
0.5	g_h	0	g_l	20
0.7	0	g_h	g_l	20
1	0	g_l	g_h	10

The last group has access to a private substitute and never uses the publicly provided good. Therefore the members of this groups wants as little expenditure of the good as possible. The members in the groups 2-4 only use the public good if sufficient resources are spent on this service. Therefore, these groups prefer high spending to low spending, if there is to be any spending. They do, however, differ in the way they rank the alternative with no spending at all on the good. The ranking of this alternative is higher the later the group members start using the public good. The first group uses the public good from the start. However, at expenditure above g_l, the members would rather use additional money on private consumption than on more spending on this service.

c. $g_h \succ g_l$ since groups 2-4 prefers g_h, $g_h \succ 0$ since groups 1-3 prefers g_h, $0 \succ g_l$ since groups 3-5 prefers 0. In a pairwise election the policy g_l would loose against both other alternatives.

d. There exists an equilibrium in which groups 1, 2, and 5 each have one candidate. In this equilibrium, the members of group 1, 2, and 5 vote for their respective candidates. The members of group 3 votes for candidate 2 and the members of group 4 vote for candidate 5. Candidate 1 wins the election and policy g_l is implemented.

Although candidates 2 and 5 cannot win the race, they both have incentives to stay in the race so that their least preferred candidate does not win the election. Candidate 2 runs because if he dropped out of the race, then policy 0 would win. This possibility he dislikes more than policy g_l. Candidate 5 runs because if he dropped out then policy g_h would win. This possibility he dislikes more than policy g_l.

5.5   The agenda-setting model

A committee has to propose a level of spending, g, of a government-provided good. If the proposition passes a vote in the legislature, g will be the policy enacted, otherwise a status quo policy $\bar{g}$ will be implemented. The preferences for the spending are described by $w(g; \alpha^i) = -\left|g - \alpha^i\right|$. The preference parameter are α^c and α^m for the members of the committee and the median voter in the legislature respectively, where $\alpha^m < \alpha^c$.

a. Plot how the proposed policy g changes with the position of the status quo policy $\bar{g}$.

b. Assume that if the proposed policy g does not gain a majority in the legislature, then the leader of the majority party, with preference parameter $\alpha^l < \alpha^m$, will make a new proposal. If this amended proposal does not gain a majority, then the status quo policy $\bar{g}$ will be implemented. Plot how the equilibrium policy will depend on the status quo policy.

c.   Often, the status quo policy is determined endogenously. A typical status quo policy for the budget of the subsequent year is the budget of the current year. Consider again the setup in question (a) in which the status quo policy is implemented if the policy proposed by the committee fails to gather a majority in the legislature. Suppose that the present budget is \$1 million. Suppose further that the legislature becomes more favorable to spending on this issue as time passes, perhaps because of an increasing tax base. The legislature serves for four years, and the preference parameter of the median voter in the legislature is \$2 million, \$3 million, \$3.5 million, \$4 million in each of the four years, respectively. Assume that the voters in the legislature are myopic: they treat each vote as a one-shot game. Neither the members of the committee nor the legislature discounts the future. Can the committee do better by not maximizing the budget each year separately. What is the best strategy for the committee over the four years?

d. Now assume that the voters are not myopic, and for simplicity limit the game to the first two years. Do the committee members gain or loose when voters are myopic?

Answer

a. If the median voter in the legislature prefers the committee members' most preferred point to the status quo, then the committee proposes its most preferred policy α^c which is enacted. If the status quo policy lies between α^c and α^m then there is direct disagreement between the committee and the median voter in the legislature in which way policy should move and the committee have no choice but to propose the status quo policy. If the median voter in the legislature prefers the status quo policy to the committees most preferred point, but the status quo is smaller than α^m, then the best the committee can do is to propose a policy which is equally disliked by the legislature, but which is higher than α^m.

b. First, solve the last period game where the majority party leader has the proposal power. The result is the line labelled b' in the figure underneath. Then, solve the first stage of the game where the solution to the second stage acts in the same way as the status quo. The policy proposed by the committee is thus as described by the line labelled (b).

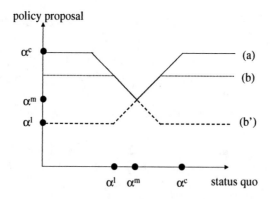

c. A committee which maximizes the budget for each year separately would propose, 3, 3, 4, and 4 million dollars for the four years respectively. This would amount to a total budget of 14 million dollars over the four years. A better strategy, indeed the best, is to propose no increase in the first year. This makes the status quo very unattractive, and in the next year an increase in the budget to 5 million dollars will pass against the status quo. This budget can be increased no further and is kept through years 2-4, amounting to a total budget of 16 million dollars for the four year period. The possibility to manipulate the status quo thus increases the power of the agenda setter.

d. If the voters are myopic, then the committee can either propose a budget of 1+5 million dollars, or 3+3 million dollars both yielding 6 million dollars. However, if voters are not myopic, then the committee can propose a budget of 4 million dollars in the first period. The median voter in the legislature realizes that if the status quo wins then the budget will be 1+5 million dollars over the two years and he will suffer a loss of 6 utils. If he accepts the 4 million dollar budget, then the budget will be 4+4 million dollars over the two years and he will suffer a loss of 6 utils. Therefore the 4+4 million dollar budget passes and the committee gets 8 million dollars worth of spending. The improved position of the committee depends on the fact that they can threaten the legislature with the loss during the whole supergame instead of small losses in each period.

5.6   Rents with endogenous value of being in office

This question is inspired by Baron and Ferejohn (1989). Consider a legislature with n members that have to divide rents of size r among themselves. The members are the consumption value of the rents $w^i(r) = r$. A member of the legislative body has propose an allocation of r, and the legislature votes on the proposition. If the proposition is not passed, then a new member is given the right to propose an allocation of r. The discount rate is $\beta \in [0, 1]$. This member is chosen randomly, and the chance of any one member to make the proposal is $\frac{1}{n}$. This proposal is voted on, and if it does not pass then all rents are dissipated.

a. What allocation will the first proposition imply? Discuss the proposed allocation: is it even or uneven, how does the advantage of the member making the first proposition related to the size of the legislature, will all propositions receive support in the legislature?

b. Now suppose that the stage game in which a member is chosen randomly to make a new proposal is instead repeated infinitely many times. Restrict attention to equilibria in which the continuation values for each structurally identical subgame are the same. In these equilibria, the proposed division of r will be the same at any stage of the game. Show that the allocation proposed in (a) is an equilibrium in the infinitely repeated game.

Answer

a. In the last stage of the game, the member will propose to give all of r to himself. This will be accepted by the other members since they will get no rents whether the proposition wins or looses. Therefore the continuation value of the game at stage 1 is $\frac{\delta}{n}$. The member selected to divide that budget in the first period will therefore choose to give $\frac{\delta}{n}$ to a minimal winning coalition of $\frac{n-1}{2}$ members of the legislature, and keep $1 - \frac{\delta}{n}\left(\frac{n-1}{2}\right)$ to himself.

The resulting allocation of rents in the legislature is very uneven as a result of the proposer seeking a minimum winning coalition. Making the first proposition is beneficial, the agenda setter always receives at least half the rents. The other members in expectation receive $\frac{\delta}{2n}$, therefore the difference between the agenda setters and the other members rents is $1 - \frac{1}{2}\delta$. This implies that as the number of members in the legislature grows, both the agenda setter and the other members receive less rents. All propositions receive a majority in the legislature.

b. In the infinite horizon game, the proposing member need to give at least the continuation value to a minimum winning coalition. Let the continuation value of the game of member i be v^i. Any member will support a proposed allocation giving him at least δv^i. The continuation values are

$$v^i = \frac{1}{n}\left[1 - \frac{n-1}{2}\delta v^i\right] + \left(\frac{n-1}{2n}\right)\delta v^i.$$

With probability $\frac{1}{n}$ the member gets to propose an allocation in the next stage and receives rents $1 - \frac{n-1}{2}\delta v^i$. With probability $\frac{n-1}{n}$ the member does not get to propose, in which case with probability $\frac{1}{2}$ he is part of the winning coalition and receives δv^i. This simplifies to $v^i = \frac{\delta}{n}$.

Part II

Redistributive politics

Chapter 6

General-interest politics

6.1 The Meltzer-Richard model

Consider an economy in which a proportional tax on labor income is used to finance lump sum transfers to the citizens. The preferences over consumption, c, and leisure, x, of individual i are described by

$$w^i = c^i - a\left(b - x^i\right)^2.$$

The private budget constraint is $c^i = (1 - \tau)l^i + f$, and the government budget constraint is $f = \tau l$. The individual is also subject to a time constraint $1 + e^i = l^i + x^i$. The individual productivity parameters e^i are distributed with density function linearly decreasing from 2 at $e^i = 0$ to 0 at $e^i = 1$.

a. Compute each individual's labor supply as well as the total labor supply, given the tax rate. Compute the equilibrium tax level.

b. Assume that only citizens with incomes above 0.05 are allowed to vote, this excludes approximately 10% of the lowest-income earners from the electorate. Compute the new equilibrium tax rate.

c. Now suppose that 10% of the citizens of each income level were to retire and thus be moved to productivity $e^i = 0$. Compute the new equilibrium tax rate.

Answer

a. Individuals choose work hours, l, to maximize

$$w^i = (1 - \tau)l^i + f - a\left(b - 1 - e^i + l^i\right)^2.$$

The first order condition is

$$(1 - \tau) = 2a\left(b - 1 - e^i + l^i\right)$$

57

$$l^i(\tau) = 1 + e^i - b + \frac{(1-\tau)}{2a}$$

$$L(\tau) = 1 + e - b + \frac{(1-\tau)}{2a}.$$

The most preferred tax rate is

$$\tau = \frac{e^m - e}{L'(\tau)} = 2a(e - e^m).$$

The mean productivity is

$$e = \int_0^1 2(1-x)x\,dx = \frac{1}{3}.$$

The median productivity e^m is defined by

$$\int_0^{e^m} 2(1-x)\,dx = \frac{1}{2}$$

$$x = 1 - \frac{1}{\sqrt{2}} = .29289.$$

The equilibrium tax is thus

$$\tau^m = \left(\frac{1}{\sqrt{2}} - \frac{2}{3}\right)2a.$$

$a = 0.3$ implies that a tax of $\tau = 2.4$ percent finances redistributive spending.

b. If only people with productivity above 0.05 are allowed to vote. Then the size of the electorate decreases to 0.9025, and the median income in the electorate increases to

$$\int_{0.05}^{e^m} 2(1-x)\,dx = \frac{.9025}{2}$$

which holds for $e^m = .32825$. The new equilibrium tax is

$$\tau^m = \left(\frac{1}{3} - 0.32825\right)2a = 0.3 \text{ percent}.$$

c. In this case, the median productivity level is defined by

$$0.1 + 0.9\int_0^{e^m} 2(1-x)\,dx = \frac{1}{2}$$

which holds for $e^m = .25464$. The new equilibrium tax is

$$\tau^m = \left(\frac{1}{3} - 0.25464\right)2a = 4.7 \text{ percent}.$$

6.2 Pensions

Consider the model of subsection 6.2. There are three generations: young, middle-aged, and old. The population grows at rate n. The government runs a pension scheme with lump sum transfers f to the old generation financed through a proportional tax, τ, on labor. The government budget constraint is

$$f = \tau l^{iY} (1+n)^2 + \tau l^{iM} (1+n).$$

The subjective discount rate β equals the real interest rate ρ, and all individuals may save assets at the real interest rate. A young individual i's lifetime utility from the pension scheme is

$$w^{iY} = U\left(c^{iY}\right) + \frac{1}{1+\beta} U\left(c^{iM}\right) + \frac{1}{(1+\beta)^2} c^{iO} + V\left(x^{iY}\right) + \frac{1}{1+\beta} V\left(x^{iM}\right),$$

and a young individual's intertemporal budget constraint is

$$c^{iY} + \frac{c^{iM}}{1+\beta} + \frac{c^{iO}}{(1+\beta)^2} = l^{iY}(1-\tau) + \frac{l^{iM}(1-\tau)}{1+\beta} + \frac{f}{(1+\beta)^2}.$$

When individuals work, they are subject to a time constraint $1 + e^i = l^i + x^i$.

a. Solve for the individual's optimal consumption path and labor supply.

b. What is the total present value of the pension scheme to a young person of productivity e^i? What is the pension scheme's net value to a young person of average productivity. How much larger is the net present value of an individual of productivity $e^m < e$ relative to that of an individual of average productivity? Describe how these two values relate to redistribution between and within generations. Write down the equation describing the tax rate preferred by a young individual with productivity e^i and relate the terms in this expression to the above discussion.

c. Suppose that productivity is higher for middle-aged individuals than for young individuals. In particular, a young individual with productivity e^{iY} will achieve productivity

$$e^{iM} = e^{iY} + \frac{(1+n)(2+n)}{2+\beta}\left[L\left(\tau^i\right) + \tau L\left(\tau^i\right)\right]$$

when middle aged (τ^i is the tax rate preferred by the individual with productivity e^{iY}). Therefore the share of young voters with productivity lower than e^{iY} equals the share of young voters with productivity lower than

$$e^{iY} + \frac{(1+n)(2+n)}{2+\beta}\left[L\left(\tau\right) + \tau L\left(\tau\right)\right].$$

The distribution of productivities is $F(e^{iY})$ for the young.

Show how the share of young and middle-aged voters who support higher taxes in equilibrium depends on n. Discuss how large share of the young and middle-aged voters will support higher taxes in equilibrium when $n = 0$ and when n becomes very large.

d. Suppose that voting rights are extended to a generation of very young who have no labor income and receive no pension transfers. These individuals will be young in the next period and know what their productivity parameters will be. Find the tax rate that an individual with productivity e^{iY} in this group would prefer. Describe how the productivity of the new median voter will differ from the productivity of the median voter before the extension of voting rights. Discuss the equilibrium tax rate.

e. Suppose that voting rights are curtailed to exclude people with very low incomes. The people excluded from the franchise exist in equal proportion among the young, middle-aged, and old. Describe how the equilibrium tax rate would change. Discuss the relation to within- and between-generation redistribution.

Answer

a. The first order condition to the consumption decision is

$$U'\left(c^{iY}\right) = \left[\frac{1+\rho}{1+\delta}\right]^2,$$

$$U'\left(c^{iM}\right) = \frac{1+\rho}{1+\delta}.$$

Given the condition $\delta = \rho$, this implies that $U'\left(c^{iY}\right) = U'\left(c^{iM}\right) = 1$. The first order condition to the labor choice is

$$U'\left(c^{iY}\right)(1-\tau) - V'\left(1+e^i - l^{iY}\right) = 0$$

$$U'\left(c^{iM}\right)(1-\tau) - V'\left(1+e^i - l^{iM}\right) = 0,$$

and thus $l^{iY} = l^{iM} = 1 + e^i - V'^{-1}(1-\tau) = L(\tau) - e + e^i$.

b. The present value of the individuals pension payments is

$$l^{iY}\tau + \frac{l^{iM}\tau}{1+\delta},$$

whereas the present value of the benefit is

$$\frac{l^M\tau(1+n) + l^Y\tau(1+n)^2}{(1+\delta)^2}.$$

Since $l^i = L(\tau) + e^i - e,$ the present value of the net benefits are

$$L(\tau)\tau\left[\frac{(1+n)(2+n) - (1+\delta)(2+\delta)}{(1+\delta)^2}\right] + (e - e^i)\tau\frac{2+\delta}{1+\delta}.$$

Of this present value,

$$L\left(\tau\right)\tau\left[\frac{\left(1+n\right)\left(2+n\right)-\left(1+\delta\right)\left(2+\delta\right)}{\left(1+\delta\right)^{2}}\right]$$

is what a generation on average gains from having the younger generations pay its pension. This is positive if n is larger than δ, in this case the larger payments from the more numerous younger generations is worth the interest forgone by making payments when young and middle aged into the pension system. The second term, $\left(e-e^{i}\right)\tau\frac{2+\delta}{1+\delta}$, describes the redistribution towards people with low productivity within the generation.

The first order condition determining the optimal tax for a young individual is

$$L\left(\tau\right)\tau\left[\frac{\left(1+n\right)\left(2+n\right)-\left(1+\delta\right)\left(2+\delta\right)}{\left(1+\delta\right)^{2}}\right]$$

$$+\left(e-e^{i}\right)\tau\frac{2+\delta}{1+\delta}+\frac{\left(1+n\right)\left(2+n\right)}{\left(1+\delta\right)^{2}}\tau L'\left(\tau\right)=0.$$

The individual balances his gains due to increased redistribution between generations, the first term, and increased redistribution within generations, to the costs in terms of decreasing tax base, the last term. If $n=\delta$, then the first term vanishes and the preferred tax rate is as in Meltzer and Richard's model.

c. The middle aged voter who prefers the same tax rate as the young voter with income e^{iY} has productivity

$$e^{iM}=e^{iY}+\frac{\left(1+n\right)\left(2+n\right)}{2+\delta}\left[L\left(\tau^{i}\right)+\tau L\left(\tau^{i}\right)\right].$$

Under the assumption that middle aged voters are richer than young, the share of middle aged voters who prefer a higher tax than e^{iY} is $F^{M}\left(e^{iM}\right)=F\left(e^{iY}\right)$. On one hand, the older are closer to receiving the benefits from the pension, so they are more in favor of higher pensions, on the other hand they are richer so they are less in favor of redistribution within generations. With the assumed increase in incomes, these effects exactly cancel and the proportion in favor of taxes higher than τ is the same among the young and among the middle aged.

The equilibrium requirement, equation (6.15) may be rewritten as

$$1+\left(1+n\right)F\left(e^{iY}\right)+\left(1+n\right)^{2}F\left(e^{iY}\right)$$

This implies that $F\left(e^{mY}\right)=\frac{1}{2}-\frac{1}{2\left(1+n+\left(1+n\right)^{2}\right)}$. If there is no population growth, then $n=0$, and $F\left(e^{mY}\right)=\frac{1}{4}$. The total population is 3, and the whole old generation plus $\frac{1}{4}$ of the young and middle aged make up half the electorate that prefers higher taxes. If $n>0$, then the young and middle aged make up an increasing part of the electorate and thus a larger share of these groups need to support lower taxes in order to make up half the electorate.

d. Voting rights to young. The very young vote exactly as the young, conditional on their productivity. Therefore the new median voter is determined by $F\left(e^{mY}\right) = \frac{1}{2} - \frac{1}{2\left(1+n+(1+n)^2+(1+n)^3\right)}$. The new share F is larger than the old share, therefore the new median voter must be more productive. On the other hand, each individual's most preferred tax rate is unchanged. Therefore, taxes and pensions will decrease. Giving a new generation voting rights decreases the possibilities of the old to redistribute from the young, and this lowers the pensions.

e. Excluding the poor. Suppose that $\frac{1}{2} - \frac{1}{2\left(1+n+(1+n)^2\right)} = 0.3$. In equilibrium the 30 percent least productive young and middle aged voters must supports higher taxes. Excluding the poor from the electorate make the voter which has 30 percent less productive workers in the electorate more productive. Therefore e^{mY} will be higher and pensions lower. Excluding the poor will make the median voters more productive and thus decrease their incentives for higher pensions as they will carry a larger share of the cost.

6.3   Pensions and probabilistic voting

Consider again the setup of subsection 6.2. There are three generations: young, middle-aged, and old. The population grows at rate n. The government finances a pension scheme with lump sum transfers f to the old generation with a proportional tax, τ, on labor. The government budget constraint is

$$f = \sum_{iY} \tau l^{iY} \left(1 + n\right)^2 + \sum_{iM} \tau l^{iM} \left(1 + n\right).$$

The subjective discount rate, β, equals the real interest rate ρ , and all individuals may save assets at the real interest rate. The lifetime utility of a pension scheme to a young individual is

$$w^{iY} = U\left(c^{iY}\right) + \frac{1}{1+\beta}U\left(c^{iM}\right) + \frac{1}{(1+\beta)^2}c^{iO} + V\left(x^{iY}\right) + \frac{1}{1+\beta}V\left(x^{iM}\right),$$

and a young individual's intertemporal budget constraint is

$$c^{iY} + \frac{c^{iM}}{1+\rho} + \frac{c^{iO}}{(1+\rho)^2} = l^{iY}\left(1-\tau\right) + \frac{l^{iM}\left(1-\tau\right)}{1+\rho} + \frac{f}{(1+\rho)^2}.$$

There are two political candidates, A and B, who try to maximize votes by choosing an election platform consisting of a tax to finance the pension scheme. Individual i receive utility σ^i from other policies if candidate B is elected. The preference parameter, σ^i, is uniformly and symmetrically distributed around zero with densities f^Y, f^M, and f^O, for the young, middle-aged, and old respectively. The individuals choose labor and the consumption path given the tax rate. $W^{iY}\left(\tau\right)$ denotes a young individual's utility of tax rate given optimal savings and labor decisions.

a. Suppose that there is a vote on the pension system in every period and that there is no commitment. Write the equation determining the equilibrium level of pensions. Compare this with the equilibrium level of pensions in the median-voter model.

b. Suppose that there is commitment so that an enacted pension schemes will remain in place forever. Write the equation determining the equilibrium tax rate?

Answer

a. The first order condition to the consumption decision is

$$U'\left(c^{iY}\right) = \left[\frac{1+\rho}{1+\delta}\right]^2,$$

$$U'\left(c^{iM}\right) = \frac{1+\rho}{1+\delta}.$$

Given the condition $\delta = \rho$, this implies that $U'\left(c^{iY}\right) = U'\left(c^{iM}\right) = 1$. The first order condition to the labor choice is

$$U'\left(c^{iY}\right)(1-\tau) - V'\left(1+e^i - l^{iY}\right) = 0$$

$$U'\left(c^{iM}\right)(1-\tau) - V'\left(1+e^i - l^{iM}\right) = 0,$$

and thus $l^{iY} = l^{iM} = 1 + e^i + V'^1(1-\tau) = L(\tau) - e + e^i$.
  The young voter i will vote for candidate A if

$$\sigma^i \le W^{iY}\left(\tau^A\right) - W^{iY}\left(\tau^A\right),$$

and event to which the candidates assign probability $F^Y\left(W^{iY}\left(\tau^A\right) - W^{iY}\left(\tau^A\right)\right)$. The candidates maximize the expected number of votes

$$E\left[v\right] = \sum_{iY} F^Y\left(W^{iY}\left(\tau^A\right) - W^{iY}\left(\tau^B\right)\right) + \sum_{iM} F^M\left(W^{iM}\left(\tau^A\right) - W^{iM}\left(\tau^B\right)\right)$$
$$+ \sum_{iO} F^O\left(W^{iO}\left(\tau^A\right) - W^{iO}\left(\tau^B\right)\right)$$

subject to the budget constraint

$$L(\tau)\tau(1+n)(2+n) = f.$$

The first order condition to this problem is

$$-f^{YM}L + f^O\left(\tau L_\tau + L\right) = 0,$$

where

$$f^{YM} = \frac{(1+n)^2}{(1+n) + (1+n)^2}f^Y + \frac{(1+n)}{(1+n) + (1+n)^2}f^M,$$

is the population weighted average of the density of the young and middle aged.
The equilibrium tax rate is

$$\tau = \max\left(\left(f^O - f^{YM}\right) \frac{L}{|L_\tau|}, 0 \right).$$

If the votes of the old are more sensitive to pension spending than the average of
the votes of the young and middle aged, then there will be positive pensions in
equilibrium. This question shows a fundamental difference between this model and
the median voter model. If less than 50 percent of the voters gain from spending
on an issue in the median voter model, there will be no spending at all. In the
Lindbeck and Weibull model, politicians compete for votes by allocating money
to areas where they can gain more votes on the margin, and small groups with
politically effective voters may get large per capita redistribution.

b. The candidates again maximize votes. Now however, the indirect utilities, W, are
computed for the whole life span of the individuals. The new equilibrium conditions
are

$$\sum_{iY} f^Y \left[-l^{iY} - \frac{l^{iM}}{1+\delta} + \frac{f_\tau}{(1+\delta)^2} \right] + \sum_{iM} f^M \left[-l^{iM} + \frac{f_\tau}{1+\delta} \right] + \sum_{iO} f^O f_\tau = 0,$$

or equivalently

$$-L \left[f^Y (1+n)^2 \left(\frac{2+\delta}{1+\delta} \right) + f^M (1+n) \right] + f_\tau \left[f^O + f^M \frac{1+n}{1+\delta} + f^Y \frac{(1+n)^2}{(1+\delta)^2} \right] = 0$$

$$\tau = \frac{L}{|L_\tau|} \frac{f^O + f^Y (1+n)^2 \frac{(2+n)(1+n)-(2+\delta)(1+\delta)}{(1+\delta)^2} + f^M (1+n) \left(\frac{(1+n)(2+n)}{1+\delta} - 1 \right)}{f^O + f^M \frac{(1+n)}{1+\delta} + f^Y \frac{(1+n)^2}{(1+\delta)^2}}.$$

If the population grows rate exceeds the real interest rate, all generations gain from
the pension program and taxes will be positive. As in the median voter case, the
reason for the positive pension scheme is that only the present generation is voting.
Consider the case when $n = \delta$. The equilibrium condition then becomes

$$\tau = \frac{L}{|L_\tau|} \frac{f^O + f^M \left(n^2 + 3n + 1\right)}{f^O + f^M + f^Y}.$$

6.4 Unemployment insurance

Consider the model of subsection 6.4.1. Individuals maximize lifetime utility of consumption over an infinite horizon:

$$V^J = E_0 \left[\sum_{t=0}^{\infty} \beta^t U\left(c_t^I\right) \mid I = J \text{ at } t = 0 \right], \quad I, J \in \{E, U\},$$

where β is a subjective discount factor, and the E and U superscripts denote the state of being employed or unemployed respectively. If employed, individuals consume their real wage, net of taxes, $l(1 - \tau)$. In each period a currently employed becomes unemployed with probability φ, whereas a currently unemployed becomes employed with probability ϑ.

a. Assume that $U(c) = \ln(c)$. Compute the equilibrium tax and benefit size.

b. Discuss how the tax rate and the unemployment benefit depend on the firing rate and hiring rates.

c. Show that an increase in both firing and hiring rates, keeping unemployment constant will increase the unemployment benefit. Discuss the results.

Answer

a. The utility of the employed then takes the form

$$V^E = c \left(\beta\varphi \ln\left(\tau \frac{\vartheta}{\varphi}\right) + (1 - \beta(1 - \vartheta)) \ln(1 - \tau) \right).$$

The first order condition is

$$\frac{\beta\varphi}{\tau} - \frac{1 - \beta(1 - \vartheta)}{1 - \tau} = 0,$$

which yields the equilibrium tax

$$\tau = \frac{\beta\varphi}{1 - \beta + \beta\varphi + \beta\vartheta}.$$

and equilibrium benefits

$$f = \tau \frac{\vartheta}{\varphi} = \frac{\beta\vartheta}{1 - \beta + \beta\varphi + \beta\vartheta}.$$

b. The tax rate is clearly increasing in the firing rate and decreasing in the hiring rate. The reason is that an increase in the firing rate makes it more likely that an employed worker will be unemployed soon. Therefore the employed want more insurance. The tax rate is decreasing in the hiring rate since a higher hiring rate makes unemployment spells shorter.

To isolate the effect from the hiring rate rewrite the equation as

$$f = \frac{\beta}{\frac{1}{\vartheta}\left(1 - \beta + \beta\varphi\right) + \beta}.$$

Increasing the hiring rate increases the benefit, increasing the firing rate decreases the benefit.

c. Holding unemployment constant and increasing the hiring and firing rates proportionally yields

$$f = \frac{\beta}{\frac{1}{\vartheta}\left(1 - \beta\right) + \beta\frac{1}{1-u} + \beta}.$$

Therefore, increasing the hiring an firing probabilities simultaneously increases the unemployment benefit. The reason is that an increase in the firing probability makes the employed median voter care more about insurance since he is more likely to become unemployed.

6.5   Unemployment insurance with multiple equilibria

This question is based on Hassler and Rodriguez Mora (1999). Unemployment insurance may be more valuable when expected unemployment spells are long. Individuals may, for example, have precautionary savings that are depleted if the spells are long. To model this idea in an analytically simple fashion, assume that a fired worker receives a severance payment of s/d per period where d is the average duration of the unemployment spell. With long unemployment spells, this payment per period thus becomes smaller. Given the hiring rate ϑ, the expected duration of the unemployment spell is $\frac{1}{\vartheta}$. Use the model specified in the previous question, but include this feature.

a. Compute the equilibrium tax and show that it is decreasing in the hiring rate, and decreasing in the firing rate.

b. Assume that the unemployment rate $u = 0.06$, that the discount factor $\beta = \frac{4}{5}$ and that the severance payment $s = \frac{4}{5}$. By plotting the unemployment benefit as a function of the firing rate, show that an increase in both firing and hiring rates, keeping unemployment constant may decrease the unemployment benefit. Discuss the results.

c. Now suppose that the firing rate is constant at $\varphi = 0.05$ whereas the unemployment may vary. Show that the unemployment benefit is lower when the hiring rate is high and unemployment is low.

d. It has been argued that higher unemployment benefits, will make unemployed workers more reluctant to accept job offers. Assume for this reason that higher unemployment benefits makes hiring more difficult, so that hiring is decreasing in the level of benefits. More precisely, assume that

$$\vartheta = \frac{1}{15f}.$$

Show that there are two equilibria: one in which the unemployment is high, the unemployment benefit is high, and duration is long, and another in which unemployment is low, unemployment benefits are low, and duration long. Explain the equilibria.

Answer

The utility of the employed then takes the form

$$V^E = c\left(\beta\varphi U\left(s\vartheta + \tau\frac{\vartheta}{\varphi}\right) + (1 - \beta(1 - \vartheta))U(1 - \tau)\right).$$

The first order condition is

$$\frac{\beta\vartheta}{s\vartheta + \tau\frac{\vartheta}{\varphi}} - \frac{1 - \beta(1 - \vartheta)}{1 - \tau} = 0.$$

The first term in this expression shows that the value of the unemployment insurance payments is higher under a long unemployment spell (a low hiring rate). The equilibrium tax is

$$\tau = \frac{\varphi(\beta - s + \beta s - \beta\vartheta s)}{1 - \beta + \beta\varphi + \beta\vartheta}$$

Increasing both hiring and firing rates proportionally implies

$$\varphi = \frac{u}{(1 - u)}\vartheta$$

$$\tau = \frac{\frac{u\vartheta}{(1-u)}(\beta - s + \beta s - \beta\vartheta s)}{1 - \beta + \beta\frac{u\vartheta}{(1-u)} + \beta\vartheta}$$

$$f = \frac{(1 - u)}{u}\frac{\frac{u\vartheta}{(1-u)}(\beta - s + \beta s - \beta\vartheta s)}{1 - \beta + \beta\frac{u\vartheta}{(1-u)} + \beta\vartheta}.$$

b. Given that $u = 0.06$, $s = \frac{4}{5}$,   and $\beta = \frac{4}{5}$

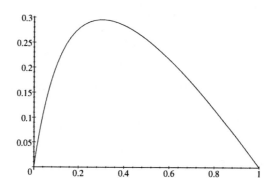

The unemployment benefits are the highest when the hiring probability is around 0.2, i.e. when the average unemployment duration is about 5 years. At an unemployment of 6 percent, this implies that the firing rate is 1.27×10^{-2} and the average employment duration is around 80 years. Thus in contrast to the standard model, in this type of model higher turnover means lower unemployment benefits because the unemployment insurance has lower value in this case.

c. The tax level is

$$\tau = \frac{\varphi(\beta - s + \beta s - \beta \vartheta s)}{1 - \beta + \beta \varphi + \beta \vartheta},$$

and the unemployment benefit is

$$f = \tau \frac{(1-u)}{u} = \frac{\vartheta(\beta - s + \beta s - \beta \vartheta s)}{1 - \beta + \beta \varphi + \beta \vartheta}.$$

The unemployment benefit plotted against the hiring rate is shown in the figure below.

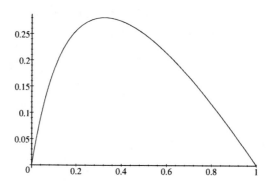

Again the unemployment benefit is decreasing for average unemployment spells of three years or larger.

d. By plotting the political determination of the benefit, given the hiring rate, and the market determination of the hiring rate, given the unemployment benefit, it is clear that two equilibria exist. In one equilibrium, average duration of unemployment is about 3 years, the unemployment level is 17 percent and the benefits are about 27 percent of the mean income. In the other equilibrium, the average unemployment spell is 1.2 years, the unemployment level is 6 percent and the unemployment benefit is about 7 percent of the average wage.

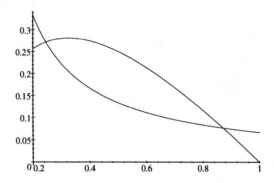

The intuition is that given that short unemployment spells are expected, low unemployment benefits are needed. The low unemployment benefits in turn forces unemployed workers to get jobs quickly, causing short unemployment spells.

Chapter 7

Special-interest politics

7.1 Legislative bargaining with amendment rights

This question is based on Baron and Ferejohn (1989). Consider a legislature with 3 members that have to divide rents of size 1 among themselves. The consumption value of the rents to legislator i is $w^i(r) = r$. The rents are divided according to the following procedure. A member of the legislature is randomly selected to propose a division of the rents. If a majority of the members in the legislature do not accept the proposition, then another member is randomly selected to make a new proposition. Each time a new proposition is made, the payoffs are discounted by a factor δ. The game continues until a proposition is accepted.

a. Compute the equilibrium with stationary (that is history-independent) strategies in this game.

b. Now consider what happens when amendments are allowed. First one member of the legislative body has been selected to be the agenda setter and to propose an allocation of the rents, r_1, that will be named the proposition on the floor. Then another member is randomly selected among the legislators other than the agenda setter. This other member can let the legislative body vote on implementing r_1. He may also propose an amended allocation r_2. In this case there is a vote between r_1 and r_2. The winner becomes the proposition on the floor. Then a new member is randomly chosen. This other member can let the legislative body vote on implementing the proposition on the floor. He may also propose an amended allocation r_3. In this case there is a vote between the proposition on the floor and r_3. The winner becomes the proposition on the floor. The process continues until an allocation is implemented. The members are assumed to have a common discount factor $\delta \in [0,1]$. Every the allocation is amended, the value of the payoffs is discounted by δ.

Consider stationary equilibria of the following form: the member proposing the allocation keeps a share y of the budget to himself and gives $1 - y$ to one other member and nothing to the remaining member. If a member is indifferent between a bill and an amendment, he will vote for the amendment. Compute the optimal stationary strategy y for the member proposing an allocation.

c. Now consider stationary equilibria of the following form: the member proposing the allocation keeps a share y of the budget to himself and gives $\frac{1-y}{2}$ to each of the two remaining members. Compute the optimal strategy y.

d. Discuss when it is optimal for the agenda setter to offer positive rents to only one other member (a minimum winning coalition, as in question (b)) and when it is optimal to offer rents to all members of the legislature (universalism, as in question (c)). Discuss how allowing for amendments affects the agenda-setting power.

e. Suppose there was prior stage where in which the legislative body chose by majority decision whether to use an open or a closed rule. Assume that it is known who would be the first agenda setter and who would be included in prospective coalitions. Which rule would prevail?

Answer

a. The proposer keeps y and offers one randomly chosen other member of the legislative body $1 - y$. For this member to accept, his payoff must be $1 - y \geq \delta V_c$, where V_c is the continuation value of the game. The agenda setter optimally makes this inequality bind, so that the other member just accepts. The continuation value thus equals $V_c = \frac{1}{3}y + \frac{1}{3}(1-y) = \frac{1}{3}$. Therefore, $y = 1 - \frac{\delta}{3}$. The value of being agenda setter is $V_a = y = 1 - \frac{\delta}{3}$.

b. The agenda setter suggests an allocation vector $(y, 1-y, 0)$, where the first vector component denotes the agenda setters share, the second, the second members share and the third, the third members share. Then one of the other two members are given the opportunity to amend the proposition. With probability $\frac{1}{2}$, the second member is chosen. He will bring the proposition to a vote for implementation given that his share is larger than the value of being the agenda setter in the following period: $1 - y \geq \delta V_a$. The agenda setter will set the highest y that satisfies this inequality. If the third member is given the opportunity to amend, then he will amend the allocation and suggest $(0, 1 - y, y)$. This amendment will receive the support of the second and third member and be the new proposition on the floor. Then either member 1 or member 2 are given the opportunity to amend the proposition. If member 2 is chosen, then he will bring the proposition to a vote for implementation in which case this allocation will be implemented. If member 1 is chosen then he will again be the agenda setter and propose $(y, 1 - y, 0)$.

The value of being an agenda setter is thus

$$V_a = \frac{1}{2}y + \frac{\delta^2}{4}V_a.$$

Together with the constraint $1 - y = \delta V_a$, this yields

$$V_a = \frac{1}{2\left(1 + \frac{1}{2}\delta - \frac{1}{4}\delta^2\right)}.$$

$$y = 1 - \frac{\delta}{2\left(1 + \frac{1}{2}\delta - \frac{1}{4}\delta^2\right)} = \frac{4 - \delta^2}{4 + 2\delta - \delta^2}.$$

c. In this case, the agenda setter proposes $(y, \frac{1-y}{2}, \frac{1-y}{2})$. This is not amended if $\frac{1-y}{2} \geq \delta V_a$, and the agenda setter will make this inequality bind. Given that the inequality is satisfied, $V_a = y$. Thus in equilibrium,

$$V_a = \frac{1}{1 + 2\delta} = y.$$

The agenda setter will choose to have a minimum winning coalition if the discount factor is large enough: $\delta \geq \sqrt{3} - 1 = 0.73$. If the discount factor is very small, then it is very risky for the agenda setter to give rents to only one other member of the electorate. The agenda setter is then better off by offering something to everyone in the legislature and being sure receiving some rents in the first period. Therefore universalism should be expected in areas when the need for quick implementation is large.

For all positive values of δ, the value of being an agenda setter is higher without amendments. Amendments therefore undermines the agenda setting power.

d. With the closed rule, the equilibrium payoffs are $(1 - \frac{\delta}{3}, \frac{\delta}{3}, 0)$. With the open rule and with minimum winning coalitions, the values of the game to the agenda setter, the coalition partner to the agenda setter and the member excluded from the coalition are (V_a^a, V_c^a, V_x^a) respectively, where

$$V_a^a = \frac{1}{2\left(1 + \frac{1}{2}\delta - \frac{1}{4}\delta^2\right)},$$

$$V_c^a = \frac{1}{2}(1 - y) + \frac{1}{2}\delta\left(\frac{1}{2}(1 - y) + \frac{1}{2}\delta V_c^a\right),$$

$$V_c^a = \frac{\delta}{4\left(1 + \frac{1}{2}\delta - \frac{1}{4}\delta^2\right)} \frac{\left(1 + \frac{\delta}{2}\right)}{\left(1 - \frac{\delta^2}{4}\right)},$$

$$V_x^a = \frac{\delta}{4\left(1 + \frac{1}{2}\delta - \frac{1}{4}\delta^2\right)}.$$

The value of being included is thus higher than the value of being excluded in the coalition. With open rule and universal coalitions, the values of the games are (V_a, V_c, V_c)

$$V_a = \frac{1}{1 + 2\delta},$$

$$V_c = \frac{\delta}{1 + 2\delta}.$$

The agenda setter prefers the closed rule for all values of the discount factor. The person that is not in the coalition weakly prefers the open rule, and strictly prefers the open rule for $\delta < 0.73$. For the legislative member who is part of the coalition both under the closed and the open rule things are less clear. This member prefers the open rule to the closed rule for $\delta < 0.73$. Between $0.73 < \delta < 0.79$, he prefers the closed rule and for $\delta > 0.19$ he prefers the open rule. The diagram below depicts the coalition members value of the game under the closed rule (straight line), the open rule with minimum winning coalitions (convex curve), and the open rule with universal coalitions (concave curve).

Therefore, the open rule would prevail for $\delta < 0.73$. The closed rule would prevail for $0.73 < \delta < 0.79$. Which rule would prevail for $\delta > 0.19$ depends on how the member who would not be part of any coalition in this range would vote.

7.2   Budgetary powers and amendments rights in legislatures

Suppose that individuals receive utility from private consumption, c, and consumption of a publicly provided private good, g, described by the utility function $v = u(c) + g$. The public good is financed through a proportional income tax τ. There are three groups each of size 1, and all individuals receive income 1. The budget constraint is thus $3\tau = g_1 + g_2 + g_3 = G$.

a. What is the socially optimal level of taxes?

b. Suppose now that a representative from one of the groups chooses taxes in a first stage. In the next stage, a representative from another group proposes an allocation of G. It is not known whether the agent setting taxes will receive positive allocation from this proposal. If the proposed allocation is not accepted, then one of the two other groups is randomly chosen to have its representative propose a new allocation. The discount rate is δ. Compute the level of taxes and the allocation of G. Are taxes too high or too low in equilibrium?

c. Now suppose that G is allocated using a rule with amendment rights, as described in question (b) of problem 7.1. Further assume that the discount rate is greater than 0.73, so that only one group other than the agenda setter receives publicly provided services. It is not known whether the agent setting taxes will be included in the winning coalition. Compute the level of taxes and the allocation of G. Are taxes too high or too low in equilibrium?

d. Now suppose that G is allocated using a rule with amendment rights, but that the discount rate is smaller than 0.73, so that there is a universalistic equilibrium in which all groups receives publicly provided services. Compute the level of taxes and the allocation of G. Are taxes too high or too low in equilibrium?

e. Finally, assume that the first stage proposer, a_τ, is elected by the members of all groups and thus cares about all groups. For example, imagine a president being elected in national election, and state representatives deciding of over the state allocation of G. What level of taxes would be chosen under each rule.

Answer

a. A social planner maximizes $\sum_{i=1}^{3} u(c_i) + g_i$. This problem has the solution $u'(1 - \tau) = 1$.

b. In this game, we know from the above exercise that the agenda setter a_g offers one of the other members a share $\frac{\delta}{3}G$. Realizing that in expectation his group will receive $\frac{\delta}{6}G$ at any spending level G, a_τ sets taxes to satisfy

$$u'(1 - \tau) = 3\frac{\delta}{6} < 1.$$

When the allocation is made under a closed rule, then the level of taxes will be too low.

c. In this game, we know from the above exercise that the agenda setter a_g offers a_τ a share $\frac{\delta}{2\left(1+\frac{1}{2}\delta-\frac{1}{4}\delta^2\right)}G$. that in expectation his group will receive $\frac{\delta}{4\left(1+\frac{1}{2}\delta-\frac{1}{4}\delta^2\right)}G$ at any spending level G, a_τ sets taxes to satisfy

$$u'(1 - \tau) = 3\frac{\delta}{4\left(1 + \frac{1}{2}\delta - \frac{1}{4}\delta^2\right)} < 1.$$

Taxes are still lower than optimal. Taxes are, however, higher than under a closed rule since $\frac{\delta}{3} < \frac{\delta}{2\left(1+\frac{1}{2}\delta-\frac{1}{4}\delta^2\right)}$, for all values of $\delta \in (0, 1]$.

d. In this game, we know from the above exercise that the agenda setter a_g offers a_τ a share $\frac{\delta}{1+2\delta}G$. Realizing this, a_τ sets taxes to satisfy

$$u'(1 - \tau) = 3\frac{\delta}{1 + 2\delta}.$$

Taxes are still lower than optimal. The basic intuition is that the agenda setter has power that allows him to get a share that is larger than $\frac{1}{3}$ of the government revenue to his district. Therefore the remaining two legislators always on average will receive less than $\frac{1}{3}$ of any increase in government spending and taxes will be suboptimally low. Taxes are decreasing in agenda setting power. Amendments undermine the agenda setting power and therefore increase taxes.

e. Irrespectively of how the benefits from government spending are allocated, the president internalizes them and sets the optimal level of taxes.

7.3   Truthful strategies in the lobbying model

Consider the simple lobbying model of subsection 7.3.1. A subset L of groups are organized in lobbies. Each lobby j simultaneously and non cooperatively presents a contribution schedule, $C_j(\mathbf{g})$, to the incumbent. Each of the lobbies maximizes the net welfare of its members: $N_j(W_j(\mathbf{g}) - C_j(\mathbf{g}))$. The incumbent sets $\mathbf{g}$ to maximize the weighted sum of social welfare and contributions:

$$W(g) = \eta \sum_j N_j W_j(\mathbf{g}) + (1 - \eta) \sum_{j \in L} N_j C_j(\mathbf{g}),$$

where $\eta \in [0, 1]$.

a. Explain why an equilibrium must be jointly Pareto optimal for the government and the lobbies.

b. Now suppose that the lobbies set contribution schemes that are differentiable. Show that the truthful strategy

$$C_j(\mathbf{g}) = \max[W_j(\mathbf{g}) - b_j, 0]$$

satisfies the condition for an optimal strategy.

Answer

a. It must be the case that the equilibrium is jointly Pareto optimal for the incumbent and each lobby separately

$$g \in \arg \max W(g) + N_j(W_j(\mathbf{g}) - C_j(\mathbf{g})),$$

for all j. Suppose that g' is not Pareto optimal between the government and lobby j. Then there exists some g^{*j} that Pareto dominates g'. But then g' can not be an equilibrium. The reason is that lobby group j could offer the government a contribution schedule which for any allocation vector g, contributed the difference between its welfare at g and its welfare at g^{*j}, plus something extra for choosing g^{*j}. With these new contribution schedule, both the government and the lobby group would be better off.

b. For interior solutions (positive C_j), by the Pareto optimality condition of the contribution schemes,

$$\nabla W(g) + \nabla N_j(W_j(\mathbf{g}) - \nabla C_j(\mathbf{g})) = 0,$$

for all i and all j, and by the governments first order condition

$$\nabla W(g) = 0,$$

for all i. Thus

$$\nabla C_j(\mathbf{g}) = \nabla W_j(\mathbf{g}),$$

for all i and all j. Let the policy $\mathbf{g}^0$ be the policy that gives members of group j the lowest utility,

$$C_j(\mathbf{g}) - C_j(\mathbf{g}^0) = \int_{g^0}^{g} \nabla W_j(\mathbf{g}) \cdot d\mathbf{g} = W_j(\mathbf{g}) - W_j(\mathbf{g}_0).$$

The contribution scheme

$$C_j(\mathbf{g}) = W_j(\mathbf{g}) - W_j(\mathbf{g}_0) = W_j(\mathbf{g}) - b_j,$$

is the least expensive scheme that satisfies the above condition.

7.4 Coalition formation in a three-party legislature

This question is based on Austen-Smith and Banks (1988). Suppose that three parties in a parliament are indexed L, M, R, corresponding to "leftist", "middle" and "rightist" respectively. The parties set a policy $y \in [0, 1]$ and divide the exogenous rents of being in office, that is they select a vector $\mathbf{r} = (r_L, r_M, r_R)$, subject to $r_L + r_M + r_R \leq \bar{r}$. The parties have preferences over policy described by utility function $u_k = r_k - (x_k - y)^2$, $k \in \{L, M, R\}$, where $x_L = 0$, $x_M = \frac{1}{2}$, and $x_R = 1$.

Prior to the parliamentary session, an election has been held, giving the parties vote shares $w_L > w_M > w_R$. As is often the case in practice, the largest party may propose a policy and allocation of rents that is implemented if it receives support from a government coalition in the parliament. If the suggested policy is not accepted, then the second-largest party is asked to try to form a coalition. If the policy is again not accepted, then the smallest party is asked to form a coalition. If this fails then all parties receive a payoff of 0.

a. Describe the equilibrium proposals. Explain why a large leftist party may wish to form coalition with a small rightist party (or vice versa).

b. Now suppose that $w_L > w_R > w_M$. Compute the equilibrium outcome. Assume that M attempts to form a coalition with R in the last period (M is indifferent between coalition partners). Compute the party members equilibrium utilities.

c. Assume that the members of the electorate either have bliss points x_L, x_M, or x_R. Further assume that there are more voters with bliss points x_L than with bliss points x_M and one more voter with bliss points x_M than with bliss points x_R. Could there be an equilibrium in which all voters vote for the party whose policy platform they most prefer?

d. An argument for having a proportional electoral system with more than two parties is that the legislature's composition, and therefore policy, in such a system better represents the voters preferences than first-past-the-post system with only two parties. Discuss this argument in the light of the answers to questions (a) through (c).

   Remark. The analysis in this question could be expanded, first by finding strategies that are optimal for the voters given the mapping from electoral outcomes to policy outcomes in the legislature, and second finding the three parties' optimal policy platforms, given the voters strategies and the policy outcomes they induce. Austen-Smith and Banks (1988) gives an example of this type of full equilibrium.

Answer

a. The game is solved by backwards induction. In the last stage, the R party gets to form a coalition. Given coalition partner k, Party R solves

$$\max u_R = r_R - (1 - y)^2$$

subject to the condition that the coalition partner accepts the proposal

$$u_k = r_k - (x_k - y)^2 \geq 0,$$

and subject to the total constraint on rents

$$r_k + r_R \leq \bar{r}.$$

The best policy is thus characterized by

$$2(1 - y) + \lambda_1 2(x_k - y) = 0,$$

$$1 = \lambda_2,$$

$$\lambda_1 = \lambda_2.$$

Where the lambdas are Lagrange-multipliers on the two constraints respectively.

Solving for y and r_k yields

$$y_3 = \frac{1 + x_k}{2},$$

$$r_k = \left(\frac{x_k - 1}{2}\right)^2.$$

It is better for R to form a coalition government with M, both because R needs to compromise less on policy, and because she has to give up less rents. Thus in the third stage, R, forms a coalition with M, sets policy $y = \frac{3}{4}$, and rents $r = (0, \frac{1}{2}, \overline{r} - \frac{1}{2})$. The utilities are $u_L = -\frac{9}{16}, u_M = 0, u_R = \overline{r} - 1$.

In the second stage, M gets to form a coalition. Since R gets to form a coalition if this attempt fails, R has a higher reservation utility than L. Therefore, it is cheaper for M to form a coalition with L. M maximizes his utility subject to the constraint that L receives at least his reservation utility. The solution is

$$y_2 = \frac{1}{2},$$

$$r_k = 0.$$

M can choose his most preferred point and give L no rents. M still prefers this to receiving no rents and having policy $y = \frac{3}{4}$ implemented. The utilities under this coalition are $u_L = -\frac{1}{16}, u_M = 1, u_R = -\frac{1}{16}$.

In the first stage, L chooses R as coalition partner. Had L chosen M as coalition partner, then he would have had to promise M's optimal policy and given M all the rents. By choosing R as coalition partner, L optimally sets $y = \frac{1}{2}$ and $r_L = 1$. The utilities under this coalition for L, M, and R are $(\overline{r} - \frac{1}{4}, 0, -\frac{1}{4})$ respectively. Although M is closer to L ideologically, L can not hope to convince M to join the coalition. The reason is that M has so much to gain if the coalition formation fails and M gets to form government.

b. In equilibrium, party L forms a coalition with party M, sets policy equal to $y = \frac{1}{4}$, and rents $(\overline{r}, 0, 0)$. The utilities are $(\overline{r} - \frac{1}{16}, -\frac{1}{16}, -\frac{9}{16})$.

c. No, a voter from group M would prefer to change his vote to R to make it the larger party.

d. In this model, the influence over policy is not monotonically increasing in the number of seats a party has in the parliament. Therefore, the policy outcome would not necessarily reflect preferences well if all voters voted for their most preferred party. Further, some voters may have incentives not to vote for their most preferred party, but instead strategically for some other party. Therefore it is not clear that the multiparty proportional representation system produces a legislature whose composition reflects the preferences of the electorate.

7.5   Legislative bargaining and lobbying

Consider the following game of lobbying and legislative bargaining, which is a slight modification of that presented in subsection 7.5.3. A legislature has three members who allocate a fixed set of public expenditures, G, to three electoral districts. The policy vector is thus $\mathbf{g} = (g_1, g_2, g_3)$, and $g_1 + g_2 + g_3 = G$. In each representative's electoral district there is a lobby group that lobby this representative exclusively. The lobby group in district i has utility $g_i - C_i$, where C_i is the contribution paid to the representative. The legislators care only about the contributions they get from the lobbies.

Each legislative session takes the following form. First, Nature randomly selects an agenda setter. Then the lobby groups present their representative with a truthful contribution schedule: $C_i(\mathbf{g}) = \max[g_i - b_i, 0]$. These schedules are simultaneously announced and observed by all legislators. Finally, the agenda setter formulates a take-it-or-leave-it offer, and the legislature votes on this proposal. If the proposal is not accepted, then a new legislative session begins in which Nature randomly draws another agenda setter. For each legislative session, the payoffs are discounted by the discount factor δ.

a. Compute the policies, contributions, and payoffs in the stationary equilibrium.

b. Suppose that the legislators also care about the amount of public spending that benefits their electoral district. Compute the stationary equilibrium in the game as above, but assume that the legislators also care about public spending in their district and have utilities $u_i = g_i + \eta C_i$.

c. Suppose the game is changed so that the legislature may amend the agenda setter's proposal. The legislative game is the same as in question 7.1.b but now the lobby groups may set truthful contribution schedules during each session. More precisely, each legislative session now takes the following form. First, Nature randomly selects an agenda setter. Then the lobby groups present their representative with a truthful contribution schedule: $C^J(\mathbf{g}) = \max[g_i - b^J, 0]$. These schedules are simultaneously announced and observed by all legislators. The agenda setter proposes an allocation $\mathbf{g}^1$. Finally, Nature selects another member of the legislature, who either let the legislative body vote on implementing $\mathbf{g}^1$ or makes a new amended proposition $\mathbf{g}^2$, in which case there is a vote on whether to keep $\mathbf{g}^1$ or to accept the amended proposition $\mathbf{g}^2$. For each amendment, the payoffs are discounted by the discount factor δ.

Consider stationary equilibria of the following form: the member proposing the allocation keeps g_a to himself and gives $g_p = G - g_a$ to one other member, and nothing to the remaining member. If a member is indifferent between a bill and an amendment, he will vote for the amendment. Compute the optimal stationary strategy g_a for the member proposing an allocation.

d. Now consider stationary equilibria of the following form: the member proposing the allocation keeps a share g_a of the budget to himself and gives $\frac{1-g_a}{2}$ to each of the two remaining members. Compute the optimal strategy g_a. Discuss when it is optimal for the agenda setter to offer positive rents to only one other member (a minimum winning coalition) and when it is optimal to offer rents to all members of the legislature (universalism). Discuss how allowing for amendments and lobbying affects the agenda setting power.

Answer

a. In equilibrium the agenda setter allocates g_a to his own constituency and offers one other coalition partner, indexed by p, of the legislature $G - g_a$. This other member receives the contribution $G - g_a - b_p$ from his lobby group and accepts if $G - g_a - b_p \geq \delta \left(\frac{1}{3} V_a + \frac{1}{3} V_p \right)$. Since the continuation value is the same for all members of the legislature, the agenda setter selects the member with the smallest b_i. Competition among the lobby groups drive down b_i to zero. The equilibrium value of being an agenda setter is the contribution of the agenda setter's lobby group $V_a = g_a - b_a$. The equilibrium value of being a member of the coalition is $V_p = G - g_a$. To maximize his pay-off, the agenda setter sets g_a so that the above inequality binds:

$$g_a^* = G - \delta \left(\frac{1}{3} V_a + \frac{1}{3} V_p \right).$$

The group who lobby the agenda setter in turn set b_a to minimize their costs: $b_a = g_a^*$, and thus $V_a = 0$. Therefore

$$g_a^* = G - \delta \left(\frac{1}{3} (G - g_a^*) \right).$$

The only equilibrium is therefore $g_a^* = G$. One might have thought that if it had positive value to be a coalition member, then the coalition member might demand this value. But this could not be an equilibrium since the coalition member would accept $\frac{\delta}{3}$ of this value today. The only equilibrium is that $g = (G, 0, 0)$, and no rents are paid in equilibrium. Notice that in this equilibrium, two factors drive the result of maximal concentration of public spending. First as before that lobby groups compete to be in the coalition. Second that the lobby group of the agenda setter brings the utility of being an agenda setter down to zero.

b. The agenda setter again offers $G - g_a$ to one other member of the legislature. This other member accepts if

$$G - g_a + \eta \max (G - g_a - b_p, 0) \geq \delta \left(\frac{1}{3} V_a + \frac{1}{3} V_m \right).$$

Since the continuation values of the game are the same, the agenda setter will make the offer to the legislative member with the lowest b_i. Competition among the lobby groups will bring down b_i to zero. The agenda setter will set g_a so that the above inequality is just satisfied. The lobby group of the agenda setter will set their schedule so that there are no contributions in equilibrium. Thus $b_a = g_a^*$, which implies $V_a = g_a^*$. Similarly , $V_p = (1 + \eta)(G - g_a^*)$. Solving for g_a^*

$$(1 + \eta)(G - g_a) = \delta \left(\frac{1}{3} g_a^* + \frac{(1 + \eta)}{3} (G - g_a^*) \right)$$

$$g_a^* = \left(1 + \frac{\delta}{3(1+\eta)\left(1 - \delta(1+\eta)\frac{1}{3}\right)}\right)^{-1} G.$$

The share of spending that goes to the agenda setters district when $\eta = 1$ is depicted by the solid line in the graph below. The dashed line shows that level of spending without lobbying. With lobbying, the district of the agenda setter receives more public spending than without. No lobby contributions are made to the agenda setter. The legislative member who is not agenda setter, receive positive contributions amounting to $G - g_a^*$, and thus receive utility $2(G - g_a^*)$.

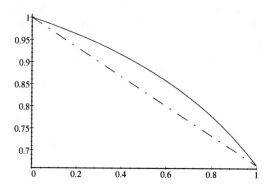

c. The agenda setter makes the proposal, g_p, to a coalition partner. The coalition partner chooses to move this to a vote for implementation if

$$g_p + \eta \max[g_p - b_p, 0] \geq \delta V_a.$$

Since the value of being an agenda setter is the same for all, the present agenda setter chooses the member of the legislature with the lowest b_i as his coalition partner. Anticipating this, the lobby groups bid down b_i to zero. The agenda setter chooses g_p so that the coalition partner just accepts, that is $g_p = \frac{1}{1+\eta}\delta V_a$. The value of being an agenda setter is

$$V_a = \frac{1}{2}\left(G - g_p + \eta \max[G - g_p - b_a, 0]\right) + \frac{\delta^2}{4}V_a.$$

Inserting the value for g_p, assuming that $G - g_p - b_a \geq 0$, and solving for V_a yields:

$$V_a = \frac{1}{2}\frac{(1+\eta)\,G - \eta b_a}{1 + \frac{\delta}{2} - \frac{\delta^2}{4}}.$$

In equilibrium, the lobby group of the agenda setter will set $b_a = G - g_p$. This will provide the right incentives for the agenda setter and will result in no payments in equilibrium. Inserting this and solving for g_p yields

$$g_p = \frac{\delta}{2\left(1 + \frac{\delta}{2} - \frac{\delta^2}{4}\right) + \eta\left(2 - \frac{\delta^2}{4}\right)}G.$$

As η approaches zero, this approaches the solution to the equilibrium with no lobby groups under open rule. When η approaches infinity, the solution approaches the simple case with no contributions and all public goods going to the agenda setter's district.

The value of being the agenda setter in this game is

$$V_a = \frac{(1+\eta)}{\delta} g_p = \frac{(1+\eta)}{2\left(1+\frac{\delta}{2}-\frac{\delta^2}{4}\right)+\eta\left(2-\frac{\delta^2}{4}\right)} G.$$

d. Now consider an agenda setter who will give offers to both the two other members of the legislature. For both of them to accept if they are chosen to decide on whether or not to amend, it must be the case that

$$g_2 + \eta \max[g_2 - b_2, 0] \geq \delta V_a,$$

$$g_3 + \eta \max[g_3 - b_3, 0] \geq \delta V_a.$$

The agenda setter will choose to just satisfy these inequalities, so that, assuming that $g_2 \geq b_2, g_3 \geq b_3$,

$$g_2 = \frac{1}{1+\eta}\left(\delta V_a + \eta b_2\right),$$

$$g_3 = \frac{1}{1+\eta}\left(\delta V_a + \eta b_3\right).$$

The value being the agenda setter in this equilibrium is

$$V_a = (G - g_2 - g_3) + \eta\left(G - g_2 - g_3 - b_a\right).$$

Inserting the expressions for g_2 and g_3 yields

$$V_a = (1+\eta)\left(G - g_2 - g_3\right) - \eta b_a.$$

$$V_a = -\delta V_a - \eta b_2 - \delta V_a - \eta b_3 + (1+\eta)G - \eta b_a.$$

$$V_a = \frac{1}{1+2\delta}\left((1+\eta)G - \eta b_2 - \eta b_3 - \eta b_a\right).$$

All three lobby groups have incentives to set their b's as high as possible.

$$g_2 = \frac{\delta}{1+2\delta}G + \frac{\eta}{1+\eta}\left(\frac{(1+\delta)b_2 - \delta(b_3 + b_a)}{1+2\delta}\right),$$

$$g_3 = \frac{\delta}{1+2\delta}G + \frac{\eta}{1+\eta}\left(\frac{(1+\delta)b_3 - \delta(b_2 + b_a)}{1+2\delta}\right),$$

$$g_a = \frac{1}{1+2\delta}G + \frac{\eta}{(1+\eta)(1+2\delta)}\left(2\delta b_a - b_2 - b_3\right).$$

This is under the assumption that $b_a \leq g_a, b_2 \leq g_2, b_3 \leq g_3$. The lobby groups will always want to keep these inequalities satisfied. If they did not, then their contribution schemes would not have any incentive effects for the legislators. In the above expressions, this would amount to setting the b of that lobby group equal to zero, which is not in the interest of the lobby group. Since

$$\frac{dg_2\,(b_a, b_2, b_3)}{db_2} < 1,$$

the largest b_2 for which $b_2 \leq g_2\,(b_a, b_2, b_3)$ is the $b_2\,(b_a, b_3)$ which satisfies $b_2 = g_2\,(b_a, b_2, b_3)$. This $b_2\,(b_a, b_3)$ is the best reply of b_2 to b_a, b_3. It may be computed by inserting $b_2 = g_2$ in the above equation and solving for b_2. Similarly, the best replies $b_a\,(b_2, b_3)$ and $b_3\,(b_a, b_2)$ may be computed. The unique equilibrium is

$$g_a = \frac{1}{1 + 2\delta} G,$$

$$g_2 = g_3 = \frac{\delta}{1 + 2\delta} G.$$

This can be checked by inserting $b_a = g_a = g_a^*$, $b_2 = g_2 = g_2^*$, and $b_3 = g_3 = g_3^*$ into the above equations defining $g_a\,(b_a, b_2, b_3)$ etcetera.

The conclusion is thus that with the possibility to lobby under universal coalitions, lobbying has no effect on the allocation of G. Further there are no contributions paid in equilibrium.

The value of being the agenda setter is

$$g_a = \frac{1}{1 + 2\delta} G.$$

This should be compared with the value of being an agenda setter under minimum winning coalitions

$$V_a = \frac{(1 + \eta)}{\delta} g_p = \frac{(1 + \eta)}{2\left(1 + \frac{\delta}{2} - \frac{\delta^2}{4}\right) + \eta\left(2 - \frac{\delta^2}{4}\right)} G.$$

The value of being an agenda setter is not influenced by the existence of lobby groups when the coalition includes all members of the legislature. On the other hand the value of being agenda setter is increasing in the weight that the legislators attach to the lobby groups contributions. Therefore the existence of lobby groups make minimum winning coalitions more likely. When $\eta = 0$ the agenda setter will choose maximum coalitions when $\delta < \sqrt{3} - 1 = 0.73$ when $\eta \to \infty$, the agenda setter will choose maximum coalitions when $\delta < 2\sqrt{5} - 4 = 0.47$.

Part III

Comparative Politics

Chapter 8

Electoral Rules and Electoral Competition

8.1 Proportional elections and concave utility

Consider a society with three distinct groups of voters, denoted $J = 1, 2, 3$. Each group has a continuum of voters with unit mass. Preferences over government policy are identical for every member of group J and given by the utility function

$$W^J = u(c^J) + H(g) = u(1 - \tau + f^J) + H(g).$$

Here, c^J is the private consumption of the average individual in group J, τ is a common tax rate, f^J is a transfer targeted to individuals in group J, and g is the supply of a (Samuelsonian) public good, evaluated by the concave and monotonically increasing function $H(g)$. Assume $u(\cdot)$ to be concave as well.

The public policy vector $\mathbf{q}$ is defined by

$$\mathbf{q} = [\tau, g, r, \{f^J\}] \geq 0,$$

where all components are constrained to be non negative. Any feasible policy must satisfy the government balanced budget constraint

$$3\tau = \sum_J f^J + g + r.$$

The component r reflects (endogenous) rents to politicians and is a deliberate object of choice. Rent extraction is associated with some transaction costs $(1 - \gamma)$, such that only γr benefit the politician.

Consider proportional elections:

Before the elections, two parties or candidates (A and B) commit to policy platforms $\mathbf{q}_A$ and $\mathbf{q}_B$. They act simultaneously and do not cooperate. The winning party's platform is implemented. Party P maximizes the expected value of rents, namely

$$E(v_P) = p_P \cdot (R + \gamma r),$$

where R denotes the (exogenous) ego rents associated with winning the elections, and p_P denotes the (endogenous) probability that P wins the right to set policy, given $\mathbf{q}_A$ and $\mathbf{q}_B$.

We assume probabilistic voting. Thus the election outcome is uncertain when platforms are chosen, and different voters evaluate these candidate's ideological or personal attributes in different ways. Specifically, let $W^J(\mathbf{q})$ denote the preferences of voters in group J over government policy. Then voter i in group J votes for party A if

$$W^J(\mathbf{q}_A) > W^J(\mathbf{q}_B) + (\delta + \sigma^{iJ}),$$

where the term $(\delta + \sigma^{iJ}) \lessgtr 0$ reflects voter i's ideological preference for party B. δ is common to all voters and σ^{iJ} is idiosyncratic.

Assume that δ is uniformly distributed on $\left[-\frac{1}{2\psi}, \frac{1}{2\psi}\right]$, σ^{iJ} differs across groups J, and it is uniformly distributed on $\left[-\frac{1}{2\phi^J} + \overline{\sigma}^J, \frac{1}{2\phi^J} + \overline{\sigma}^J\right]$, $J = 1, 2, 3$. Assume further that $\overline{\sigma}^1 < \overline{\sigma}^2 = 0 < \overline{\sigma}^3$, $\phi^2 > \phi^1, \phi^3$, and that $\overline{\sigma}^1\phi^1 + \overline{\sigma}^3\phi^3 = 0$.

a. Compute the social planner's policy choice.

b. How do transfers in the proportional election model compare with the social optimum?

c. Write down the condition for the choice of rents, r, in equilibrium.

d. How does the provision of the public good differ from that of the model with linear utility of voters?

Answer

a. The social optimum is given by

$$\max_{q=\{\tau,\{f^j\}_{j=1}^3,g,r\}} \sum_{j=1}^3 W^j(q)$$

$$\text{s.t. } q \geq 0 \text{ and } 3\tau = \sum_j f^j + g + r, \text{ or}$$

$$\max_{q=\{\tau,\{f^j\}_{j=1}^3,g,r\}} \sum_{j=1}^3 (u(1 - \tau + f^j) + H(g))$$

$$\text{s.t. } q \geq 0 \text{ and } 3\tau = \sum_j f^j + g + r$$

The first order condition describes the trade-off between the choice of τ and g:

$$\frac{1}{3}u'(c^j) = H_g(g). \tag{8.1}$$

Marginal utility of consumption is equalized across groups. As all individuals are equal, there is no need for transfers. Note that rents, r, are also zero as they are wasteful from the social view point. Thus, the social optimum will be given by the solution of (8.1) and the budget constraint

$$3\tau = g$$

which together imply

$$\frac{1}{3}u'(1 - \frac{g}{3}) = H_g(g).$$

b. Now the objective of party A becomes:

$$\max_{\substack{\tau_A, \{f_A^j\}, \\ g_A, r_A}} E(u^P) \quad s.t. \quad 3\tau_A = \sum_j f_A^j + g_A + r_A \quad \text{or}$$

$$\max_{\substack{\tau_A, \{f_A^j\}, \\ g_A, r_A}} \{\frac{1}{2} + \frac{\psi}{3\phi} \sum_j \phi^j [u(1 - \tau_A - f_A^j) + H(g_A) - W^j(q^B)]\}(R + \gamma r)$$

$$s.t. \quad 3\tau_A = \sum_j f_A^j + g_A + r_A$$

Let us look at the first order condition describing the choice of transfers, f_A^j and f_A^i :

$$\phi^2 u'(c_A^2) = \phi^1 u'(c_A^1) = \phi^3 u'(c_A^1).$$

As $\phi^2 > \phi^1, \phi^3$ more transfers go to group 2. Instead of marginal utility being equalized among groups, as it was the case in the social optimum, transfers are now used by candidates to attract voters from groups with a high density of swing voters. The result is that a mixed measure of marginal utility and group density is equalized across groups, resulting in some groups gaining higher consumption that others.

c. The condition for the choice between rents, r_A, and f_A^2 provides us with the condition for the choice of rents:

$$p\gamma = \frac{\psi}{3\phi}\phi^2 u'(c_A^2)(R + \gamma r).$$

d. The condition for choosing between g_A versus f_A^2 gives us the following condition which helps pinning down the choice of g:

$$H_g(g_A) = \frac{\phi^2 u'(c_A^2)}{\sum_j \phi^j u'(c_A^j)} = \frac{1}{3}.$$

In the model with linear preferences we had

$$H_g(g_A) = \frac{\phi^2}{3\phi} > \frac{1}{3}$$

so that more public good is provided in this model.

8.2   Existence of majoritarian equilibria

For the same model as in problem 8.1, now assume multiple-district (majoritarian) elections: Assume that the three groups of voters, $j = 1, 2, 3$, correspond to three electoral districts, each with one seat. Earning the right to set policy now requires winning at least two seats out of three. Assume further that voter's utility for consumption is linear $(u(c) = c)$.

Let g^* be the solution to $H_g(g^*) = 1$.

a. Show that the level of transfers provided to group 2 voters is given by $f^{2*} = 3 - g^* - \frac{1}{2\psi} + \frac{R}{\gamma}$ in an equilibrium in which both parties compete only for district two.

b. Show that such an equilibrium exists if and only if $\bar{\sigma}^3 \geq 3 - g^* - \frac{1}{2\psi} + \frac{R}{\gamma}$ and $\bar{\sigma}^1 \leq -(3 - g^* - \frac{1}{2\psi} + \frac{R}{\gamma})$.

Answer

a. In equilibrium, only group 2 is targeted and thus this group receives all transfers. By the budget constraint we have that

$$f^{2*} = 3\tau^* - g^* - r^*.$$

It can be seen by the f.o.c. that $\tau^* = 1$ and the condition for r is given by

$$p\gamma = [R + \gamma r^*]\psi$$

As $p = \frac{1}{2}$ we find:

$$r^* = \frac{1}{2\psi} - \frac{R}{\gamma}.$$

b. Suppose

$$\bar{\sigma}^3 < f^{2*} = 3 - g^* - \frac{1}{2\psi} + \frac{R}{\gamma}.$$

Given that party B behaves in accordance to the equilibrium strategies, consider the following deviation for party A. Party A takes all the transfers to group 2 and moves them to group 3. Note that the level of g and of taxes does not change. Now the probability party A wins the election is given by

$$
\begin{aligned}
P^{3,A} &= \Pr(\pi^{3,A} > \frac{1}{2}) = \psi(W^3(q^A) - W^3(q^B) - \bar{\sigma}^3) + \frac{1}{2} \\
&= \psi(f^{2*} - \bar{\sigma}^3) + \frac{1}{2} > \frac{1}{2}
\end{aligned}
$$

Thus, this deviation increases the probability that party A wins the election without affecting the rents it extracts. Therefore, this is a profitable deviation for party A.

Now suppose that the prescribed equilibrium exists. Party A should not be able to deviate to group 3 and gain. Consider any such deviation. Let $\tilde{p}$ and $\tilde{r}$ be the new probability of winning the election and the new rents for this deviation. The deviation is not profitable if

$$\tilde{p}(R + \gamma\tilde{r}) < \frac{1}{2}(R + \gamma r).$$

Using the first order conditions for r and $\tilde{r}$ we have:

$$\tilde{p} < \frac{1}{2}.$$

Thus, we need to check that such a deviation lowers the probability of winning. Let us look at the first order condition for setting rents when focusing on group 3.

$$\tilde{p}\gamma = [R + \gamma\tilde{r}]\psi$$

Replacing $\tilde{p}$ with its expression we get

$$(\psi(\tilde{f} - \bar{\sigma}^3) + \frac{1}{2})\gamma = [R + \gamma\tilde{r}]\psi.$$

Now we show that if $f^{2*} < \bar{\sigma}^3$ we would get that $\tilde{p} < \frac{1}{2}$ which would guarantee that the deviation is not profitable. If $f^{2*} < \bar{\sigma}^3$ then for $\tilde{f} = f^{2*}$ and $r = r^*$ we would get

$$(\psi(f - \bar{\sigma}^3) + \frac{1}{2})\gamma < \frac{1}{2}\gamma = [R + \gamma r]\psi.$$

Thus rents must be lowered and f must be increased to satisfy the first order condition. But if we increase f to equal $\bar{\sigma}^3$ we get

$$(\psi(f - \bar{\sigma}^3) + \frac{1}{2})\gamma = \frac{1}{2}\gamma = [R + \gamma r^*]\psi > [R + \gamma(r^* - (\bar{\sigma}^3 - f^{2*})]\psi.$$

Thus, the solution to the first order condition is with $\tilde{f} \in (f^{2*}, \bar{\sigma}^3)$ and this in turn implies

$$\tilde{p} = (\psi(\tilde{f} - \bar{\sigma}^3) + \frac{1}{2}) < \frac{1}{2}.$$

8.3   Distortionary taxes and electoral competition

Examine the two models, those of proportional and majoritarian elections (problem 8.1 and problem 8.2), with distortionary taxes: Consider a model with distorting taxation to compare majoritarian and proportional elections. Voters now have to choose e (effort). The amount of effort chosen determines the amount of income earned according to the production function $y = e$. Effort is a costly activity with a cost function $c(e) = \frac{e^2}{2}$. The tax rate is proportional, so that a voter with income y pays τy. Assume further that utility for consumption of voters is linear $(u(c) = c)$.

a. Characterize the voters' choice of effort, their income, and the resulting government revenue as functions of the tax rate τ.

b. Show that taxes in the majoritarian model are higher and that public-good provision is lower than in the model with proportional elections.

Answer

a. Given a tax rate of τ, voters solve

$$\max_e \{(1 - \tau)e - \frac{1}{2}e^2\}.$$

The solution for this is given by

$$y(\tau) = e(\tau) = (1 - \tau)$$

and government revenue becomes

$$T(\tau) = 3\tau(1 - \tau) = 3(\tau - \tau^2).$$

b. First, let us characterize the equilibrium under proportional elections. The objective of party A is to maximize $E(u^p)$:

$$\max_{\tau_A, \{f_A^j\}, g_A, r_A} \{\frac{1}{2} + \frac{\psi}{3\phi} \sum_j \phi^j [\frac{(1 - \tau_A)^2}{2} + f_A^j + H(g_A) - W^j(q^B)]\}(R + \gamma r)$$

$$s.t \ \ 3(\tau_A - \tau_A^2) = \sum_j f_A^j + g_A + r_A$$

Thus, the choice between f_A^j and f_A^i is determined by comparing ϕ^j and ϕ^i. Therefore only group 2 will enjoy transfers, i.e.,

$$f_A^2 > 0 \text{ and } f_A^1, \ f_A^3 = 0.$$

How about g_A versus f_A^2? The condition for this choice is given by

$$H_g(g_A) = \frac{\phi^2}{\sum_j \phi^j}$$

The condition for the choice between τ_A versus f_A^2 is given by

$$\tau_A = \frac{3\frac{\phi^2}{\sum_j \phi^j} - 1}{6\frac{\phi^2}{\sum_j \phi^j} - 1}$$

and this pins down the tax rate.

With majoritarian elections, the problem of party A becomes,

$$\max_{\tau_A, \{f_A^j\}, g_A, r_A} \{\frac{1}{2} + \psi[\frac{(1-\tau_A)^2}{2} + f_A^2 + H(g_A) - W^2(q^B)]\}(R + \gamma r)$$

$$s.t \quad 3(\tau_A - \tau_A^2) = \sum_j f_A^j + g_A + r_A$$

Conditions for the solution become

$$H_g(g_A) = 1 > \frac{\phi^2}{\sum_j \phi^j}$$

Therefore, we get a smaller g in the majoritarian model! As for taxes we get:

$$\tau_A = \frac{2}{5} > \frac{3\frac{\phi^2}{\sum_j \phi^j} - 1}{6\frac{\phi^2}{\sum_j \phi^j} - 1}$$

and thus the tax rate is higher.

8.4 Districts and voter groups that do not coincide

In the same model as problem 8.3 suppose districts and groups do not overlap and that $n^{2,district2} > \frac{1}{3}$ and $n^{1,district2} < \frac{1}{3}$, $n^{3,district2} < \frac{1}{3}$, where $n^{j,district-i}$ denotes the share of voters of group j in district i. Assume parameters are such that there exists an equilibrium in which parties compete only in district 2.

a. Show that the majoritarian equilibrium corresponds to a proportional equilibrium with different weights for the groups. Compute these weights.

b. Compare the majoritarian model (question (a)) and the proportional model in this context. Compare the weights given to the different groups in both equilibria.

Answer

a. To win a district, the parties need to have more than a half the votes in that district. The vote shares in district k are given by

$$\pi^{k,A} = \frac{1}{2} + \sum_j n^{j,k} \phi^j (w^j(q^A) - w^j(q^B) - \delta - \bar{\sigma}^j).$$

Therefore the probability of winning district k is given by

$$p^{k,A} = \Pr(\pi^{k,A} \geq \frac{1}{2}) = \frac{1}{2} + \psi(\sum_j n^{j,k}\phi^j(w^j(q^A) - w^j(q^B) - \bar{\sigma}^j).$$

The parties solve the following maximization problem

$$\max_{\substack{q^A \\ s.t. \ BC}} (\frac{1}{2} + \psi(\sum_j n^{j,k}\phi^j(w^j(q^A) - w^j(q^B) - \bar{\sigma}^j))(R + \gamma r).$$

So the solution to this is the solution to the problem

$$\max_{q^A}(\frac{1}{2} + \psi(\sum_j \phi'^j(w^j(q^A) - w^j(q^B) - \bar{\sigma}^j))(R + \gamma r)$$

where $\phi'^j = n^{j,k}\phi^j$.

b. As $\frac{\phi'^2}{\sum_j n^{j,k}\phi^j} > \frac{\phi^2}{\sum_j \phi^j}$, more emphasis is given to group 2 in the majoritarian elections than in the proportional elections. The reason for this is that the majoritarian equilibrium focuses attention on district 2 in which group 2 has a majority. The proportional election forces candidates to disregard the different districts and look only at the different groups. Thus, only the fact that group 2 has the most swing voters comes into play.

8.5   Broad vs. Targeted policy

Consider the following modification of the model analyzed in problems 8.1-8.5. Again, there are three regions, $J = 1, 2, 3$. The economic model is different, however. Voters are employed or unemployed. Employed individuals consume $c = y(1 - \tau)$, where y is income and τ a non distorting tax. Unemployed individuals receive an unemployment subsidy, f. Individuals are risk averse and evaluate private consumption with a concave utility function $U(\cdot)$. Let us also assume that individuals differ in the probability of being employed. Let n^k denote the probability that an individual of type k is employed. The average value of n^k in the population is n, which also denotes the fraction of employed individuals. There are K different types: $k = 1, 2...K$ and each type forms a continuum. Individuals also draw utility from *local* public consumption, and g^J denotes local public consumption per capita in region J. At present, suppose that the utility from the local public consumption is linear. Thus, an individual of type k residing in region J has preferences:

$$w^{kJ} = n^k U(c) + (1 - n^k)U(f) + H(g^J).$$

Where $H(g^j)$ is a concave utility function for the local good. Summing over risk types k, the government budget constraint can be written as:

$$ny\tau = (1 - n)f + \frac{1}{3}\sum_J g^J.$$

As before, individuals trade off economic benefits and ideology when deciding how to vote. Let $W^{kJ}(q)$ be the indirect utility function of voter of type k in region J, as a function of the policy vector $\mathbf{q} = \left[\tau, f, \{g^J\}\right]$. Then the swing voter of type k in region J is defined as usual, namely as a voter with an ideological bias given by:

$$\sigma^{kJ} = W^{kJ}(\mathbf{q}_A) - W^{kJ}(\mathbf{q}_B) - \delta.$$

Finally, suppose that the distribution of individual ideological preferences is uniform and specific to each region *cum* risk type, with density ϕ^{kJ} for type k in region J. Different regions also differ in the mean of the distribution, and these means are sufficiently different that the conditions for existence of a political equilibrium under majoritarian elections are satisfied (see problem 8.2 above). Under majoritarian elections, regions and voting districts coincide. Region 2 is the middle district, with zero mean and the highest density. Compare proportional and majoritarian elections in this model. Assume $\phi^{k,j} = \phi^j$.

a. Show that group 2 enjoys more public good provision under the majoritarian elections than under proportional elections.

b. Assume that $U(c) = \ln c$ and $H(g) = \ln g$. Show that the amount of total spending on public goods and the amount of spending on unemployment insurance are equal in the two election models.

Answer

Now voters' utility is given by:

$$W^{k,j}(q^A) = n^k U(y(1 - \tau^A)) + (1 - n^k)U(f) + H(g^j).$$

And as before parties' objective boils down to maximizing

$$\sum_k \sum_j \phi^{j,k} W^{k,j}(q^A)$$

under the proportional elections, and

$$\sum_k \phi^{2,k} W^{k,2}(q^A)$$

under the majoritarian elections.

Let us first start by characterizing the equilibrium under the proportional elections. Party A solves

$$\max_{\tau^A, f, \{g^j\}_J} \left\{ \sum_k \sum_j \phi^j [n^k U(y(1 - \tau^A)) + (1 - n^k)U(f) + H(g^j)] \right\}.$$

The corresponding conditions are:
– Between τ^A and f:

$$y(1 - \tau^A) = f$$

as marginal utilities of consumption are equalized. Thus, we have full insurance against unemployment.

– Between g^j and f:

$$3H_g(g^1)\frac{\phi^1}{\sum_j \phi^j} = 3H_g(g^2)\frac{\phi^2}{\sum_j \phi^j} = 3H_g(g^3)\frac{\phi^3}{\sum_j \phi^j} = U'(f).$$

Thus $g^2 > g^1, g^3$.

Last, we use the budget constraint to pin down the values

$$ny\tau = (1-n)f + \frac{1}{3}\sum_j g_j.$$

Now, let us check the equilibrium under the majoritarian elections. Party A now solves

$$\max_{\tau^A, f, \{g^j\}} \left\{ \sum_k \phi^2 [n^k U(y(1-\tau^A)) + (1-n^k)U(f) + H(g^2)] \right\}.$$

The conditions for this are:

– Between τ^A and f:

$$y(1-\tau^A) = f$$

Again we have full insurance.

– Between g^2 and f:

$$3H_g(g^2) = U'(f).$$

But now only group 2 has public good provided. The amount of g^2 provided is larger than the amount provided to group 2 under proportional as the left–hand side of this condition is multiplied by $\frac{\phi^2}{\sum_j \phi^j}$ in the proportional elections. Finally the budget constraint,

$$ny\tau = (1-n)f + \frac{1}{3}\sum_j g_j,$$

will pin down equilibrium values.

b. The first order condition in the majoritarian model becomes

$$\frac{3}{g^2} = \frac{1}{f} \Rightarrow g^2 = 3f$$

While in the proportional election model we have

$$\forall j \quad \frac{3}{g^j}\frac{\phi^j}{\sum_i \phi^i} = \frac{1}{f} \Rightarrow g^j = 3f\frac{\phi^j}{\sum_i \phi^i} \Rightarrow \sum_j g^j = 3f\sum_j \frac{\phi^j}{\sum_i \phi^i} = 3f.$$

As expenditures on public goods enter as a sum in the budget constraint, we see that the solution for f is the same in the two models, and thus total expenditures on public goods are equalized.

Chapter 9

Institutions and Accountability

9.1 Local vs. national elections and externalities among local public goods

Consider the following career concerns model with different localities. There are two periods, no redistributive transfers among voters, and local — rather than national — public goods. Tax revenue is fixed at $\bar{\tau}$ and the government budget must be balanced in both periods. There are three localities, indexed by J, which may or may not coincide with voting districts, depending on the electoral rule. Each locality has a population of identical voters, the size of which is normalized to unity. Localities differ only in that each of them enjoys utility from a different local public good, g^J. Voters' preferences in locality J and period t are:

$$w_t^j = y - \bar{\tau} + \alpha g_t^j + \beta(g_t^i + g_t^k),$$

where $\alpha > \beta$ and $\alpha > 1$ as before. Assume voters in each district can observe the public goods in all the other districts.

Politicians choose how to allocate tax revenues between public goods and rents. A separate government budget constraint applies in each locality and in each period, irrespective of the degree of centralization or of the form of the electoral system:

$$g_t^J = \eta^J(\bar{\tau} - r_t^J).$$

where, η^J denotes the competence of the politician in charge of providing the public good and r_t^J denotes rents in locality J. Rents are constrained to be non negative and have an exogenous upper bound $\bar{r}$; $0 \leq r_t^J \leq \bar{r}$. Competence is a random variable, uniformly and independently distributed in each locality, with an expected value of 1 and with density ξ in all localities. Politicians' preferences are given by:

$$E[v] = r_1 + p_I \delta(R + r_2),$$

97

where p_I is the probability that the incumbent is reappointed. The exact meaning of endogenous and exogenous rents depends on the institutional arrangement. With decentralization, r_t is given by r_t^J, rents in locality J, while in a centralized set up, r_t is the sum of rents in all localities: $r_t = \sum_J r_t^J$.

The timing of events is as follows: (i) An incumbent politician is in office in period 1 and chooses rents for that period, r_1^J, without knowing his own competence η^J. (ii) The value of η^J is realized and public good provision g_1^J is residually determined. Voters observe their own utility, but do not directly observe η^J or r_1^J. (iii) Elections are held. If the incumbent wins, his competence in locality J remains η^J. If he loses, his opponent's competence in locality J is drawn at random from the same distribution. (iv) Period 2 rents r_2^J are set, and public goods are residually determined.

In a regime of national elections, one policy maker runs for office in the three regions and wins if he gets more than half the votes of the whole population. Under local elections, three different elections are held in three different localities.. A candidate who gets more than half the shares in his locality wins the election for that locality.

a. Solve the equilibrium for national and local elections. Determine the expression for the probability that the incumbent is reelected in the national elections model.

b. Show that when $\alpha > \beta$, re-electing the incumbent in the national election does not correspond to the social optimum rule (when constrained to choose only one policy maker).

c. Show that when $\alpha = \beta$, re-electing the incumbent in the national election is socially optimal (when constrained to choose only one policy maker). Is this re-election rule better than that in the local elections?

Answer

a. First note that the analysis for the local elections is not affected by the externalities. The reason for this is that the re-election choice does not change. As voters in group j cannot affect the reelection of politicians in other districts, they base their reelection decision solely on the performance of their politician. Thus, the same equilibrium (and therefore have the same equilibrium rents) will prevail in each locality:

$$\tilde{r}^j = \bar{\tau} - \xi\delta(R + \bar{r}).$$

In the national elections, the re-election decision is now changed, as each voter in each group is affected by the levels of the three goods, and they can affect the reelection of the politician who chooses these three goods. Now a voter in group j will choose the incumbent with competencies (η^j, η^i, η^k) if and only if this candidate will give him a higher utility than the expected utility from a new draw. Thus this voter will re-elect the incumbent if and only if

$$\alpha \frac{\bar{\tau} - \bar{r}}{\eta^j} + \beta(\frac{\bar{\tau} - \bar{r}}{\eta^i} + \frac{\bar{\tau} - \bar{r}}{\eta^k}) \geq (\alpha + 2\beta)(\bar{\tau} - \bar{r})$$

$$\Leftrightarrow$$

$$\frac{\alpha}{(\alpha + 2\beta)}\eta^i\eta^k + \frac{\beta}{(\alpha + 2\beta)}\eta^j\eta^k + \frac{\beta}{(\alpha + 2\beta)}\eta^i\eta^j \geq \eta^i\eta^j\eta^k.$$

Given this re-election decision by voters, incumbents again set their choice of rents according to the maximization of

$$\sum r^j + p\delta(R + 3\bar{r}),$$

where again

$$p = p_1 p_2 + p_1 p_3 + p_3 p_2 - 2 p_1 p_2 p_3$$

and $p_1 = p_2 = p_3 = \gamma$, with γ given by

$$\gamma = \Pr\left[\frac{\alpha}{\alpha + 2\beta}\eta^i\eta^k + \frac{\beta}{\alpha + 2\beta}\eta^j\eta^k + \frac{\beta}{\alpha + 2\beta}\eta^i\eta^j \geq \eta^i\eta^j\eta^k\right].$$

Therefore rents are given by the first order condition

$$1 - \frac{\delta(R + 3\bar{r})}{\bar{\tau} - \tilde{r}^j}(2\gamma - 2\gamma^2) = 0 \Rightarrow \tilde{r}^j = \bar{\tau} - \delta(R + 3\bar{r})2\gamma(1 - \gamma).$$

b. When there is only one incumbent, a reelection rule is optimal if and only if, for every draw of $(\eta'^i, \eta'^j, \eta'^k)$, the incumbent is replaced when

$$\sum_j w_{t+1}^j(\eta'^i, \eta'^j, \eta'^k) \geq E[\sum_j w_{t+1}^j(\eta^i, \eta^j, \eta^k)].$$

This expression can be simplified to

$$\eta^i\eta^k + \eta^j\eta^k + \eta^i\eta^j \geq \eta^i\eta^j\eta^k.$$

In the national election the incumbent is replaced if and only if at least two of the following hold:

$$\frac{\alpha}{(\alpha + 2\beta)}\eta^i\eta^k + \frac{\beta}{(\alpha + 2\beta)}\eta^j\eta^k + \frac{\beta}{(\alpha + 2\beta)}\eta^i\eta^j \geq \eta^i\eta^j\eta^k$$

$$\frac{\alpha}{(\alpha + 2\beta)}\eta^j\eta^k + \frac{\beta}{(\alpha + 2\beta)}\eta^i\eta^k + \frac{\beta}{(\alpha + 2\beta)}\eta^i\eta^j \geq \eta^i\eta^j\eta^k$$

$$\frac{\alpha}{(\alpha + 2\beta)}\eta^i\eta^j + \frac{\beta}{(\alpha + 2\beta)}\eta^j\eta^k + \frac{\beta}{(\alpha + 2\beta)}\eta^i\eta^k \geq \eta^i\eta^j\eta^k$$

Obviously, if $\alpha \neq \beta$, one can find a draw that satisfies this condition but not the social optimum condition.

c. If $\alpha = \beta$, the three above conditions collapse to the social welfare condition, i.e.

$$\eta^i\eta^k + \eta^j\eta^k + \eta^i\eta^j \geq \eta^i\eta^j\eta^k.$$

Thus, the re-election rule is optimal. However, his rule is not superior the re-election rule under local elections, as in the latter case we are allowed to replace bad incumbents while keeping the good ones.

9.2   Yardstick competition

Consider the same framework as in problem 9.1 without externalities and with two localities. Therefore group j voters' preferences are given by

$$w_t^j = y - \bar{\tau} + \alpha g_t^j,$$

where $\alpha > 1$. Now let $g_2^j = (\eta^j + \varepsilon)(\bar{\tau} - \bar{r})$, where η^j and ε are distributed normally with $\mu_\eta = 1$ and $\mu_\varepsilon = 0$ as means and σ_η and σ_ε as standard deviations respectively. Assume elections are held locally.

a. Show that voters' optimal voting rule should depend both on the level of public goods in their own district and on the level of public goods in the other district.

b. Show that the voting rule for voters in district j has the property that the incumbent's re-election probability is increasing in district $j's$ public good provision and decreasing in district $i's$ public good provision.

c. Show that for a high variance of ε, voters rely less on district j's public good.

Answer

a. Voters observe g_2^i and g_2^j. They update their beliefs about η^j upon observing these values. Voters will base their voting decision on the prospect that the incumbent's expected ability $E[\eta^j | g_2^i, g_2^j]$ is larger than 1. First, we use the following manipulation of conditional probabilities:

$$E[\eta^j | g_2^i, g_2^j] \geq 1 \Leftrightarrow E[E[\eta^j | (\eta^j + \varepsilon_{|g_2^i})] | g_2^i] \geq 1$$

To determine the voting rule we need to find the distribution of η^j conditional on the observation of g_2^i and g_2^j. By the above equation we can first find the distribution of ε conditional on g_2^i (the only useful information for a voter in group j upon observing g_2^i is about ε). Then we can compute the distribution of η^j given $\varepsilon_{|g_2^i}$ and g_2^i.

By the signal extraction property we have: $\varepsilon_{|g_2^i}$ is distributed normally with mean $(\frac{g_2^i}{(\bar{\tau} - \bar{r}^i)} - 1)\frac{\sigma_\eta^2}{\sigma_\eta^2 + \sigma_\varepsilon^2}$ and variance $\sigma^2 = \frac{\sigma_\eta^2}{\sigma_\eta^2 + \sigma_\varepsilon^2}$. Now we can compute the distribution of $\eta^j_{|\eta^j + \varepsilon_{|g_2^i} = \frac{g_2^j}{(\bar{\tau} - \bar{r}^i)}}$. Again by the signal extraction property this is a normal distribution with mean $((\frac{gj}{(\bar{\tau} - \bar{r}^i)} - (\frac{g_2^i}{(\bar{\tau} - \bar{r}^i)} - 1)\sigma^2)\frac{\sigma^2}{\sigma_\eta^2 + \sigma^2})$ and variance $\frac{\sigma^2}{\sigma_\eta^2 + \sigma^2}$. Now we are ready to write the expression for the optimal voting rule: Vote for the incumbent if and only if

$$((\frac{gj}{(\bar{\tau} - \bar{r}^i)} - (\frac{g_2^i}{(\bar{\tau} - \bar{r}^i)} - 1)\sigma^2)\frac{\sigma^2}{\sigma_\eta^2 + \sigma^2}) \geq 1. \qquad (9.1)$$

By (9.1), in the optimal voting rule, voters take account both their own districts' public good level and the other districts'. The reason for this is that the other districts' public good level is informative about the common shock affecting both districts. This additional information allows the voters to glean more precisely the information about their incumbent's ability in the level of public good in their district. In the literature, the voters' use of the information in other districts is referred to as yardstick competition.

b. By (9.1) the higher the public good provided in the other district the lower is the probability the incumbent will be chosen. The reason for this is that a higher public good in the other district is a signal that the common shock was higher and therefore voters must lower their expectation of the ability of their incumbent.

c. Again by (9.1) a higher variance of the common shock diminishes the informativeness of the other district's public good. This can be seen by the fact that the term $\sigma^2 = \frac{\sigma_\eta^2}{\sigma_\eta^2 + \sigma_\varepsilon^2}$ becomes smaller and this term represents the relative weight that the voters put on the public good of the other district.

9.3   Groups with coordinated voting

There are N voters. Voter j has preferences:

$$w^J = c^J + H(g) = y - \tau + f^J + H(g) \ .$$

with g denoting a general public good benefiting all voters and f^J denoting non-negative lump sum transfers to voter j. An exogenous state of nature, θ, captures the cost of converting private goods into public. Thus, the government budget constraint is:

$$\theta g = N\tau - r - f,$$

with $f = \sum_J f^J$. We restrict all policy instruments to be non-negative and assume that appropriating rents entails some transaction costs $(1-\gamma)$. Thus, the incumbent maximizes:

$$E(v_I) = \gamma r + p_I R,$$

where R is the exogenous rents from office.

The timing of events is: (i) The state of nature θ is realized and observed by everyone. (ii) All voters simultaneously choose a retrospective voting rule. (iii) The incumbent chooses policy: $\{f^J\}, g, \tau$ and r, which is fully observed by voters. (iv) Elections are held.

Assume that M voters are organized so that they coordinate their votes to maximize the sum of utilities in the group.

a. Assume $M > \frac{n}{2}$. Characterize the equilibrium that ensues.

b. Assume $M < \frac{n}{2}$. Characterize the equilibrium that ensues.

c. Compare the results in questions (a) and (b) and discuss the relation between group size and political power.

Answer

a. A candidate must gain the support of half of the electorate and so must gain the support of group M. As voters in M coordinate their strategies, they can demand the maximum payoff given that the incumbent's participation constraint is met. The incumbent can always set $\tau = y$, $f_j = 0$ for all j, $g = 0$ and $r = Ny$. This warranties him a payoff γNy.

Thus in equilibrium, group M must leave rents to the incumbent at

$$\gamma r^* + R = \gamma Ny$$

and therefore equilibrium rents satisfy

$$r^* = \max[0, Ny - \frac{R}{\gamma}].$$

Now group M will maximize its utility

$$\max\{\sum_{j \in M} f_j + MH(g)\} \text{ s.t. } \theta g = Ny - r^* - \sum_{j \in M} f_j$$

The first order condition for this problem is given by

$$H_g(g^*(\theta)) = \frac{\theta}{M} \text{ and}$$

$$f_j(\theta) = Ny - r^* - \theta g^*(\theta) \text{ for all } j \text{ in } M.$$

b. If $M < \frac{n}{2}$, it is not sufficient to win only this group's support. Now, the competition between voters will work in the favor of the politician. In equilibrium, the incumbent will have the support of $\frac{n}{2}$ voters which may or may not include the voters in M. Hence, $H_g(g^*(\theta)) = \frac{2\theta}{N}$, and the Bertrand competition keeps transfers at zero.

c. In this model, there is a discontinuous relation between group size and political power. When the group consists of more than half the voting population it has all the bargaining power and thus leaves the politician at his lowest possible payoff. When group size is smaller than half the population, the politician has the full bargaining power as voters compete with each other. In this case, the politician can extract the maximum rents.

9.4   Checks and balances with bilateral bargaining

Consider the following model of separation of powers. There are two political offices, the holders of which are both subject to re-election. We label them the executive, X, and the legislature, L. The voters now choose retrospective voting strategies for X and L separately. Total rents from office are split between the two office holders, $r_L + r_X = r$, and a specific policy decision must be made with regard to the allocation. Each incumbent office holder has an objective of the form

$$E(v_I) = \gamma r_I + p_I R_I,$$

where $I = X, L$. As before, a budget constraint limits the policy choice $\theta g = N\tau - r$, where θ is observable to voters.

The structure of the game is the following: (i) θ is realized and observed by everyone. (ii) The voters choose a retrospective voting rule. (iii) The incumbent X proposes a tax rate, τ, and public spending, g. (iv) The allocation of rents, $\{r^X, r^L\}$, is then decided upon through bargaining between the two politicians. Specifically assume that the rents available to the politicians, after τ and g have been set, are divided between the politicians with a share α of total rents going to X. (v) Voters observe g and τ. (vi) Elections are held where each incumbent runs against an opponent identical to himself.

a. What is the minimum utility that X can always guarantee himself?

b. Can voters guarantee optimal public-good provision? If yes characterize such an equilibrium. If no, why not?

c. What are the total rents the politicians appropriate?

Answer

a. $X's$ utility is always greater or equal to $\alpha\gamma Ny$ in any equilibrium. X can always set $\tau = y$ and $g = 0$ and get $\alpha\gamma Ny$.

b. As we saw in (a) X can always get $\alpha\gamma Ny$. Thus in an equilibrium in which X is forced to choose an optimal level of g we have

$$\alpha\gamma Ny \le \gamma r^x + R^X$$

which can be written as

$$r^X \ge \frac{\alpha\gamma Ny - R^x}{\gamma}.$$

As L gets $(1 - \alpha)$ of total rents we have that

$$r^L = r^x \frac{1-\alpha}{\alpha} = \frac{\alpha\gamma Ny - R^x}{\gamma} \frac{1-\alpha}{\alpha}.$$

In equilibrium voters will want to lower rents as much as possible and thus we will have these two inequalities satisfied with equality. The government budget constraint is given by:

$$\theta g + r^x + r^y = N\tau$$

Denote the optimal public good choice by $G(\theta)$, thus

$$\theta G(\theta) + \frac{\alpha\gamma Ny - R^x}{\alpha\gamma} = N\tau$$

And voters, to achieve this equilibrium, must set

$$w(\theta) = \frac{R^x}{\alpha\gamma N} - \frac{\theta G(\theta)}{N} + H(G(\theta))$$

c. Total rents are given by $r = r^x + r^y = Ny - \frac{R^x}{\alpha\gamma}$. In the model with checks and balances in the text, rents were zero while they are positive here. This is a result of the fact that in this modification of the model, X, upon choosing taxes and public spending, is a claimant of the rents that are left.

9.5   Separation of powers and the common pool problem

As suggested in the text consider the case in which separation of powers creates a common-pool problem. In the framework of problem 9.4 suppose that first X chooses r^X $(r^X \le Ny)$, then L chooses r^L (such that $r^L \le Ny - r^X$). Given these two values, taxes and public goods are chosen (namely maximizing voters' utility subject to the constraint of providing the politicians with the rents chosen). Suppose that $R^X > R^L$.

a. Can the voters enforce the optimal outcome of $r^X = r^Y = 0$ and $g = G(\theta)$? If yes under what conditions? If no, why not?

b. Suppose both politicians get rents in equilibrium. Characterize such an equilibrium and specify the conditions for the public good to be set at the optimal level.

c. Compare the total rents of politicians in this model and in the model with a single politician.

Answer

a. If voters enforce the optimal outcome, it must be that X does not wish to deviate and take all rents, Ny. Thus

$$\gamma Ny \leq R^X$$

and the same for L: $\gamma Ny \leq R^L$.

If these two conditions hold then, if voters set their cutoff utility at $y - T(\theta) + H(G(\theta))$ for electing both candidates, politicians will have to comply.

b. If the conditions in (a) are both violated then voters must give some rents to the politicians in equilibrium. Consider an equilibrium with $\{r^X, r^L, g, \tau\}$. Let us analyze the choice of X. On the one hand, he can comply to the equilibrium and choose r^X, get re-elected, and thus receive a utility $\gamma r^X + R^X$. On the other hand, X can deviate and appropriate all of voters' income. The benefit of this will be a gain of γNy, whereas the cost comes from the fact that X will not be re-elected. Thus, in equilibrium we must have

$$\gamma Ny \leq \gamma r^X + R^X.$$

The same reasoning will apply to L with the difference that he has a smaller share of the income to appropriate. Thus in equilibrium

$$\gamma(Ny - r^X) \leq \gamma r^L + R^L.$$

Obviously, voters will want the rents of both politicians to be small so that they will make constraints binding. Thus, the equilibrium entails

$$r^X = Ny - \frac{R^X}{\gamma}$$

and

$$r^L = \frac{R^X - R^L}{\gamma}$$

Moreover, voters would like to have the optimal level of g set. Thus, optimal taxes will be determined by the budget constraint (incorporating the rents above)

$$Ny - \frac{R^L}{\gamma} + \theta G(\theta) = N\tau$$

so that, to have such an equilibrium, we need this expression to be smaller than total income, yielding

$$\frac{R^L}{\gamma} \geq \theta G(\theta).$$

c. Total rents in this model are given by $r = r^X + r^L = Ny - \frac{R^L}{\gamma}$, whereas in the single politician model, rents were given by $r' = Ny - \frac{R'}{\gamma}$. Thus, if $R^L < R'$, rents are larger in this model. This assumption may be reasonable as L is a claimant of only part of total rents while a single politician claims all the rents. So in a dynamic setting one would expect L to have a smaller continuation value than a single politician.

Chapter 10

Political Regimes

10.1 A model with a prime minister

Assume the following model of policy choice. The are three groups of voters, $J = 1, 2, 3$, all of size (mass) unity. Groups coincide with electoral districts, each represented by a single legislator, $l = 1, 2, 3$. Moreover a prime minister, P, heads the government. Elections are majoritarian. Voters in district J have preferences

$$w^J = c^J + H(g) = y - \tau + f^J + H(g),$$

where τ denotes taxes and f^J denotes transfers to group j. g denotes a general public good benefiting all voters.

Politicians can appropriate rents and must choose how these should be allocated. This is done by a legislative decision. Denoting by r_i the rents captured by legislator i or the prime minister, we write the government budget constraint as

$$3\tau = g + \sum_J f^J + \sum_l r_l + r_P = g + f + r,$$

where f denotes aggregate transfers. Items in the government budget constraint must all be non negative, and $\mathbf{q}$ denotes the full policy vector.

The prime minister, P, proposes a policy vector, $\mathbf{q}$, and his proposal is subject to a vote in the legislature. The prime minister remains in office only if his proposal is accepted in parliament. Let $\bar{r}$ be the default rents of legislators and the prime minister if the proposal fails. What will the level of public goods provision be in this regime? Who will end up with positive rents, transfers?

Answer

The prime minister has to please only two districts. Therefore, faced with voting strategies of voters, $(\varpi_1, \varpi_2, \varpi_3)$ he will always choose to please those districts with a lower reservation utility. The Bertrand competition between districts will therefore lead to equal reservation utilities at least among the two districts in the coalition. With out loss of generality assume it is districts 1 and 2 that form the coalition. Therefore we have that in any equilibrium $\varpi_1 = \varpi_2 = \varpi^* \leq \varpi_3$. Moreover the Bertrand competition will also imply that at ϖ^* transfers to the districts are zero.

The prime minister will need the vote of two legislators, 1 and 2. For this he will have to provide these legislators with rents, r_1 and r_2, so that $\gamma r_i + R = \gamma \bar{r}$ for $i = 1, 2$. Therefore $r_i^* = \max\{\bar{r} - \frac{R}{\gamma}, 0\}$ for $i = 1, 2$ if $\varpi^* < \varpi_3$.

Given $\varpi_1 = \varpi_2 = \varpi^* \leq \varpi_3$ the maximization problem faced be the prime minister will be given by

$$\max \quad \gamma r_p + R$$
$$\text{s.t.} \quad f_1 + y - \tau + H(g) \geq \varpi^*$$
$$f_2 + y - \tau + H(g) \geq \varpi^*$$
$$3\tau = g + f + r$$

The solution to this will be given by:

$$\tau^* = y \text{ and } H(g^*) \geq \frac{1}{2}$$

with interior solution at $H(g^*) = \frac{1}{2}$. Lastly

$$\varpi^* = H(g^*).$$

10.2   Adding a president

Now consider a presidential-congressional model. The framework is the same as in problem 10.1 only now, instead of a prime minister we have a president, P. The congressional policy game has the following timing, (i) Two different agenda setters, a_τ and a_g, the "finance committee" and the "expenditure committee" respectively, are appointed among the three legislators. (ii) Voters set the cut off utilities ϖ^J in their re-election rules optimally, conditional on the their legislator's status. (iii) a_τ proposes a tax rate, τ. (iv) Congress votes on the proposal: if it is approved by a majority, the tax proposal becomes law; if it is not, the default tax rate is $\bar{\tau} > 0$. (v) a_g proposes g, $\{f^J\}_{j=1,2,3}$, and $\{r_i\}_{i=1,2,3,P}$ subject to $3\tau \geq g + f + r$. (vi) Congress votes on the allocation proposal: if the proposal is rejected by a majority, the default allocation is $g = 0$, $f^J \equiv \tau - r_l \geq 0$, $r_l = \bar{r}$. (vii) The president decides whether to veto the decision of Congress. If he does the default allocation is implemented. (vii) Voters observe everything and elections are held. The president is held to national elections, and the legislators contest in their districts. Assume R is large.

a.   Construct an equilibrium in which public goods are provided at a level $H_g(g^*) = 1$.

b.   Show that there are infinitely many equilibria with $H_g(g^*) = 1$ and positive transfers for the district of a_g.

c.   Compare the results of the model with a president and the model without one. Why doesn't the addition of the president change the equilibria?

Answer

a. First, if we want an equilibrium to have public good provided at the level of g^* we must have a_g care enough about re-election so that he won't appropriate all taxes ($\tau = \frac{g^*}{3}$), i.e.,

$$\gamma(3\frac{g^*}{3} - \bar{r}) \leq \gamma r^* + R.$$

Assume that R is big enough so that this is satisfied even with zero rents, so that

$$g^* - \bar{r} - \frac{R}{\gamma} \leq 0.$$

Now set reservation utilities at a level $\varpi^* = y - \frac{g^*}{3} + H(g^*)$ for all districts and for the national election of the president as well. Now a_τ will want to set $\tau^* = \frac{g^*}{3}$ as he knows all taxes will be used to finance the public good. Any tax above this will entail rents for a_g.

Note that the inclusion of the president's veto power is redundant as we already have a coalition supporting $a_g's$ proposal. Moreover he will receive zero rents if R is large enough.

b. In (a) we have shown an equilibrium with g^*. Now any equilibrium supported by the following cutoffs can be sustained

$$\bar{w}^{a_g} = y - (\frac{g^*}{3} + x) + H(g^*) + 3x = y - \frac{g^*}{3} + H(g^*) + 2x$$

$$\bar{w}^j = y - (\frac{g^*}{3} + x) + H(g^*), \ j \neq a_g h$$

$$\tau^* = \frac{g^*}{3} + x$$

$$f^{a_g} = 3x, \ f^j = 0, \ \text{where } x > 0.$$

The reason why these are equilibria is that if group a_g insists on getting this cutoff, the other groups are forced to comply if they want any public good produced in equilibrium. Group a_g enjoys extra bargaining power as it is always in the coalition which supports the policy. The other two groups are weakened by the "Bertrand competition" result.

c. The reason why adding the president doesn't change the results is that the vote in the congress on the policy already imposes on the legislators to take into account a coalition of two groups of voters.

10.3 Infinitely repeated presidential-congressional regime

In the frame work of problems 10.1 and 10.2 now assume there is no president. Consider an infinitely repeated game in which at each period the following is played: (i) Two different agenda-setters, a_τ and a_g, the "finance committee" and the "expenditure committee" respectively, are appointed among the three legislators. (ii) Voters set the cut off utilities ϖ^j in their re-election rules optimally, conditional on their legislator's status. (iii) a_τ proposes a tax rate, τ. (iv) Congress votes on the tax proposal: if it is approved by a majority, the tax proposal becomes law; if not, the default tax rate is $\bar\tau > 0$. (v) a_g proposes $g, \{f^J\}$, and $\{r_l\}$ subject to $3\tau \geq g + f + r$. (vi) Congress votes on the allocation proposal: if it is rejected by a majority, the default allocation is $g = 0$, $f^J \equiv \tau - r_l \geq 0$, $r_l = \bar r$. (vii) Voters observe everything, and elections are held.

Assume there are no exogenous rents but there is an endogenously determined continuation value for reelection. Suppose that at the beginning of each period, each legislator is chosen with equal probability for each position a_g, a_τ and $j \neq a_g, a_\tau$.

a. Construct a stationary equilibrium for this model in which $H_g(g^*) = 1$.

b. Compute the continuation value for staying in office, the rents gained by the politicians, and reservation utilities for voters.

Answer

At time t voters set reservation utilities $\{\bar w_t^j\}_{j=1,2,3}$ and a_τ and a_g choose τ_t and $\{g_t, \{f_t^j\}_{j=1,2,3}\}$ respectively. We will construct a stationary equilibrium such that $\bar w_t^j = \bar w^*$ for all groups and at any period, $\tau_t = \tau^*$, $r_t = r^*$, $g_t = g^*$, and $f_t^j = f^*$.

The utility of legislator j in period t is given by

$$E[u^j] = \gamma r_t^j + \delta V_t,$$

where $V_t = V^*$ is the value of being re-elected.

Let g^* be defined by

$$H_g(g^*) = 1.$$

We will now construct an equilibrium in which $g_t = g^*$ at any period. Every period taxes must be collected to pay for g^* and $r_t^{a_g} = r^*$. Thus

$$\tau_t^* = \tau^* = \frac{g^* + r^*}{3}.$$

If a_g doesn't want to be re-elected he might as well appropriate all taxes and get

$$\gamma(3\tau^* - \bar r)$$

This should be smaller than playing along equilibrium path, receiving

$$\gamma r^* + \delta V^*$$

Thus in equilibrium we will have

$$\gamma(3\tau^* - \bar{r}) \leq \gamma r^* + \delta V^*$$

In equilibrium this will hold with equality, i.e.,

$$r^* = 3\tau^* - \bar{r} - \frac{\delta}{\gamma}V^*.$$

From the budget constraint

$$g^* = 3\tau^* - r^* = \bar{r} + \frac{\delta}{\gamma}V^*$$

So that in equilibrium we must have

$$\bar{r} + \frac{\delta}{\gamma}V^* = g^* \Rightarrow V^* = \frac{\gamma}{\delta}(g^* - \bar{r})$$

on the other hand, if re-elected, a politician is chosen with equal probability to any position. As rents are positive only for a_g we get the following expression for the continuation value

$$V^* = \frac{1}{3}\gamma r^* + \delta V^* \Rightarrow V^* = \frac{1}{3(1-\delta)}\gamma r^*$$

and therefore combining expressions we pin down the rents

$$r^* = \frac{3(1-\delta)}{\delta}(g^* - \bar{r})$$

and we get an expression for the value of re-election

$$V^* = \frac{\gamma}{\delta}(g^* - \bar{r})$$

This equilibrium will be supported by

$$\bar{w}^j = y - (\frac{g^* + r^*}{3}) + H(g^*).$$

10.4   The "caretaker government" subgame

In this problem we consider a continuation game following the breakdown of a parliamentary coalition. In the same framework as that of the last three problems assume now that a "caretaker government", a single legislator, is picked at random after the breakdown, voters reformulate their re-election rules, the caretaker legislator makes the entire budget proposal, and this is approved or not by the legislature. Assume that if the coalition breaks down after this subgame the defaults are given by $r^j = \bar{r}$ to all legislators and $g = 0$, $f = 0$ and $\tau = 0$. Solve the subgame and compute the expected payoffs for entering into this subgame.

Answer

With equal probability a legislator j is chosen to act as caretaker government. If he doesn't consider being reelected he will buy one of the legislator and give him $\bar{r}$. Then he can set $\tau = y$ and get $(3y - \bar{r})$ as rents. Thus in equilibrium we must have equilibrium rents, r^*, satisfying

$$\gamma(3y - \bar{r}) = \gamma r^* + R^j$$

therefore

$$r^* = 3y - \bar{r} - \frac{R^j}{\gamma}.$$

The care taker government is faced with the problem

$$\max_{\tau, g, \{f_i\}} r \quad s.t. \quad 3\tau = g + r + \sum f_i$$

$$w^j = y - \tau + f^j + H(g) \geq \bar{w}^j$$
$$\exists i \text{ s.t. } w^i = y - \tau + f^i + H(g) \geq \bar{w}^i \text{ where } i \neq j$$

Thus $H_g(g^*) \geq \frac{1}{2}$, $f^j \geq 0$, and $f^i = 0$. Now, group j can set:

$$\bar{w}^j = y - \frac{g^* + 3y - \bar{r} - R^j/\gamma + f^{*j}}{3} + f^{*j} + H(g^*) = -\frac{g^*}{3} + \frac{\bar{r} + \frac{R^j}{\gamma}}{3} + f^{*j} + H(g^*)$$

and the other groups set the same

$$\bar{w}^i = -\frac{g^*}{3} + \frac{\bar{r} + R^j/\gamma - f^{*j}}{3} + H(g^*)$$

and this is an equilibrium.
Thus expected payoffs to legislators are

$$r' \equiv E[r^i] = \frac{3y - \bar{r} - \frac{R^j}{\gamma}}{3} = y - \frac{\bar{r} + \frac{R^j}{\gamma}}{3}.$$

Taxes are given by

$$\tau = \frac{g^*}{3} + y - \frac{\bar{r} + \frac{R^j}{\gamma}}{3} + \frac{f^{*j}}{3}.$$

10.5 Calculating the equilibria in the Parliamentary regime

Using the results of problem 10.4 you are now asked to compute the equilibria of the full model of parliamentary regimes (as in the text): (i) Two incumbent legislators, a_g and a_τ, are appointed to act as expenditure and finance ministers, respectively. (ii) Voters set their reservation utilities conditional on their legislators' status. (iii) The finance minister, a_τ, proposes a tax rate τ. (iv) The expenditure minister proposes expenditures $(g, \{f^J\}, \{r_l\})$ subject to the budget constraint and the proposed tax rate. (v) Either member of the government can veto the proposal. If neither does, the proposal passes and elections are held. (vi) If at least one of them vetoes, the government breaks down and a default policy is implemented with payoffs as in problem 10.4. Under what conditions does an equilibrium with public good provided at a level of $H_g^{-1}(1/2)$ exist?

Answer

Suppose τ is set as the tax rate. How does the expenditure minister choose g? The minister solves the problem,

$$\max_{g,\{f_j\},\{r^\tau,r^g\}} r^g \quad s.t. \quad 3\tau = g + r^g + r^\tau + \sum f_j$$

$$y - \tau + f^g + H(g) \geq \bar{w}^g$$
$$(\gamma r^\tau + R^\tau \geq \gamma r' \text{ and } y - \tau + f^\tau + H(g) \geq \bar{w}^\tau)$$
$$\text{or } (r^\tau \geq r' \text{ and } y - \tau + f^\tau + H(g) < \bar{w}^\tau)$$

Note that the expenditure minister must give the finance minister at least r' as rents and will always give him enough rents to satisfy

$$r^\tau = r'/3 - R^\tau/\gamma.$$

If $f^g, f^\tau > 0$ in equilibrium it must be that $H_g(g) = 1/2$. If $f^\tau = 0$ the equilibrium can have $1 \geq H_g(g^*) \geq 1/2$. The condition for $H_g(g^*) = 1/2$ to hold in equilibrium is that total rents left for politicians are large enough so that

$$3y - r^g - r^\tau \geq g^*.$$

If this is not satisfied the politicians would just appropriate all income and forgo reelection. Total rents are given by the two constraints for the politicians to be interested in reelection,

$$\gamma\left(3y - \left(\frac{r'}{3} - \frac{R^\tau}{\gamma}\right)\right) \leq \gamma r^g + R$$

$$\gamma\left(\frac{r'}{3} - \frac{R^\tau}{\gamma}\right) \leq \gamma r^\tau + R \Rightarrow r = r^g + r^\tau \geq 3y - \frac{2R}{\gamma}$$

Finally the condition becomes

$$\tfrac{2R}{\gamma} \geq H_g^{-1}(1/2).$$

10.6 Presidential regime with line-item veto

Consider a presidential-congressional model with line-item veto. The framework is the same as in question 10.1 only now, instead of a prime minister we have a president, P. The congressional policy game has the following timing, (i) One agenda-setters, a_g, is appointed among the three legislators. (ii) Voters set the cut-off utilities ϖ^J for re-electing their representative in the congressional elections, conditional on the status of their legislator. (iii) a_g proposes a tax rate, τ, $g, \{f^J\}_{j=1,2,3}$, and $\{r_i\}_{i=1,2,3,P}$ subject to $3\tau \geq g + f + r$. (iv) Congress votes: if rejected by a majority, the default allocation is $\bar{\tau} > 0$, $g = 0$, $f^J \equiv \tau - r_l \geq 0$, $r_l = \bar{r}$. (v) Voters set cut-off utilities w^J in their re-election in the presidential election.(vii) The president decides whether to veto the whole public goods program, g, or any of the specific cash transfers, f^J. If he vetoes, he may take the resources saved as private rents, r^P, or to lower taxes. (vii) Voters observe everything and elections are held. The president is elected in national elections and the legislators contest in their districts. It is assumed that the benefits from the public goods program is such that $H(g) - H(0) \geq \frac{2}{3}g$. Starting with the veto stage, the president may at this stage default and use all available resources for private rents. In order to avoid this, he must at least be given rents satisfying

$$\gamma r^P + R \geq \gamma \left(g + \sum_J f^J \right).$$

We will first assume that the rents R are large enough so that this is always satisfied. Disregard equilibria in which the politician can never satisfy the demands of any two groups.

a. Show that the president will not veto the public goods program.

b. Show that in the veto stage, the president will veto the transfer to group that would receive the largest cash transfers under the allocation of the legislative game.

c. Show that the president must return all the funds saved from cancelling the transfer program to the tax payers.

d. Compute the equilibrium allocation of rents, public goods provision, transfers, and taxes in the legislative game and discuss the results.

Answer

a. If the president chooses to please the voters, he must satisfy the re-election demands from at least two groups. The president will veto the public goods program if the freed resources will be more valuable in utility terms to the voters in the coalition, than the public goods provided, that is if

$$H(g) - H(0) \geq \frac{g}{3} + \frac{g}{6} = \frac{2}{3}g.$$

If the program is cancelled, then the group members do not pay the contribution $\frac{g}{3}$, in addition, they may split the resources provided by the third group. The assumption $H(g) - H(0) > \frac{2}{3}g$, ensures that the president does not want to cancel the program.

b. The president maximizes his rents given that he satisfies the re-election demands of two groups. Since the president does not need the votes of the third group, he will veto the program benefiting this group.

Conditional on being in the coalition and not having the cash transfer program , f^L, vetoed, setting a reservation utility, $\overline{w}^L$, corresponds to setting the level of tax returns demanded, $\overline{\tau}_r^L$, defined by:

$$y - \tau + \frac{1}{3}\overline{\tau}_r^L + f^L + H(g) = \overline{w}^L.$$

We will discuss voter demands in terms of tax returns rather than in terms of reservation utilities.

Number the legislators so that $f^1 < f^2 < f^3$. The president has three options, satisfying groups 1 and 2; 1 and 3; or 2 and 3, in which case he recieves utility

$$\gamma\left(f^3 - \max\left(\overline{\tau}^1, \overline{\tau}^2\right)\right) + R,$$
$$\gamma\left(f^2 - \max\left(\overline{\tau}^1, \overline{\tau}^3\right)\right) + R,$$
$$\gamma\left(f^1 - \max\left(\overline{\tau}^2, \overline{\tau}^3\right)\right) + R,$$

respectively.

We first show that only group 3 will get their transfer program vetoed. If 1 is not part of the coalition, then it must be the case that $f^1 - \max\left(\overline{\tau}^2, \overline{\tau}^3\right) > f^3 - \max\left(\overline{\tau}^1, \overline{\tau}^2\right)$, or equivalently

$$\max\left(\overline{\tau}^1, \overline{\tau}^2\right) - \max\left(\overline{\tau}^2, \overline{\tau}^3\right) > f^3 - f^1 > 0,$$

which implies $\overline{\tau}^1 > \overline{\tau}^3$. But then voters in group 1 have incentives and possibility to lower their demands on tax cuts and enter the coalition. Therefore group 1 must be in the coalition. By an identical argument, group 2 will be part of the coalition. The reason 1 and 2 will be in the coalition is that by having lower cash transfer programs, they have a comparative advantage in undercutting group 3 by lowering their reservation utilities.

c. When the president keeps the transfer programs to groups 1 and 2, their pay-offs are

$$y - \tau + \frac{1}{3}\max\left(\overline{\tau}^1, \overline{\tau}^2\right) + f^1 + H(g)$$

$$y - \tau + \frac{1}{3}\max\left(\overline{\tau}^1, \overline{\tau}^2\right) + f^2 + H(g).$$

The maximal amount of tax returns given that the transfer program to group 3 is cancelled is f^3. Given any value of $\overline{\tau}^2 < f^3$, the best reply of group 1 is to set

$$\overline{\tau}^1 = \max\left(f^3 - f^1 + \max\left(\overline{\tau}^2, \overline{\tau}^3\right), f^3\right).$$

This is the highest feasible reservation utility that keeps 1 in the coalition. While for $\bar{\tau}^2 = f^3$, any point $\bar{\tau}^1 \in \left[0, f^3\right]$ is a best reply.

Similarly for group 2, the best reply is

$$\bar{\tau}^2 = \max\left(f^3 - f^2 + \max\left(\bar{\tau}^1, \bar{\tau}^3\right), f^3\right).$$

for $\bar{\tau}^1 < f^3$, and $\bar{\tau}^2 \in \left[0, f^3\right]$, for $\bar{\tau}^2 = f^3$. In equilibrium, either 1 or 2, or both, set $\bar{\tau}^L = f^3$. Both 1 and 2 are included in the coalition while the transfer program to group 3 is cancelled. The president receives no rents. All the funds saved from the cancelled program are used to lower taxes.

The reason that all taxes must be returned is that the coalition consists of more than 1 member and that these collectively push up demands on the president. Either 1 or 2 must be in the coalition, so although group 3 may have lower demands on tax returns, the tax returns required in a coalition including 3 is based on the tax demands of the other group. This improves the bargaining power of 1 and 2.

d. The legislative bargaining stage. Given the outcome after the veto stage, all participants understand that the highest transfer $f^{\max}$ will consequently be vetoed by the president and used for tax returns. The expected utility of a group that does not receive the highest transfer is

$$y - \tau + \frac{1}{3}f^{\max} + f^K + H\left(g\right),$$

while the government budget constraint is

$$3\tau = g + \sum_L r^L + \sum_L f^L.$$

After the agenda setter has been selected, the other two legislators compete not to be offered the highest transfer. In the competition to be in the coalition, voters underbid each other up to the point where $f^m = 0$ for the group in the coalition, that is up to the point where $w^m = w^n = y - \tau + \frac{1}{3}f^{\max} + H(g)$. Again, assume that $\bar{r} \leq R/\gamma$, so that the rents r^m needed to satisfy $\gamma r^m + R = \gamma\bar{r}$ is never positive. In order to give the agenda setter incentives not to use the whole budget for rents, r^a must satisfy

$$\gamma r^a + R \geq \gamma\left(3y - \bar{r}\right).$$

Legislator a will get cash transfers f^a to her district and $f^a + \varepsilon$, where ε is a small number, to the district of the member who is not in the coalition. The policy maximizing the utility of the voters in district a is therefore the solution to

$$\max\left[f^a + y - \tau + \frac{1}{3}\left(f^a + \varepsilon\right) + H(g)\right],$$

subject to the budget constraint

$$3\left(\tau - y\right) + \bar{r} + \frac{R}{\gamma} = g + 2f^a.$$

The solution implies

$$
\tau = y,
$$
$$
g = \min\left[H_g^{-1}(2/3), \overline{r} + \frac{R}{\gamma}\right],
$$
$$
f = \frac{1}{2}\left(\overline{r} + \frac{R}{\gamma} - g\right),
$$
$$
r^a = 3y - \overline{r} - \frac{R}{\gamma}.
$$

With line-item veto, public goods provision, g, is higher, transfers, f, are lower and taxes $\tau - f$, are lower than without line-item veto.

Part IV

Dynamic politics

Chapter 11

Dynamic policy problems

11.1 Debt structure, labor taxation and money

This problem is adapted from section 7.2. in Persson and Tabellini 1990. Consider the following two-period model. At date 1, the agent's initial assets are 0. The agent consumes an amount c_1 of private good, he supplies labor l_1 and he can invest in bonds d_1 or hold money balances m_1. We assume the real wage to be unity. Moreover, the return from bonds is $R = 1$. Money balances pay a zero nominal wage of return and depreciate. The per unit depreciation in the real value of money is $\pi = \frac{p_2 - p_1}{p_2}$, where p_t is the market price at date t. Finally, government consumes an exogenous per capita amount g and taxes labor income. We call τ_1 the tax rate. In period 2, the agent consumption level is c_2, his labor supply is l_2 and his demand for money balances is m_2. Labor is also taxed in period 2 and the tax rate is τ_2. Then, the government finances g by raising taxes in periods 1 and 2 and by using its revenues from bonds and money balances. We assume that one unit of labor is necessary to produce one unit of good, then the resource constraints in periods 1 and 2 are $c_1 + g = l_1$ and $c_2 = l_2$, respectively. The individual's preferences are summarized by

$$w = c_1 + c_2 - V(l_1) - V(l_2) + U(m_1) + U(m_2),$$

where $V(\cdot)$ is increasing and convex and $U(\cdot)$ is increasing and concave.

a. Determine the agent's intertemporal budget constraint. Determine the agent's supply of labor and demand for money functions.

b. Determine the government's budget constraint as well as its optimization program, when it is committing to future policy rules at the beginning of date 1. What is the optimal policy?

c. Suppose now that the government cannot commit. Determine the implemented policy. Compare your result with that of question (b).

Answer

a. The budget constraint in period 1 is:

$$c_1 + d_1 + m_1 \leq l_1(1 - \tau_1)$$

and in period 2:

$$c_2 + m_2 \leq l_2(1 - \tau_2) + m_1(1 - \pi) + d_1$$

The intertemporal budget constraint is then:

$$c_1 + c_2 = l_1(1 - \tau_1) + l_2(1 - \tau_2) - m_2 - m_1\pi$$

The agent maximizes his utility under the budget constraints. The first order conditions are:

$$1 - \tau_1 = V_l(l_1) \qquad 1 - \tau_2 = V_l(l_2)$$
$$U_m(m_1) = \pi \qquad U_m(m_2) = 1$$

Then, in equilibrium:

$$l_t(\tau_t) = V_l^{-1}(1 - \tau_t) \qquad t = 1,2$$
$$m_1(\pi) = U_m^{-1}(\pi) \qquad m_2 = U_m^{-1}(1) \tag{11.1}$$

Note that the demand for real balances in period 2 is constant. This is only due to our specification of the preferences.

b. The budget constraint of the government at date 1 is:

$$g \leq \tau_1 l_1 + m_1 + d_1 \tag{11.2}$$

at date 2, the budget constraint is:

$$d_1 + m_1 \leq \tau_2 l_2 + \pi m_1 + m_2 \tag{11.3}$$

Note that inflation provides the government with revenues. Basically, π acts as a tax on nominal wealth. Besides, note that the government's intertemporal budget constraint is $g \leq \tau_1 l_1 + \tau_2 l_2 + \pi m_1 + m_2$. Since m_2 is constant, we have to assume that $m_2 < g$ for the problem to be interesting. If this condition is not satisfied, public expenditures are financed by money balances m_2 only. In addition to the budget constraints, the government must satisfy the following resources constraints:

$$c_1 + g = l_1 \tag{11.4}$$

and:

$$c_2 = l_2 \tag{11.5}$$

Its objective is to maximize the agent's utility under the constraints (11.1)-(11.5). This program can be written as:

$$\max_{l_1,l_2,m_1} l_1 - g + l_2 - V(l_1) - V(l_2) + U(m_1) + U(m_2)$$
$$\text{s.t. } g \leq [1 - V_l(l_1)]l_1 + [1 - V_l(l_2)]l_2 + U_m(m_1)m_1 + m_2 \text{ and } U_m(m_2) = 1$$

Denoting by μ the multiplier of the first constraint, the first order conditions are:

$$
\begin{aligned}
1 - V_l(l_1) + \mu[1 - l_1 V_{ll}(l_1) - V_l(l_1)] &= 0 \\
1 - V_l(l_2) + \mu[1 - l_2 V_{ll}(l_2) - V_l(l_2)] &= 0 \\
U_m(m_1) + \mu[U_{mm}(m_1)m_1 + U_m(m_1)] &= 0
\end{aligned}
$$

Then, the optimal labor supply and demand of money when the government can commit satisfy the following rule:

$$
\frac{1 - V_l(l_1)}{1 - l_1 V_{ll}(l_1) - V_l(l_1)} = \frac{1 - V_l(l_2)}{1 - l_2 V_{ll}(l_2) - V_l(l_2)} = \frac{U_m(m_1)}{m U_{mm}(m_1) + U_m(m_1)} \qquad (11.6)
$$

Let $\epsilon_{l_t} = \frac{V_l(l_t)}{l_t V_{ll}(l_t)}$ be the elasticity of the labor supply function at date t and $\epsilon_{m_1} = \frac{-U_m(m_1)}{m_1 U_{mm}(m_1)}$ be the elasticity of the demand for money at date 1. The previous expression can be rewritten as:

$$
\frac{\tau_1}{1 - \tau_1} \epsilon_{l_1} = \frac{\tau_2}{1 - \tau_2} \epsilon_{l_2} = \epsilon_{m_1} \qquad (11.7)
$$

Equation (11.7) describes the relation between the three tax rates (the two taxes on labor and the inflationary tax) and the elasticities of these tax rates. Note that, under commitment and given the symmetry of preferences, the taxes on labor are the same.

c. Suppose that the government cannot commit. In period 2, his ex post budget constraint is:

$$
d_1 + m_1 = \tau_2 l_2(\tau_2) + \pi m_1 + m_2 \qquad (11.8)
$$

where m_1 is predetermined and has zero ex post elasticity. Besides, m_2 is constant and d_1 is also predetermined. Therefore, as long as $\tau_2 > 0$, it is in the interest of the government to set $\pi = 1$. With respect to the commitment case we have the following conclusions. First, the equilibrium entails a higher tax on money balances and a smaller tax on period 2 labor. Second, anticipating this, agents reduce their demand for money balances in period 1. Last, the government needs to overtax period 1 labor to satisfy its first period budget constraint.

11.2   Credibility problems in labor taxation when government consumption is endogenous

This problem is based on section 8.2. in Persson and Tabellini 1990. Consider the following two-period model. In each period $t = 1, 2$, the representative consumer has preferences over private consumption c_t and leisure x_t. His labor supply is denoted by l_t and satisfies the time constraint $x_t + l_t = 1$. Assume that the real wage is 1. The government consumes only in period 2 a quantity g_2. The agent's utility is

$$w = F(c_1, l_1, c_2, l_2) + H(g_2),$$

where $F(\cdot)$ is decreasing (respectively, increasing) and concave with respect to labor (respectively, consumption) at each period and $H(\cdot)$ is increasing and concave. Labor is taxed in each period and the tax rate is denoted by τ_t. In addition, the representative agent's initial wealth is b_1. Finally, the consumer can invest in foreign assets and government bonds in the first period, which both pay 0 return. Denote by d_1 the chosen level of investment. Government choices are made by a benevolent social planner who determines g_2 and uses the tax receipts to finance it.

a. Suppose that the government can commit. Determine the agent's intertemporal budget constraint. What is his optimization program? Write his ex ante indirect utility function, which we will denote by $W(\tau_1, \tau_2; b_1)$. Determine the government's intertemporal budget constraint and write its optimization program. Determine the optimal fiscal policy.

b. Suppose now that the government cannot commit. What is the agent's wealth b_2 at the beginning of period 2? Write the budget constraint of the representative agent in period 2 and characterize his ex post indirect utility $\tilde{W}(\tau_2; b_2)$. Determine the government budget constraint. What is the second period optimal fiscal policy?

c. When does the equilibrium under no commitment coincide with the equilibrium with commitment? What happens if $F(c_1, l_1, c_2, l_2) = U(c_1) - V(l_1) + c_2 - V(l_2)$? Do we have the same result when $F(c_1, l_1, c_2, l_2) = c_1 - V(l_1) + U(c_2) - V(l_2)$? Why or why not?

Answer

a. The budget constraint of the agent at the first period is:

$$b_1 + (1 - \tau_1)l_1 = c_1 + d_1$$

At date 2, it is:

$$d_1 + (1 - \tau_2)l_2 = c_2$$

Therefore, the intertemporal budget constraint is:

$$b_1 = c_1 + c_2 - (1 - \tau_1)l_1 - (1 - \tau_2)l_2$$

The optimization program of the agent is then:

$$\max_{c_1,c_2,l_1,l_2} F(c_1,l_1,c_2,l_2)$$

$$\text{s.t.} \quad b_1 = c_1 + c_2 - (1-\tau_1)l_1 - (1-\tau_2)l_2$$

The solution consists in labor supplies and consumption levels as functions of τ_1, τ_2 and of the initial wealth b_1. Denote the equilibrium labor supplies by $L_1(\tau_1,\tau_2,b_1)$ and $L_2(\tau_1,\tau_2,b_1)$. These functions reflect period 1 consumer decisions taken with the knowledge of the tax rates in both periods. One can easily check that they depend on both tax rates, as well as the initial wealth of the agent. In particular, we have that L_t is decreasing in the tax rate τ_t. Besides, L_2 is increasing in τ_1. The associated indirect utility function depends on the same arguments as the labor supply and is determined by:

$$W(\tau_1,\tau_2,b_1) = \max\{F(c_1,l_1,c_2,l_2)|b_1 = c_1 + c_2 - (1-\tau_1)l_1 - (1-\tau_2)l_2\}$$

Note that W increases in b_1 and decreases in both tax rates. The budget constraint of the government is simply:

$$\tau_1 L_1 + \tau_2 L_2 \geq g_2$$

and its optimization problem is:

$$\max_{\tau_1,\tau_2} W(\tau_1,\tau_2,b_1) + H(g_2)$$

$$\text{s.t.} \quad \tau_1 L_1(\tau_1,\tau_2,b_1) + \tau_2 L_2(\tau_1,\tau_2,b_1) \geq g_2$$

The first order conditions are:

$$W_{\tau_1} + [L_1 + \tau_1 L_{1_{\tau_1}} + \tau_2 L_{2_{\tau_1}}]H_{g_2} = 0 \tag{11.9}$$

$$W_{\tau_2} + [L_2 + \tau_2 L_{2_{\tau_2}} + \tau_1 L_{2_{\tau_2}}]H_{g_2} = 0 \tag{11.10}$$

which determine the optimal fiscal policy. These conditions are Ramsey formulas. Let $\epsilon_{L_t}(\tau_2)$ be the <u>ex ante</u> elasticity of labor at time t with respect to τ_2. Formally $\epsilon_{L_t}(\tau_2) = \frac{\tau_2 L_{t_{\tau_2}}}{L_t}$. Note that $\epsilon_{L_2}(\tau_2) \leq 0$ and $\epsilon_{L_1}(\tau_2) \geq 0$. Moreover, applying Roy's identity[1] to the second period labor supply, we have $L_2(\tau_1,\tau_2,b_1) = -\frac{W_{\tau_2}}{W_{b_1}}$ and (11.10) can be rewritten as:

$$\frac{W_{b_1}}{H_{g_2}} = [1 - \epsilon_{L_1}(\tau_2)\frac{\tau_1 L_1}{\tau_2 L_2} + \epsilon_{L_2}(\tau_2)] \tag{11.11}$$

b. At date 2, the wealth of the representative agent is d_1. Then, he maximizes $F(c_1,l_1,c_2,l_2)$ (where l_1 and c_1 are predetermined) under the budget constraint related to period 2, i.e.:

$$d_1 = c_2 - (1-\tau_2)l_2$$

---

[1] Recall that when $g(p,x) = \max\{U(x) : p.x \leq b\}$, where p and x are vectors, the solution of this program can be expressed as $x(p,b)$. Roy's identity describes the relationship between $x(p,b)$ and $g(p,x)$. Formally $x_i(p,b) = -\frac{\partial g}{\partial p_i}/\frac{\partial g}{\partial b}$ where i represents the ith element of p and x respectively.

He determines his second period labor supply as a function of τ_2 and d_1. Denote the second period equilibrium labor supply $\tilde{L}_2(\tau_2, d_1)$. Then, his ex post indirect utility writes as:

$$\tilde{W}(\tau_2, d_1) = \max_{l_2}\{F(c_1, l_1, c_2, l_2)|d_1 = c_2 - (1 - \tau_2)l_2\}$$

The budget constraint of the government is $g_2 + m \leq \tau_2 l_2$ where m represents the debt of the government at the beginning of date 2. The government selects τ_2 by solving:

$$\max_{\tau_2} \tilde{W}(\tau_2, d_1) + H(g_2)$$

$$\text{s.t.} \qquad g_2 = \tau_2 \tilde{L}_2(\tau_2, d_1) - m$$

The first order condition is therefore:

$$\tilde{W}_{\tau_2} + [\tilde{L}_2 + \tau_2 \tilde{L}_{2_{\tau_2}}]H_{g_2} = 0$$

Similar manipulations as in question (a) leads us to:

$$\frac{\tilde{W}_{d_1}}{H_{g_2}} = [1 + \epsilon_{\tilde{L}_2}(\tau_2)] \qquad\qquad (11.12)$$

where $\epsilon_{\tilde{L}_2}(\tau_2)$ is the <u>ex post</u> elasticity of labor supply, $\epsilon_{\tilde{L}_2}(\tau_2) = \frac{\tau_2 \tilde{L}_{2_{\tau_2}}}{\tilde{L}_2}$.

c. The left-hand sides of (11.11) and (11.12) are equal if they are evaluated at the allocation chosen under commitment. If the right-hand sides of these two expressions are equal when evaluated at this allocation, then the ex ante optimal policy is also ex post optimal under no commitment. By contrast, if the right-hand sides do not coincide (which is generally the case), then the equilibrium policy under commitment is not a rational expectation equilibrium under no commitment: there is an incentive to cheat ex post and therefore the policy is not credible.

Suppose that preferences are such that $F(c_1, l_1, c_2, l_2) = U(c_1) - V(l_1) + c_2 - V(l_2)$. In that case, the labor supply in each period depends exclusively on the tax rate set in this period. Formally, (11.11) writes simply as:

$$\frac{W_{b_1}}{H_{g_2}} = [1 + \epsilon_{L_2}(\tau_2)] \qquad\qquad (11.13)$$

and is equivalent to (11.12). The reason is that the cross elasticity $\epsilon_{L_1}(\tau_2)$ is zero while the ex ante and ex post elasticities $\epsilon_{L_2}(\tau_2)$ and $\epsilon_{\tilde{L}_2}(\tau_2)$ are equal. Therefore the policies with and without commitment are equivalent. By contrast, if $F(c_1, l_1, c_2, l_2) = c_1 - V(l_1) + U(c_2) - V(l_2)$, the ex ante and the ex post elasticities $\epsilon_{L_2}(\tau_2)$ and $\epsilon_{\tilde{L}_2}(\tau_2)$ are different. Then, the optimal allocation prescribed under commitment is not credible under non commitment.

11.3   Debt structure and labor taxation

This problem is inspired by section 8.3. in Persson and Tabellini 1990. Consider a three-period model in which the representative agent has preferences over his private consumption levels c_t, his labor supply l_t, and the government consumption levels g_t for all $t = 1, 2, 3$. The real wage is 1. In the first period, there is no production, so $l_1 = 0$. The representative agent has an initial endowment b_1 that can be spent on his private consumption c_1 and government consumption g_1. In other words, $b_1 \geq c_1 + g_1$. Government consumption is financed through borrowing, which is repaid at dates 2 and 3. In the second and third periods, the government does not consume, so $g_t = 0$ for all $t = 2, 3$. Then, the endogenous resources l_t are used only to produce, i.e. $l_t = c_t$ for $t = 2, 3$. The government repays the debt by raising taxes. Let τ_2 and τ_3 be the tax rates in periods 2 and 3. The utility of the representative agent is given by

$$w = c_1 + U(c_2) - V(l_2) + U(c_3) - V(l_3)$$

where $V(\cdot)$ is increasing and convex in labor supply and $U(\cdot)$ is increasing and concave in consumption. Let d^s (respectively, d^l) be the debt issued by the government in period 1 and maturing in period 2 (respectively, in period 3). We will refer to these as short-term and long-term debt respectively. Denote by r_t the interest rate between periods t and $t + 1$. Naturally, given the three-period model, there are only two subsequent interest rates, r_1 and r_2.

a. Determine the representative agent's overall intertemporal budget constraint. What is his maximization program? Determine his optimal choice.

b. Suppose that the government can commit to a tax policy in period 1. Determine its budget constraint at the beginning of period 1. Write its optimization program and derive the ex-ante optimal tax policy.

c. Suppose now that the government cannot commit. What is the government budget constraint in period 2? Determine its optimization program and characterize the optimal policy from the perspective of period 2.

d. What are the sources of the differences between the optimal tax policy under commitment and that under no commitment, respectively? What happens if $d^s > d^l$ and if $d^s < d^l$? In which case does the optimal tax policy under commitment coincide with the optimal tax policy under no commitment? Discuss.

Answer

a. In period 1, the budget constraint of the representative agent is $c_1 + g_1 = b_1$ where $g_1 = d^s + d^l$. In period 2, the agent faces $c_2 = (1 - \tau_2)l_2 + r_1 d^s$. Last in period 3, the budget constraint writes as $c_3 = (1 - \tau_3)l_3 + r_1 r_2 d^l$. Then, the intertemporal budget constraint is:

$$b_1 = c_1 + \frac{c_2}{r_1} + \frac{c_3}{r_1 r_2} - \frac{(1 - \tau_2)l_2}{r_1} - \frac{(1 - \tau_3)l_3}{r_1 r_2} \tag{11.14}$$

The representative agent maximizes his utility under the intertemporal budget constraint. The first order conditions are:

$$\frac{1-\tau_2}{r_1} - V_l(l_2) = 0 \qquad \frac{1-\tau_3}{r_1 r_2} - V_l(l_3) = 0$$

$$U_c(c_2) = \frac{1}{r_1} \qquad U_c(c_3) = \frac{1}{r_1 r_2}$$

which can be rewritten as:

$$
\begin{array}{ll}
r_1 = \frac{1}{U_c(c_2)} & r_2 = \frac{U_c(c_2)}{U_c(c_3)} \\[2mm]
\tau_2 = 1 - \frac{V_l(l_2)}{U_c(c_2)} & \tau_3 = 1 - \frac{V_l(l_3)}{U_c(c_3)}
\end{array}
\qquad (11.15)
$$

b. The budget constraint of the government is:

$$g_1 \leq \frac{\tau_2 l_2}{r_1} + \frac{\tau_3 l_3}{r_1 r_2}$$

Given the previous question, it can be rewritten as:

$$g_1 \leq U_c(l_2) - V_l(l_2)]l_2 + [U_c(l_3) - V_l(l_3)]l_3$$

The government maximizes the utility under the previous budget constraint as well as the resource constraints. This leads to:

$$\max \ b_1 - g_1 + U(l_2) - V(l_2) + U(c_3) - V(l_3)$$
$$\text{s.t. } g_1 \leq [U_c(l_2) - V_l(l_2)]l_2 + [U_c(l_3) - V_l(l_3)]l_3$$

Call λ the multiplier of the constraint, then the first order conditions are:

$$
\begin{array}{l}
(1+\lambda)[U_c(l_2) - V_l(l_2)] + \lambda l_2[U_{cc}(l_2) - V_{ll}(l_2)] = 0 \\
(1+\lambda)[U_c(l_3) - V_l(l_3)] + \lambda l_3[U_{cc}(l_3) - V_{ll}(l_3)] = 0
\end{array}
\qquad (11.16)
$$

The optimal tax policy under commitment is such that the labor supply is the same in both periods. Since $r_2 = \frac{U_c(c_2)}{U_c(c_3)}$ and given the resource constraints $c_t = l_t$ for all $t = \{2,3\}$, we have $r_2 = \frac{U_c(l_2)}{U_c(l_3)} = 1$.

c. In period 2, c_1 is predetermined and the behavior of the agent remains the same as in question (a). The government budget constraint is:

$$d^s + \frac{d^l}{r_2} \leq \tau_2 l_2 + \frac{\tau_3 l_3}{r_2}$$

The government maximizes the utility of the representative agent under the budget constraint. The latter can be rewritten as:

$$d^s U_c(l_2) + d^l U_c(l_3) \leq [U_c(l_2) - V_l(l_2)]l_2 + [U_c(l_3) - V_l(l_3)]l_3$$

Call μ the multiplier of this constraint, the first order conditions are:

$$(1 + \mu)[U_c(l_2) - V_l(l_2)] + \mu l_2[U_{cc}(l_2) - V_{ll}(l_2)] - \mu U_{cc}(l_2)d^s = 0$$
$$(1 + \mu)[U_c(l_3) - V_l(l_3)] + \mu l_3[U_{cc}(l_3) - V_{ll}(l_3)] - \mu U_{cc}(l_3)d^l = 0 \tag{11.17}$$

d. To determine the differences between the optimal tax policy under commitment and no commitment, we have to compare (11.16) and (11.17). First, the marginal cost of public funds may differ ex ante and ex post, i.e. we can have $\lambda \neq \mu$. Second, the debt carried out over from period 1 appears in (11.17) but not in (11.16). This is the case because any change in the tax structure in period 2 affects the value of the government's outstanding debt.

Suppose that the optimal tax policy under commitment is such that $d^s > d^l$. If the government sticks to the ex ante optimal tax structure, then $l_2 = l_3$ so that $\tau_2 l_2 = \tau_3 l_3$ and $r_2 = 1$. Then, the budget constraint is $d^s + d^l = 2\tau_2 l_2$ and $d^s - \tau_2 l_2 > 0$. In other words, the debt that the government has to reimburse at date 2 is higher than the taxes that it collects at date 2. The government has an incentive to sell some new debt. For simplicity, we consider the case in which $d^l = 0$. Then, the ex post first order conditions write as:

$$(1 + \mu)[U_c(l_2) - V_l(l_2)] + \mu l_2[U_{cc}(l_2) - V_{ll}(l_2)] - \mu U_{cc}(l_2)d^s = 0$$
$$(1 + \mu)[U_c(l_3) - V_l(l_3)] + \mu l_3[U_{cc}(l_3) - V_{ll}(l_3)] = 0$$

Let $f(l_2, \mu) = (1 + \mu)[U_c(l_2) - V_l(l_2)] + \mu l_2[U_{cc}(l_2) - V_{ll}(l_2)]$, then $f_{l_2}(l_2, \mu) = (1 + 2\mu)[U_{cc}(l_2) - V_{ll}(l_2)] + \mu[U_{ccc}(l_2) - V_{lll}(l_2)]l_2$. The first term of the right hand side is negative while the second term has an ambiguous sign. Suppose that $U(\cdot)$ and $V(\cdot)$ are such that $f_{l_2}(l_2, \mu) < 0$. Then, it comes immediately that the optimal labor supplies under no commitment are such that $l_2 > l_3$. This implies that τ_2 (respectively, τ_3) is decreased (respectively, increased) with respect to the optimum under commitment. Besides, since $r_2 = \frac{U_c(c_2)}{U_c(c_3)} = \frac{U_c(l_2)}{U_c(l_3)}$, then we have $r_2 < 1$ at the optimum without commitment. The government has an interest to reduce r_2 in order to sell the debt at a higher price. Naturally, if $d^s < d^l$, the incentives goes in the opposite direction and $r_2 > 1$. By raising r_2, the government reduces the value of the long term debt which is bought back at a lower price.

Suppose now that $d^s = d^l$. The government has no incentives to sell short term debt or buy long term debt. In that case, the first order conditions (11.17) lead to $l_2 = l_3$ and the optimal tax schedule under commitment is implemented.

11.4   Capital taxation and inflation surprise

This problem is related to the analysis of section 6 in Persson and Tabellini 1990. Consider an economy in which the representative agent has preferences over private consumption c_t and labor l_t, where $t = 1, 2$. At date $t = 1$, the agent's initial capital endowment is b_1 and he does not work, so $l_1 = 0$. He can save part of his endowment but cannot borrow. Then if his savings are denoted by s_1, we impose $s_1 \geq 0$. At date $t = 2$, the agent works and consumes. The real wage is unity. In addition, the gross return associated with the first period savings is R. Labor and capital are taxed at rates τ and θ respectively. The government consumes an exogenous per capita amount g_2 at date 2 that is financed through taxes. The individual's preferences are summarized by

$$w = U(c_1) + c_2 - V(l_2),$$

where $U(\cdot)$ is increasing and concave and $V(\cdot)$ is increasing and convex. In addition, we assume that $U_{ccc}(\cdot) \geq 0$.

a. Would the analysis be modified if g_2 were endogenous and included in the agent's preferences? Determine the agent's intertemporal constraint. What are the agent's labor supply and savings level? How do they vary with the level of taxes?

b. Determine the government's budget constraint as well as its optimization program when it commits to future policy rules at the beginning of date 1. What is the optimal policy? [Hint: It may be convenient to write the government's program in terms of labor and consumption, rather than in terms of taxes.]

c. Suppose now that the government cannot commit. What does this imply? Again, determine the implemented policy and discuss.

Now consider the same model as before, but suppose that s_1 is constrained to be 0. Savings can take only the form of money holdings that pay a zero nominal rate of return. Let p_t be the market price at date t, then the real return is $-\pi = -\frac{p_2-p_1}{p_2}$, that is the opposite of the inflation rate. In other words, money holdings depreciate and the per unit depreciation is π. Let m_t be the demand of money at date $t = 1, 2$. The individual's preferences are now

$$w = U(c_1) + c_2 - V(l_2) + H(m_2),$$

where $H(\cdot)$ is increasing and concave. The government finances g_2 by raising taxes on labor and by printing money. Let M_2 be the nominal quantity of money in the economy; the equilibrium in the money market at date 2 is $M_2 = p_2 m_2$.

d. Determine the agent's supply of labor and demand for money functions. What is the optimal policy decided by a government that can commit at the beginning of period 1? Compare your results with the results obtained in the first part of the problem.

e. Suppose now that the government cannot commit. What are its ex post incentives? Discuss.

Answer

a. Since g_2 is an exogenous amount, including it or not in the preferences of the representative agent does not modify the analysis. If g_2 were endogenous, including it in the utility function would be necessary. The first period budget constraint of the agent is:

$$c_1 + s_1 \leq b_1$$

In the second period, his budget constraint is:

$$c_2 \leq (1 - \tau)l_2 + s_1 R(1 - \theta)$$

Both constraint are binding in equilibrium and the intertemporal budget constraint is:

$$b_1 = c_1 + \frac{c_2}{R(1 - \theta)} - \frac{(1 - \tau)l_2}{R(1 - \theta)} \tag{11.18}$$

Since the government can commit, the level of taxes that are fixed at the beginning of the game will be implemented in the future. Then, for given announced τ and θ, the agent solves the following problem:

$$\max_{c_1, c_2, l_2} U(c_1) + c_2 - V(l_2)$$

$$\text{s.t.} \quad b_1 = c_1 + \frac{c_2}{R(1 - \theta)} - \frac{(1 - \tau)l_2}{R(1 - \theta)}$$

which can be rewritten as:

$$\max_{c_2, l_2} U\left(b_1 - \frac{c_2}{R(1 - \theta)} + \frac{(1 - \tau)l_2}{R(1 - \theta)}\right) + c_2 - V(l_2)$$

If an interior solution exists, the first order conditions with respect to c_2 and l_2 are respectively:

$$U_c(c_1) \frac{1}{R(1 - \theta)} = 1$$

$$U_c(c_1) \frac{1 - \tau}{R(1 - \theta)} = V_l(l_2)$$

Therefore, the solution entails:

$$U_c(b_1 - s_1) \begin{cases} = R(1 - \theta) & \text{if} & s_1 > 0 \\ > R(1 - \theta) & \text{if} & s_1 = 0 \end{cases} \tag{11.19}$$

$$V_l(l_2) = 1 - \tau$$

In other words:

$$s_1 = \max[0, s(\theta)] \quad \text{where} \quad s(\theta) = b_1 - U_c^{-1}(R(1 - \theta)) \tag{11.20}$$

$$l_2 = V_l^{-1}(1 - \tau) \tag{11.21}$$

Note that $s(\theta)$ is decreasing in θ and l_2 is decreasing in τ. The higher the taxes, the smaller the incentives to save and to work.

b. The budget constraint of the government is:

$$g_2 \leq \tau l_2 + \theta R s_1$$

Replacing the equilibrium value of τ and θ into that constraint, it becomes:

$$g_2 \leq l_2[1 - V_l(l_2)] + s_1[R - U_c(b_1 - s_1)]$$

The problem of the government is to maximize the utility of the representative agent under its budget constraint, which is binding at the equilibrium. Then, the optimization program can be written as:

$$\max_{l_2, s_1} U(b_1 - s_1) + l_2 + R s_1 - l_2[1 - V_l(l_2)] - s_1[R - U_c(b_1 - s_1)] - V(l_2)$$

The first order conditions are:

$$1 - (1 - V_l(l_2)) + l_2 V_{ll}(l_2) = V_l(l_2)$$

$$-U_c(b_1 - s_1) + R - [R - U_C(b_1 - s_1)] - s_1 U_{cc}(b_1 - s_1) = 0$$

Then, in equilibrium, we have:

$$\frac{1 - V_l(l_2)}{1 - V_l(l_2) + l_2 V_{ll}(l_2)} = \frac{U_c(b_1 - s_1) - R}{U_c(b_1 - s_1) - R - s_1 U_{cc}(b_1 - s_1)} \tag{11.22}$$

The numerators in (11.22) measure the marginal tax distortions. More precisely, the numerator on the left-hand side is the marginal distortion of the tax on labor and the numerator on the right-hand side represents the marginal distortion of the tax on capital. The denominators measure the increase in revenue of higher tax rates: on labor on the left-hand side and on capital on the right-hand side. Let ϵ_l (respectively, ϵ_s) be the elasticity of the labor supply function (respectively, savings supply function). Formally $\epsilon_l = \frac{V_l}{l_2 V_{ll}}$ and $\epsilon_s = \frac{-U_c(b_1 - s_1)}{s_1 U_{cc}(b_1 - s_1)}$. We can rewrite (11.22) as:

$$\frac{1 - \tau}{\tau} / \frac{1 - \theta}{\theta} = \frac{\epsilon_l}{\epsilon_s} \tag{11.23}$$

From (11.23) it comes that the most inelastic tax base is taxed more heavily. Moreover, if both elasticities are positive, both labor and capital are taxed at the equilibrium with commitment.

c. If the government cannot commit, then the tax policy that is effective in period 2 cannot be decided upon in period 1. Then the representative agent chooses how much to save based on his expectations about future tax policy. Since there is no commitment, the problem has to be solved backward. Once the tax τ is selected, the agent chooses l_2 that maximizes his utility under his second period budget constraint. This is:

$$\max_{l_2} U(b_1 - s_1) + R s_1(1 - \theta) + (1 - \tau) l_2 - V(l_2)$$

Therefore, l_2 is such that:

$$V_l(l_2) = 1 - \tau \tag{11.24}$$

Then, the government chooses the tax policy so as to maximize the utility of the representative agent under (11.24) and the budget constraint $g_2 \leq \tau l_2 + \theta R s_1$, where s_1 is predetermined. For the budget constraint to be satisfied, θ must be such that $\theta \geq \frac{g}{Rs_1} - \frac{\tau l_2}{Rs_1}$. In other words, we must have:

$$\theta = \min\{1, \frac{g_2}{Rs_1} - \frac{\tau l_2}{Rs_1}\}$$

Suppose that the government selects $\theta = \frac{g}{Rs_1} - \frac{\tau l_2}{Rs_1} < 1$, then its program turns to:

$$\max_{l_2} U(b_1 - s_1) + Rs_1 - g_2 + l_2 - V(l_2)$$

Therefore, we get $V_l(l_2) = 1$, which implies $\tau = 0$ and $\theta = \frac{g_2}{Rs_1}$. As a consequence, we have in equilibrium:

$$\theta = \min\{1, \frac{g_2}{Rs_1}\} \tag{11.25}$$

We now turn to the decision of the agent in period 1. In the first period, the optimal level of savings satisfies:

$$U_c(b_1 - s_1) \quad \begin{cases} = R(1 - \theta^e) & \text{if} \quad s_1 > 0 \\ > R(1 - \theta^e) & \text{if} \quad s_1 = 0 \end{cases}$$

where θ^e denotes the expectation of θ. In addition, the agent anticipates that the tax will satisfy (11.25).

Suppose that consumers do not save, so that $s_1 = 0$. Therefore, $\theta = 1$ by (11.25). Then, it is optimal for agents not to save. As a consequence $s_1 = 0$ is an equilibrium: when everybody expects everyone else to anticipate $\theta = 1$, then $\theta = 1$ (or full expropriation) emerges in equilibrium. Besides, since nobody saves, the government relies exclusively on labor taxation. Therefore, labor is overtaxed with respect to the commitment solution.

Let $\overline{g_2} = \max_\theta Rs_1(\theta)$. For all $g_2 > \overline{g_2}$, we have that $\frac{g_2}{Rs_1} > \frac{\overline{g_2}}{Rs_1} \geq 1$, then $\theta = 1$ is the unique equilibrium when $g_2 > \overline{g_2}$. By contrast, if $g_2 < \overline{g_2}$, there exist other equilibria such that $\theta < 1$. Indeed, there exists θ^e such that $\theta^e = \frac{g_2}{Rs(\theta^e)} < 1$. If agents anticipate θ^e, then they invest $s(\theta^e)$ and θ^e is selected by the government at date 2. Note that in that case, $\tau = 0$. In other words, labor is undertaxed with respect to the commitment solution.

d. The intertemporal budget constraint of the agent is:

$$c_2 + m_2 = l_2(1 - \tau) + (b_1 - c_1)(1 - \pi)R$$

Maximizing his utility function under the previous constraint, his optimal decisions are obtained:

$$\begin{aligned} U_c(b_1 - m_1) &= R(1 - \pi) \quad &\text{if} \quad m_1 > 0 \\ V_l(l_2) &= 1 - \tau \\ H_m(m_2) &= 1 \end{aligned} \tag{11.26}$$

The budget constraint of the government is $g_2 \leq \tau l_2 + m_2 + \pi m_1 R$. Note that inflation provides the government with revenues. Besides, if we label m_1 as s_1 and π as θ, it is easy to verify that the current model is almost identical to the first model in this problem. The main difference is that π is not under the direct control of the government. On the money market, the equilibrium is $M_2 = p_2 m_2$. Besides, m_2 satisfies $H_m(m_2) = 1$. Combining the previous two expressions, we get that $p_2(M_2) = \frac{M_2}{H_m^{-1}(1)}$. Moreover $\pi(p_2) = \frac{p_2 - p_1}{p_2}$ and therefore, $\pi_{p_2} = \frac{1}{p_2 H_m^{-1}(1)} - \frac{p_2 - p_1}{p_2} \frac{1}{p_2 H_m^{-1}(1)}$. Therefore, $\pi_{p_2} = \frac{1-\pi}{M_2}$. In other words, if the government controls directly the quantity of money M_2, then it controls indirectly π.

When the government can commit, the optimal labor and money supplies verify:

$$1 - (1 - V_l(l_2)) + l_2 V_{ll}(l_2) = V_l(l_2)$$

$$-U_c(b_1 - m_1) + R - [R - U_C(b_1 - m_1)] - m_1 U_{cc}(b_1 - m_1) = 0$$

with the same interpretation as before. More precisely, the government collects some revenue through the inflation tax and some through the tax on labor according to (11.23) in which we replace ϵ_s by the elasticity of the money supply ϵ_m.

e. When commitment is not possible, the government has an ex post incentive to create an inflation surprise to collect revenues without distorting savings decisions. However, agents anticipate the ex post incentives of the government to create inflation. Then, the equilibrium entails more inflation than in the commitment case but no surprise. As before, $\pi = 1$ (i.e. $p_2 = +\infty$) and $m_1 = 0$ is an equilibrium: the government raises the second period price to infinity (full expropriation of the existing nominal wealth) but agents anticipate it and do not hold any nominal wealth. Last, note that other equilibria exist as in the first part of the problem.

11.5   Labor and capital taxation when agents are heterogeneous

This problem is based on section 7.3. in Persson and Tabellini 1990. Consider a model with two types of agents. Agents of the first type live two periods. At date 1, their initial endowment in capital is b_1. They consume an amount c_1 of private good and invest an amount k. The return from capital is $R(1 - \theta)$ where θ is a capital tax. In the second period, they consume $kR(1 - \theta)$. We denote the second period consumption by c_2^1. The utility of the representative agent of the first type is

$$w^1 = c_1 + U(c_2^1),$$

where $U(\cdot)$ is increasing and concave. Agents of type 2 live only in period 2. They have no endowment and get income only from labor. The real wage is unity. Their labor supply is denoted by l_2. They consume their labor income net of taxes τ.

Their consumption is denoted by c_2^2. The representative agent in this group has the following utility function:

$$w^2 = c_2^2 - V(l_2),$$

where $V(\cdot)$ is increasing and concave. The government maximizes $\phi w^1 + w^2$ where ϕ represents the weight assigned to the first group. Moreover, he collects taxes to finance an exogenous per capita amount g_2 at date 2.

a. Determine the budget constraint of the representative agent in each group. What is the private optimal behavior for a given announced policy (τ, θ)?

b. Determine the optimal policy when the government can commit.

c. Suppose now that the government cannot commit. Which policy is implemented in that case?

Answer

a. The budget constraints of the representative agent of the first group are $c_1 + k \leq b_1$ and $c_2^1 \leq kR(1 - \theta)$. The representative agent in group 2 lives one period and faces the budget constraint $c_2^2 \leq l_2(1 - \tau)$. Agents maximize their utility function and their optimal decision for predetermined values of taxes are:

$$\frac{1}{U_c(c_2^1)R} = (1 - \theta) \tag{11.27}$$

$$V_l(l_2) = 1 - \tau \tag{11.28}$$

b. The government maximizes $\phi w^1 + w^2$ subject to (11.27), (11.28) and his budget constraint $g_2 \leq \tau l_2 + R\theta k$. Note that the government's budget constraint can be rewritten as: $g_2 \leq Rc_2^1 U_c(c_2^1) - c_2^1 + (1 - V_l(l_2))l_2$. After some manipulations, the program of the government writes as:

$$\max \phi[b_1 - c_2^1 U_c(c_2^1) + U(c_2^1)] + l_2 V_l(l_2) - V(l_2)$$
$$\text{s.t.} \quad g_2 \leq Rc_2^1 U_c(c_2^1) - c_2^1 + (1 - V_l(l_2))l_2$$

Let μ be the multiplier of the constraint, the first order conditions to that program are:

$$\phi[-U_c(c_2^1) - c_2^1 U_{cc}(c_2^1)] + \mu[Rc_2^1 U_{cc}(c_2^1) + RU_c(c_2^1) - 1] = 0$$
$$l_2 V_{ll}(l_2) + \mu[1 - V_l(l_2) - V_{ll}(l_2)l_2] = 0$$

Deriving the expressions of μ in both equations and equating them, we get that the optimum entails:

$$\frac{\phi U_c(c_2^1)}{1} = \frac{1 - \tau}{1 - \tau(1 + \epsilon_l)} \bigg/ \frac{1 - \theta}{1 - \theta(1 + \epsilon_k)} \tag{11.29}$$

where ϵ_l (respectively, ϵ_k) represents the elasticity of the labor supply function (respectively, savings supply function). This equation reflects the trade-off between economic efficiency and wealth distribution faced by the government.

c. At date 2, the first group of agents has already committed to an investment decision. The elasticity of savings with respect to θ is zero. Then, the equilibrium tax policy under no commitment satisfies:

$$\frac{\phi U_c(c_2^1)}{1} = \frac{1-\tau}{1-\tau(1+\epsilon_l)} \tag{11.30}$$

In equilibrium, τ is decreased and θ is increased with respect to the equilibrium under commitment. The first group of agents are taxed more heavily under no commitment. Note that this group is never expropriated as long as $\phi > 0$. Recall that if the government is expected to expropriate, then agents do not save, in which case $w^1 = b_1$. Since $\phi > 0$, the government does not want to tax capital too heavily, which relaxes partly the credibility constraint.

Chapter 12

Capital taxation

12.1 Multiple equilibria and credibility in taxation problems

This problem is based on Calvo 1988. Consider the following two-period model. The economy is summarized by a representative agent with an initial endowment y. In period 1, he splits his endowment between government bonds b and capital investment k. The interest factors of bonds and capital are R_b and R, respectively. In period 2, the agent works and consumes. His labor supply and his consumption are denoted by l and c, respectively. Debt can be partially defaulted (repudiated), which means that the agent receives a return $(1-\theta)R_b$ on each bond, where $\theta \in (0,1)$ represents the proportion of bonds that are repudiated. Therefore, in a perfect foresight equilibrium, the consumer is indifferent between the two assets if and only if

$$R = (1-\theta)R_b.$$

In addition, the government bears a cost of defaulting on the debt: the per capita cost per unit of repudiated debt is $\alpha \in (0,1)$. Government raises a tax τ on labor to finance debt repayment $(1-\theta)bR_b$, the cost of repudiation $\alpha\theta b R_b$ and public expenditures, g. We assume g to be exogenous. The representative agent has utility

$$w^i = c - V(l),$$

where $V(\cdot)$ is increasing and convex such that $\frac{V_l}{lV_{ll}} = \eta$ for all l.

a. Determine the agent's labor supply. Write the government's budget constraint as well as its optimization program under commitment. First, characterize the tax rate on labor by neglecting the constraint $\theta \in (0,1)$, then compute the unconstrained total amount collected through taxation.

b. How does the government have to constrain the amount of collected taxes to satisfy $\theta \in (0,1)$? Draw a graph of this amount as a function of R_b. How does the optimal repudiation share in period 2 vary with the interest rate R_b contracted in period 1? Discuss.

c. Suppose that the agent can exactly predict the repudiation share θ (then $R = (1 - \theta)R_b$ must hold). Derive the condition that must be satisfied by the budget constraint in equilibrium. Show that several equilibria exist depending on R_b, and characterize these.

d. Rank the different equilibria and discuss your results.

Answer

a. The budget constraints of the agent in period 1 and 2 are respectively:

$$y = b + k, \quad \text{and} \quad c = (1 - \theta)bR_b + kR + (1 - \tau)l.$$

Then, the optimization problem of the agent is:

$$\max_l \quad (1 - \theta)bR_b + kR + (1 - \tau)l - V(l)$$

Therefore, the equilibrium labor supply is given by:

$$l = L(\tau) = V_l^{-1}(1 - \tau)$$

which is decreasing in τ. The government budget constraint is:

$$\tau l = (1 - \theta)bR_b + g + \alpha\theta bR_b$$

If the government can precommit to τ at the beginning of the game, it solves:

$$\max_l \quad (1 - \theta)bR_b + kR + (1 - \tau)l - V(l)$$

$$\text{s.t.} \quad \tau l = (1 - \theta)bR_b + g + \alpha\theta bR_b$$
$$1 - \tau = V_l(l)$$
$$\theta \in (0, 1)$$

By the budget constraint, we know that:

$$\theta bR_b = \frac{bR_b + g - \tau l}{1 - \alpha}$$

Neglecting first the last constraint of the optimization program, we get that the equilibrium policy is given by:

$$\frac{1 - V_l(l)}{1 - \alpha} = \frac{\alpha}{1 - \alpha}V_{ll}l$$

which can be rewritten as:

$$V_l(l) = \frac{\eta}{\eta + \alpha}$$

Therefore $\tau = 1 - \frac{\eta}{\eta + \alpha}$ and the total amount of collected taxes is:

$$\tau^* L(\tau^*) = \left[1 - \frac{\eta}{\eta + \alpha}\right]V_l^{-1}\left(\frac{\eta}{\eta + \alpha}\right)$$

b. In equilibrium, the total revenue from taxes is $\tau L(\tau) \equiv [1 - V_l(l)]l = T(l)$. The condition $\theta \in (0, 1)$ is equivalent to restricting $T(l)$ in the following manner:

$$g + \alpha b R_b \leq T(l) \leq g + b R_b$$

where the left-hand side corresponds to total debt repudiation ($\theta = 1$) and the right-hand side to no repudiation ($\theta = 0$). To be in the interesting case, we assume that $\tau^* L(\tau^*) > g$. The problem of the government is depicted in Figure 1, in which we represent the unconstrained solution as well as the constraint. There exist $\underline{R_b}$ and $\overline{R_b}$ such that if $R_b \in [\underline{R_b}, \overline{R_b}]$, the government attains the unconstrained maximum. In that case, there is partial repudiation. The budget constraint yields:

$$\theta^*(R_b) = \frac{g - \tau^* L(\tau^*)}{b R_b (1 - \alpha)} + \frac{1}{1 - \alpha}$$

which is increasing in R_b. So, if $R_b < \underline{R_b}$, there is no repudiation, i.e. $\theta^*(R_b) = 0$. By contrast, if $R_b > \overline{R_b}$, repudiation is total, i.e. $\theta^*(R_b) = 1$. To sum up, the optimal repudiation share in period 2 is an increasing function of the interest rate contracted in period 1.

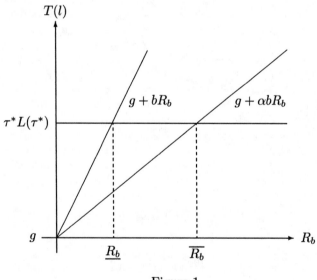

Figure 1

c. If agents are able to predict θ in period 1, then the following equality must hold:

$$(1 - \theta)R_b = R$$

which implies that R_b is greater than R. Moreover, the budget constraint must satisfy:

$$T(l) = g + (1 - \alpha)Rb + \alpha b R_b$$

We can now characterize the solution. It is depicted in Figure 2 in which we draw the equilibrium revenue from taxation $T(l)$ and the previous constraint as functions of $R_b(\geq R)$. We restrict the attention to the interesting case $\tau^* L(\tau^*) > g + bR$. There are two equilibria, E^0 and E^1.

In E^0, $R_b = R$ and the public expect no repudiation. In that case $T(l) = g + bR$. We have that $T_l(l) = 1 - [1 + \frac{1}{\eta}]V_l(l)$ and $T_{ll} = -[1 + \frac{1}{\eta}]V_{ll}(l) < 0$. Therefore $T(l)$ is concave and has a maximum in $\tilde{l}$. Since $\tau^* L(\tau^*) > g + bR$ then $T(\tilde{l}) > g + bR$. So, there exist l_1^0 and l_2^0 such that $T(l_1^0) = T(l_2^0) = g + bR$. There are two equilibria of type E^0. Naturally, the tax is smaller for l_2^0.

In E^1, $R_b > R$ and there is partial repudiation. The unconstrained optimum $\tau^* L(\tau^*)$ is implemented. Since $\tau^* L(\tau^*) > g + bR$, we have $l_1^0 < l(\tau^*) < l_2^0$.

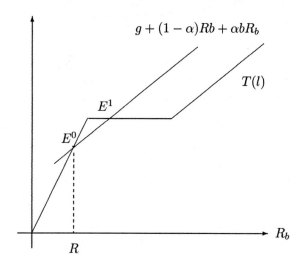

$$g + (1 - \alpha)Rb + \alpha bR_b$$

Figure 2

d. The equilibrium utility of the representative agent is $W(l, \tau) = Rb + kR + (1 - \tau)l - V(l)$. Naturally, in equilibrium $1 - \tau = V_l(l)$. Then, the utility can be written as:

$$W(l) = Rb + V_l(l)l - V(l)$$

Consider the function $H(l) = V_l(l)l - V(l)$. We have $H_l(l) = V_{ll}l > 0$. Since the labor supply is decreasing in τ in equilibrium, the equilibrium utility is decreasing in the equilibrium tax rate. Consider first type E^0 equilibria. It comes immediately that $W(l_1^0) < W(l_2^0)$. Consider now E^1. According to the previous question, we obtain:

$$W(l_1^0) < W(L(\tau^*)) < W(l_2^0)$$

We have three equilibria that can be Pareto-ranked, and the equilibrium with no repudiation and with a low tax is the dominant one.

12.2 Solving time-inconsistency problems through social contracts

This problem is an adaptation of Kotlikoff, Persson and Svensson 1988. Consider the following overlapping generations model. Each individual lives two periods. In period 1, the agent's work supply is l_1, he consumes a quantity c_1 and saves $s_1 \geq 0$ (borrowing is not allowed). The net rate of return to capital is R and the wage rate is normalized to 1. In period 2, the agent's labor supply and consumption are l_2 and c_2, respectively. There are absolute taxes on labor in period 1 and 2 as well as on savings that are denoted by τ_1, τ_2 and θ respectively. In other words, the net wage is $1 - \tau_t$ for each $t = \{1, 2\}$ and the total net return to capital is $(R - \theta)s_1$. A consumer has preferences described by

$$w^i = d(c_1 - \lambda l_1) + c_2 - \mu l_2,$$

where λ and μ are the constant marginal rates of substitution between leisure and consumption when the individual is young and old respectively and d is the gross rate of time preferences. We assume that $\lambda < 1$, $\mu < 1$ and $R > d$. Consumption and labor are constrained to be such that

$$0 \leq \underline{c_1} \leq c_1 \qquad 0 \leq \underline{c_2} \leq c_2$$

$$l_1 \in [\underline{l_1}, \overline{l_1}] \qquad \text{with } 0 \leq \underline{l_1}$$

$$l_2 \in [\underline{l_2}, \overline{l_2}] \qquad \text{with } 0 \leq \underline{l_2},$$

where $\underline{c_1}$, $\underline{c_2}$, $\underline{l_1}$, $\overline{l_1}$, $\underline{l_2}$ and $\overline{l_2}$ are exogenously given.

a. Determine each agent's savings and labor decisions. Discuss.

Assume now that each generation is represented by a council that supplies a fixed amount of public good g to its generation when the generation is old. This expenditure is financed by taxing the generation in both periods. Suppose that the council has access to lump-sum taxes and imposes a second period lump-sum tax equal to g on the old and sets all other taxes equal to 0.

b. Determine the labor and savings decisions in this case. What is the utility level for the generation? We call this equilibrium the "first best".

Suppose now that the council cannot resort to lump-sum taxes. Then, it taxes labor in the first period and saves this amount at rate R. In the second period, it taxes its generation's savings as well as labor. Moreover, the council receives the return from its own savings and spends g.

c. We first assume that the council can commit. Determine the council's intertemporal budget constraint. Characterize the maximum non-distortionary taxes. What happens if these taxes are sufficient to finance g? Suppose instead that these taxes are not sufficient to finance g. Determine the deadweight losses caused by an increase in each tax. Assume that the deadweight loss from distorting τ_2 is smaller than other distortions. What does this imply? Suppose, in addition, that distortionary taxation of l_2 raises enough revenue to finance g. Determine the "second best" optimum. What is the utility level in that case? Compare with the first best.

d. Under which condition is the second best optimum non enforceable? Suppose that this condition holds. Determine the tax the council sets on capital when it cannot commit. What then are the taxes on labor and what is the agent's equilibrium behavior? Compare the equilibrium utility with the first best and second best utilities. This equilibrium is referred to as the "third best".

Now assume that commitment is not possible. Suppose however that each young generation can set up a social contract with the following prescriptions: (i) capital taxation above the maximum non distortionary level is prohibited, and (ii) the council of the young contributes a transfer t to the council of the old, setting up the social contract costs ψ in terms of second period utility (i.e. is discounted by 1 and not by d).

e. Consider a generation. What are the budget constraints of the council when setting up the contract and if the next generation fulfills this contract. Determine the equilibrium for this generation. Characterize the conditions under which the first generation wants to set up the social contract (when young) and fulfills it (when old). Consider now the next generation. As before, determine the equilibrium when the generation fulfills the contract. Characterize the conditions under which this second generation is willing to fulfill the contract rather than creating its own and pursuing the third best optimum. Show that when all these conditions are satisfied, the contract yields a self-enforcing equilibrium.

Answer

a. The saving and labor decisions solve the following optimization program:

$$\max d(c_1 - \lambda l_1) + c_2 - \mu l_2$$

$$\text{s.t.} \quad c_1 = (1 - \tau_1)l_1 - s_1$$

$$c_2 = (R - \theta)s_1 + (1 - \tau_2)l_2$$

which gives:

$$s_1 = \begin{cases} (1 - \tau_1)l_1 - \underline{c_1} & \text{if } \frac{R-\theta}{d} \geq 1 \\ 0 & \text{if } \frac{R-\theta}{d} < 1 \end{cases}$$

$$l_2 = \begin{cases} \overline{l_2} & \text{if } 1 - \tau_2 - \mu \geq 0 \\ 0 & \text{if } 1 - \tau_2 - \mu < 0 \end{cases}$$

$$l_1 = \begin{cases} \overline{l_1} & \text{if } (1 - \tau_1) \max\left(\frac{R-\theta}{d}, 1\right) \geq \lambda \\ \underline{l_1} & \text{if } (1 - \tau_1) \max\left(\frac{R-\theta}{d}, 1\right) < \lambda \end{cases}$$

Note two things. First, the only thing that matters for saving decisions is the relation between the gross rate of time preferences and the after-tax rate of return.

A relatively high (respectively, small) after tax rate of return induces the agent to save more (respectively, less) and to consume less (respectively, more). Second, labor supplies are affected by the relation between the after tax wage rate and the rate of substitution between consumption and leisure. When the after tax wage is relatively high (respectively, small), the agent works more (respectively, less).

b. If the council has access to lump sum taxes, then the labor and saving decisions solve:

$$\max d(c_1 - \lambda l_1) + c_2 - \mu l_2$$

$$\text{s.t.} \quad c_1 = l_1 - s_1$$

$$c_2 + g = Rs_1 + l_2$$

Therefore, $s_1^* = \overline{l_1} - \underline{c_1} = \overline{s_1}$, $l_1^* = \overline{l_1}$ and $l_2^* = \overline{l_2}$. In that case, the utility level of the generation is:

$$u^* = d(\underline{c_1} - \lambda \overline{l_1}) + R(\overline{l_1} - \underline{c_1}) + \overline{l_2} - \mu \underline{l_2} - g$$

c. The council collects $\tau_1 l_1$ in period 1 and saves it . Then, it collects taxes on labor and savings in the second period and finances g. Therefore:

$$g = R\tau_1 l_1 + \tau_2 l_2 + \theta s_1$$

If the council can commit, it maximizes the utility of its generation under his budget constraint and the equilibrium savings and labor decisions determined in question (a). The maximum non-distortionary taxes are:

$$\tau_1 = 1 - \lambda, \qquad \tau_2 = 1 - \mu, \qquad \theta = R - d$$

Given these tax rates, the agent chooses the first best labor and savings levels. Then, if $g < R(1 - \lambda)\overline{l_1} + (1 - \mu)\overline{l_2} + (R - d)\overline{s_1}$, the first best is achieved. Suppose by contrast that:

$$g > R(1 - \lambda)\overline{l_1} + (1 - \mu)\overline{l_2} + (R - d)\overline{s_1} \tag{12.1}$$

In this case, the council has to increase some of the taxes to finance g. If τ_2 is increased, labor supply drops to its minimum, causing a deadweight loss equal to $(1 - \mu)(\overline{l_2} - \underline{l_2})$. If the council increases θ, savings drop to 0 which generates a deadweight loss equal to $(R - d)\overline{s_1}$. If τ_1 is increased, then the labor supply in period 1 drops to its minimum, causing a direct deadweight loss of $d(1 - \lambda)(\overline{l_1} - \underline{l_1})$ plus an indirect deadweight loss due to lower savings $(R - d)(\overline{s_1} - \underline{s_1})$ where $\underline{s_1} = (1 - \tau_1)\underline{l_1} - \underline{c_1}$.

If the deadweight loss associated to distorting τ_2 is smaller than other distortions, the council prefers to increase taxes on labor in the second period, rather than increasing θ and/or τ_1. In addition, if increasing τ_2 above the non-distortionary level provides enough revenue to finance g, then the labor and savings decisions become:

$$\hat{l}_1 = \overline{l_1}, \qquad \hat{l}_2 = \underline{l_2}, \qquad \hat{s}_1 = \overline{s_1}$$

This implies the following tax rates:

$$\tau_1 = 1 - \lambda, \qquad \theta = R - d$$

$$\tau_2 = \frac{g - R(1 - \lambda)\overline{l_1} - (R - d)\overline{s_1}}{\underline{l_2}}$$

and the utility level of the generation is:

$$\hat{u} = u^* - (1 - \mu)(\overline{l_2} - \underline{l_2})$$

Naturally, the welfare loss is generated by the deadweight loss from distorting τ_2.

d. Since capital is pre-determined in period 2, the council at that date has an incentive to deviate from the pre-announced policy in order to avoid a distortionary tax on second period labor. This happens if $R\overline{s_1}$ is sufficiently large so that τ_2 can be lowered to the nondistortionary level. i.e. if:

$$g < R(1 - \lambda)\overline{l_1} + (1 - \mu)\overline{l_2} + R\overline{s_1} \tag{12.2}$$

Then, if the capital is $\overline{s_1}$ at the beginning of the second period, the council wants to set optimally:

$$\tilde{\theta} = \frac{g - R(1 - \lambda)\overline{l_1} - (1 - \mu)\overline{l_2}}{\overline{s_1}}$$

However, a young consumer who anticipates it does not save since $\frac{R - \tilde{\theta}}{d} < 1$. This produces a deadweight loss equal to $(R - d)\overline{s_1}$. As a consequence, the council is forced to levy a distortionary tax on labor in the second period anyway. Indeed, given (12.1), g is greater than the revenue from nondistortionary taxes on labor supply. It follows that the third best is given by:

$$\tilde{l}_1 = \overline{l_1}, \qquad \tilde{l}_2 = \underline{l_2}, \qquad \tilde{s}_1 = 0$$

In that case:

$$\tau_1 = 1 - \lambda, \qquad \tau_2 = \frac{g - R(1 - \lambda)\overline{l_1}}{\underline{l_2}}, \qquad \theta = \tilde{\theta}$$

and the utility of the generation is:

$$\tilde{u} = \hat{u} - (R - d)\overline{s_1}$$

The third best optimum exhibits an additional deadweight loss due to the distortion on savings.

e. Consider the first generation. The budget constraints of the council of this generation are:

$$\tau_1 l_1 = B$$

$$g - t = \theta s_1 + \tau l_2 + RB$$

where B represents the amount collected by the council in the first period. The first generation levies:

$$\theta^1 = R - d, \qquad \tau_1^1 = 1 - \lambda, \qquad \tau_2^1 = \frac{g - t - R\tau_1^1\overline{l_1} - \theta^1\overline{s_1}}{l_2}$$

and therefore the labor and savings decisions are $l_1^1 = \overline{l_1}$, $l_2^1 = l_2$ and $s_1^1 = \overline{s_1}$. The utility level of the first generation is then $u^1 = \hat{u} + t - \psi$. The first generation institutes the social contract if $u^1 \geq \tilde{u}$, i.e. if:

$$t + (R - d)\overline{s_1} \geq \psi \tag{12.3}$$

Besides, the utility of the first generation when old is $v^1 = \hat{v} + t$ where $\hat{v}$ is the second period utility associated to the second best. Call $\tilde{v}$, the second period utility associated to the third best optimum. It is easy to verify that $\tilde{v} = \hat{v} + (1-\mu)(\overline{l_2} - \underline{l_2})$. Indeed, if the first generation breaks the social contract when old, it will impose $\tau_2 = 1 - \mu$ and $\theta = \hat{\theta}$. Therefore, the generation benefit from the elimination of the second period labor distortion with respect to the second best. However, it looses t. Now, the first generation has an incentive to fulfill the social contract when old if $v^1 \geq \tilde{v}$, i.e. if:

$$t \geq (1 - \mu)(\overline{l_2} - \underline{l_2}) \tag{12.4}$$

Consider now the second generation. If it fulfills the contract, the budget constraints of the council are:

$$t + B = \tau_1 l_1$$

$$g - t = \theta s_1 + \tau_2 l_2 + RB$$

Given these constraints, the optimal tax rates are $\tau_1 = 1 - \lambda$, $\theta = R - d$, and $\tau_2 = \frac{g + (R-1)t - R(1-\lambda)\overline{l_1} - (R-d)\overline{s_1}}{\overline{l_2}}$. The second generation achieves the second best optimum and his utility is now $u^2 = \hat{u} - (R - 1)t$. To be willing to purchase the social contract rather than create another one, we need $u^2 \geq u^1$, i.e.:

$$\psi \geq Rt \tag{12.5}$$

The second generation must also prefer to fulfill the social contract when old. Therefore, the second period utility v^2 must exceed the second period utility if the generation moves to the third best optimum, $\tilde{v}^2$. Note that $v^2 = \hat{v} - (R-1)t$. Besides, $\tau_2 = 1 - \mu$ and $\theta = \frac{g + Rt - R(1-\lambda)\overline{l_1} + (1-\mu)\overline{l_2}}{s_1} > \tilde{\theta}$ in the third best optimum . Then, $\tilde{v}^2 = \hat{v} - Rt + (1 - \mu)(\overline{l_2} - \underline{l_2})$. As a consequence, the social contract is fulfilled by the second generation when old if:

$$t \geq (1 - \mu)(\overline{l_2} - \underline{l_2}) \tag{12.6}$$

If all these constraints are satisfied, there exists an equilibrium in which the social contract is instituted once and then sold from generation to generation.

12.3   Tax competition and international cooperation

Consider a two-period and two country-model in which countries are denoted by A and B. Both countries produce the same good and have access to the same technology. Consider country A which is inhabited by individuals with preferences

$$w^i = U(c_1^i) + c_2^i,$$

where c_1^i and c_2^i denote consumption in the first and the second period, respectively. At the beginning of the first period, individual i receives an endowment $1 + e^i$ that he can invest in domestic investment d^i and foreign investment f^i. Assume that e^i is distributed on $(-1, 1)$ with zero mean and negative median e^{Am}. In the second period, individual i pays capital taxes in each country in which he has invested. We call θ^A the tax rate in country A and θ^B the tax rate in country B. He also receives a lump-sum subsidy g from the government. The individual incurs mobility costs of investing in country B, denoted by $M(f^i) = (f^i)^2$. Government finances g through the revenue received from taxes on domestic and foreign investment. The model is the same for country B, the median agent of which is denoted by e^{Bm}.

a. Suppose that $e^i = e$ for all agents in both countries. Determine the representative agent's consumption and investment decisions. Suppose that both countries cooperate and maximize their joint welfare. On which pair of taxes do they agree? Suppose now that countries do not cooperate. What is the equilibrium in that case? Compare your results under cooperation and non cooperation and discuss.

b. Suppose now that agents are heterogeneous. The game is such that agents first select a policymaker under majority rule in each country. Then each policymaker chooses the tax rate in his country by maximizing his own utility function. Suppose that a policymaker of type e^A (respectively, e^B) is elected in country A (respectively, B). Characterize the pair of taxes in equilibrium. How do they vary with the policymakers' endowments?

c. Show that the utility function of each agent in each country satisfies the intermediate preferences property. Is there a Condorcet winner in each economy? If so, who is the Condorcet winner? Characterize the endowment of the elected policymaker in each economy. Discuss your results.

d. Suppose again that $e^i = e$ and that citizens of both countries choose tax rates by majority rule by the citizens of both countries under the constraint $\theta^A = \theta^B$. Moreover, citizens in each country are called to ratify this rate before making their savings decision. Determine the tax selected in the first vote. Do citizens in country A have an incentive to deviate and not ratify the vote? Explain briefly what is expected to happen when agents are heterogeneous.

Answer

a. The budget constraints of the representative agent in country A are:

$$1 + e = c_1 + d + f$$

$$c_2 = (1 - \theta^A)d + (1 - \theta^B)f + g - M(f)$$

The representative agent maximizes his utility under these two constraints to determine his consumption and savings decisions. This yields:

$$c_1 = C^A(\theta^A) = U_c^{-1}(1 - \theta^A)$$

$$f = M_f^{-1}(\theta^A - \theta^B) = F^A(\theta^A, \theta^B)$$

$$d = 1 + e - F^A(\theta^A, \theta^B) - C^A(\theta^A) = D^A(\theta^A, \theta^B) + e$$

Note that $F_{\theta^A}^A = -F_{\theta^B}^A > 0$, $D_{\theta^A}^A = -C_{\theta^A}^A - F_{\theta^A}^A < 0$ and $D_{\theta^B}^A = -F_{\theta^B}^A > 0$. As a result the representative agent's policy preferences can be written as:

$$W^A(\theta^A, \theta^B) = U(C^A(\theta^A)) + D^A(\theta^A, \theta^B) + (1 - \theta^A)e + (1 - \theta^B)F^A(\theta^A, \theta^B)$$

$$- M(F^A(\theta^A, \theta^B)) + \theta^A F^B(\theta^B, \theta^A)$$

Naturally, the optimal behavior of the representative agent in country B is similar.

The equilibrium policy with cooperation is obtained by maximizing $W^A(\theta^A, \theta^B) + W^B(\theta^B, \theta^A)$ with respect to θ^A and θ^B. Note that, since countries are symmetric, we have $F_{\theta^B}^A = F_{\theta^A}^B$ and $F_{\theta^A}^A = F_{\theta^B}^B$. The first order conditions are:

$$-e - \theta^A C_{\theta^A}^A - 2(\theta^A - \theta^B)F_{\theta^A}^A = 0$$

$$-e - \theta^B C_{\theta^B}^B - 2(\theta^B - \theta^A)F_{\theta^B}^B = 0$$

These expressions determine the reactions functions $\theta^A(\theta^B)$ and $\theta^B(\theta^A)$. Replacing θ^A by $\theta^A(\theta^B)$ in the first expression and differentiating, we get that $\theta^A(\theta^B)$ is increasing in θ^B. Applying the same reasoning to $\theta^B(\theta^A)$, we get that $\theta^B(\theta^A)$ is increasing in θ^A. Therefore, the two taxes are strategic complements. By symmetry, the equilibrium is such that $\theta^A = \theta^B = \theta^C$, and is characterized by:

$$-e - \theta^C C_{\theta^A}^A(\theta^C) = 0$$

The equilibrium without cooperation is obtained by maximizing the welfare of each representative agent in each country. In country A, the optimal tax satisfies:

$$F^B - e - \theta^A C_{\theta^A}^A - 2\theta^A F_{\theta^A}^A = 0$$

and in country B, it is given by:

$$F^A - e - \theta^B C_{\theta^B}^B - 2\theta^B F_{\theta^B}^B = 0$$

Following the same reasoning as before, taxes are strategic complements. Given symmetry, both countries choose the same tax rate θ^{NC} which is characterized by:

$$-e - \theta^{NC} C^A_{\theta^A}(\theta^{NC}) = 2\theta^{NC} F^A_{\theta^A}(\theta^{NC}, \theta^{NC})$$

Then, it follows immediately that $\theta^C > \theta^{NC}$. In the absence of cooperation, both governments face an incentive to unilaterally reduce taxes to attract foreign capital and keep domestic capital within their borders. This incentive is measured by $F^A_{\theta^A}$ which reflects international capital mobility.

b. If the elected leader in country A has an endowment e^A, he will choose θ^A to maximize:

$$W^A(e^A, \theta^A, \theta^B) = U(C^A(\theta^A)) + D^A(\theta^A, \theta^B) + (1-\theta^A)e^A + (1-\theta^B)F^A(\theta^A, \theta^B)$$

$$-M(F^A(\theta^A, \theta^B)) + \theta^A F^B(\theta^B, \theta^A)$$

Then, the tax is such that:

$$F^B - e^A - \theta^A C^A_{\theta^A} - 2\theta^A F^A_{\theta^A} = 0$$

If the endowment of the leader in country B is e^B, then θ^B is such that:

$$F^A - e^B - \theta^B C^B_{\theta^B} - 2\theta^B F^B_{\theta^B} = 0$$

These two expressions define two reaction functions $\theta^A(\theta^B, e^A)$ and $\theta^B(\theta^A, e^B)$. Replacing θ^A (respectively, θ^B) by $\theta^A(\theta^B, e^A)$ (respectively, $\theta^B(\theta^A, e^B)$) in the first (respectively, second) expression and differentiating with respect to e^A (respectively, e^B), we obtain that the tax in country A (respectively, B) decreases in the endowment of the leader. Therefore, the reaction function shifts down when e^A (respectively, e^B) increases.

c. The policy preferences of each agent in each country satisfy the intermediate preferences property over the tax rate of his country. Therefore, there is a Condorcet winner under majority rule. Agents do not vote directly on taxes but they select a policymaker with a given endowment. Their preferences over endowments are single peaked, so they can rank policymakers endowments. Therefore, the Condorcet winner is the policymaker who is preferred by the voter with median value e^{Am}. The optimal policies from the perspective of the median voters in country A and B are respectively:

$$\theta^{Am} = \text{argmax}_\theta \quad W^A(e^{Am}, \theta, \theta^B(\theta, e^{Bm}))$$

$$\theta^{Bm} = \text{argmax}_\theta \quad W^B(e^{Bm}, \theta, \theta^A(\theta, e^{Am}))$$

In equilibrium, the median voter in country A (respectively, B) selects a policymaker who finds it ex post optimal to set $\theta^A = \theta^{Am}$ (respectively, $\theta^B = \theta^{Bm}$). Therefore, the elected policymakers are characterized by:

$$e^A = e^{Am} - \frac{\partial \theta^B(\theta^A, e^{Am})}{\partial \theta^A}[\theta^A F^B_{\theta^B} - \theta^A F^A_{\theta^B} - F^A]$$

$$e^B = e^{Bm} - \frac{\partial \theta^A(\theta^B, e^{Bm})}{\partial \theta^B}[\theta^B F_{\theta^A}^A - \theta^B F_{\theta^A}^B - F^B]$$

Given our assumptions on $M(\cdot)$, we obtain that $e^A < e^{Am}$ and $e^B < e^{Bm}$.

d. Suppose that agents have the same endowments. Moreover, assume that citizens from both countries vote over a single tax. Given symmetry, the optimal tax from the perspective of each of them maximizes:

$$U(C(\theta)) + D(\theta, \theta) + (1 - \theta)e$$

Therefore, they all agree on θ^W such that:

$$-e - \theta C_\theta = 0$$

and then $\theta^W = \theta^C$. Moreover $W^A(\theta^C, \theta^C) > W^A(\theta^A, \theta^B)$ for all $(\theta^A, \theta^B) \neq (\theta^C, \theta^C)$. Therefore, agents in each country want to ratify the vote, and θ^C is implemented.

If agents are heterogeneous and $e^{Am} \neq e^{Bm}$, the two median voters prefer different common tax rates. If it is chosen in worldwide elections, the tax rate is in between those preferred by the home and foreign medians, and depends on the distribution of e^i in the whole population. Besides, not every outcome is ratified. Formally, the decision on a common tax θ^Z is ratified if $W^A(\theta^Z, \theta^Z) \geq W^A(\theta^{Am}, \theta^{Bm})$ and $W^B(\theta^Z, \theta^Z) \geq W^B(\theta^{Bm}, \theta^{Am})$. Only such a tax can be proposed in the first round.

12.4   The effects of capital mobility on taxation

This problem is inspired by Persson and Tabellini 1992a. Consider the same model as in problem 3, in which agents have heterogeneous endowments. Moreover, assume that the mobility costs incurred by an agent of country P when investing in country $Q \neq P$ is described by the function $M(f^i; \mu^Q)$, where $\mu^Q > 0$ represents the size of the mobility costs. For simplicity, we assume that $M(f^i, \mu^Q) = \mu^Q(f^i)^2$. As in question (b) of problem 3, individuals in each country select a policymaker, who then chooses the tax rate by maximizing his own utility.

a. Determine the consumption and investment decisions of agents in both countries. Let e^A (respectively, e^B) be the endowment of the elected policymaker in country A (respectively, B). Characterize the equilibrium when $\mu^A = \mu^B$ and when $\mu^A \neq \mu^B$.

b. Suppose that $\mu^A = \mu^B$. What effects does a decrease in the size of the mobility costs have? Characterize the endowment of the policymaker who is elected under majority rule. Determine the equilibrium when $e^{Am} = e^{Bm}$ and when $e^{Am} < e^{Bm}$.

c. Answer question (b) when $\mu^A \neq \mu^B$.

Answer

a. Following the same reasoning as in the previous problem, the optimal decisions of agents in country A are:

$$c_1 = C^A(\theta^A) = U_c^{-1}(1 - \theta^A)$$

$$f = M_f^{-1}(\theta^A - \theta^B; \mu^B) = F^A(\theta^A, \theta^B; \mu^B)$$

$$d = 1 + e^i - F^A(\theta^A, \theta^B; \mu^B) - C^A(\theta^A) = D^A(\theta^A, \theta^B; \mu^B) + e^i$$

The policy preferences are:

$$W^A(e^i, \theta^A, \theta^B, \mu^A, \mu^B) = U(C^A(\theta^A)) + D^A(\theta^A, \theta^B; \mu^B) + (1 - \theta^B)F^A(\theta^A, \theta^B; \mu^B)$$

$$-M(F^A(\theta^A, \theta^B; \mu_B); \mu^B) + \theta^A F^B(\theta^B, \theta^A; \mu^A) + (1 - \theta^A)e^i$$

The policymaker in country A maximizes $W^A(e^A, \theta^A, \theta^B, \mu^A, \mu^B)$ with respect to θ^A. Similarly, the policymaker in country B maximizes $W^B(e^B, \theta^B, \theta^A, \mu^B, \mu^A)$ with respect to θ^B. The political equilibrium is therefore given by the two following conditions:

$$F^B - e^A - \theta^A[C_{\theta^A}^A + F_{\theta^A}^A - F_{\theta^A}^B] = 0$$

$$F^A - e^B - \theta^B[C_{\theta^B}^B + F_{\theta^B}^B - F_{\theta^B}^A] = 0$$

These conditions characterize the two reaction functions $\theta^A(\theta^B, e^A, \mu^B, \mu^A)$ and $\theta^B(\theta^A, e^B, \mu^A, \mu^B)$. The equilibrium conditions are formally the same when $\mu^A = \mu^B = \mu$.

b. Suppose that $\mu^A = \mu^B = \mu$. Differentiating the first order condition associated to country A with respect to μ, we obtain:

$$\frac{\partial \theta^A}{\partial \mu} \propto F_\mu^B - \theta^A[F_{\theta^A \mu}^A - F_{\theta^A \mu}^B] = F_\mu^B - \theta^A[F_{\theta^A \mu}^A + F_{\theta^B \mu}^B]$$

The first term on the right-hand side indicates that higher mobility costs reduce foreign investment. Hence the government has an incentive to maintain a high tax rate so as to tax foreign investors. We call this effect the *tax-the-foreigner effect*. The second term indicates that when both taxes increase (which discourage investment), a higher μ reduces the marginal loss of such an increase. We call this effect the *tax competition effect*. If foreign investment is positive, the two effects work in opposite directions, whereas they reinforce each other if foreign investment is negative.

Using the same reasoning as in the previous exercise, the policymaker who wins the elections in each country is the policymaker preferred by the median voter. The endowments of the policymakers are given by:

$$e^A = e^{Am} - \frac{\partial \theta^B(\theta^A, e^{Am}, \mu)}{\partial \theta^A}[\theta^A F_{\theta^B}^B - \theta^A F_{\theta^B}^A - F^A]$$

$$e^B = e^{Bm} - \frac{\partial\theta^A(\theta^B, e^{Bm}, \mu)}{\partial\theta^B}[\theta^B F_{\theta^A}^A - \theta^B F_{\theta^A}^B - F^B]$$

Consider first the case in which $e^{Am} = e^{Bm}$. In that case, $\theta^A = \theta^B$ and $F^A = F^B = 0$. Then, only the *tax competition effect* operates. Hence, $e^A < e^{Am}$ and $e^B < e^{Bm}$. Ex post, the policymaker considers a unilateral increase in the domestic tax rate, taking the foreign tax rate as given. Ex ante, voters anticipate that raising the domestic tax rate (by electing a poorer policymaker) induces the foreign country also to raise its tax. In other words, the ex ante optimal tax rate is higher than the ex post optimal tax rate, which leads voters to elect a government more to the left of the median. Suppose now that $e^{Am} < e^{Bm}$. We have $\theta^A > \theta^B$ and as a consequence $F^A > 0 > F^B$. In the low-tax country (country B), both the tax competition effect and the tax-the-foreigner effect go in the same direction. The government is therefore to the left of the median voter. However, in the high-tax country (country A), the two effects go in opposite directions. As a consequence, the elected policymaker can be either to the left or to the right of the median voter.

c. Suppose now that $\mu^A \neq \mu^B$. Then, we find:

$$\frac{\partial\theta^A}{\partial\mu^A} \propto F_{\mu^A}^B + \theta^A F_{\theta^A\mu^A}^B$$

and:

$$\frac{\partial\theta^A}{\partial\mu^B} \propto -\theta^A F_{\theta^A\mu_B}^A > 0$$

Note that $F_{\mu^A}^B > 0$ (respectively,. < 0) if $F^B < 0$ (respectively,. > 0) and $F_{\theta^A\mu^A}^B > 0$. More precisely,

$$\frac{\partial\theta^A}{\partial\mu^A} \propto -2\theta^B + 4\theta^A$$

Therefore, θ^A is not monotonically affected by an increase in μ^A.

The endowments of the policymakers are given by:

$$e^A = e^{Am} - \frac{\partial\theta^B(\theta^A, e^{Am}, \mu^A, \mu^B)}{\partial\theta^A}[\theta^A F_{\theta^B}^B - \theta^A F_{\theta^B}^A - F^A]$$

$$e^B = e^{Bm} - \frac{\partial\theta^A(\theta^B, e^{Bm}, \mu^B, \mu^A)}{\partial\theta^B}[\theta^B F_{\theta^A}^A - \theta^B F_{\theta^A}^B - F^B]$$

Note that the equilibrium is not symmetric anymore if $e^{Am} = e^{Bm}$. However, for all μ^A and μ^B, there exists e^{Am} and e^{Bm} such that $\theta^A = \theta^B$ in equilibrium.

Suppose that $e^{Am} = e^{Bm}$ and $\mu^A > \mu^B$. In that case $F^A > 0 > F^B$ and $\theta^A > \theta^B$. In the low tax country, the policymaker is to the left of the median voter. However, in the high tax country, the policymaker can be of either side of the median voter.

Chapter 13

Public debt

13.1 Preelection politics and government spending when parties are opportunistic

This problem uses the same model as in section 13.3.3 but considers the case in which politicians are purely opportunistic. There are two types of voters: $J \in \{D, R\}$, with an indirect utility function $w^{iJ} = W(b + g_2) + \sum_{t=1}^{2} H(g_t^J) + (\sigma^i + \delta_t) \cdot K_t^D$, with $W_b < 0$, and $W_{bb} < 0$. σ^i is an idiosyncratic preference parameter distributed around a zero mean according to some c.d.f. F_σ which is not group-specific. δ represents the average political preference in favor of party D at date t and follows a c.d.f. F_δ. K_t^D is an indicator variable taking on value 1 if D is elected in period $t = 1, 2$ (in the textbook, only K_2^D matters). Finally, public spending in each period is the sum of the spending on each group $J \in \{D, R\}$. That is, total borrowings, b, will be equal to first-period total spending: $b = g_1^D + g_1^R$ and $g_2 = g_2^D + g_2^R$.

The timing is as follows: (1) At the beginning of each period, parties announce their platform, that is a supply of public goods to each group. (2) Then δ_t realizes and voters cast their ballot. (3) The elected party implements its announced platform and payoffs are realized.

a. Compute the optimal provision of public goods when the share of type D voters is $d \in [0, 1]$.

b. Show that opportunistic politicians who either maximize their share of votes or maximize their probability of being elected provide the same –optimal– amount of public goods in the second period.

c. Assume d is constant over time. Show that the level of public expenditure does not affect reelection probabilities. Demonstrate that as a result, politicians also provide the optimal levels of public goods in the first period.

d. Show that if the share of D type voters changes over time, that is if $d_1 \neq d_2$, whereas individual preferences do not change, the previous result no longer applies: the debt level may be suboptimal.

Answer

a. To compute the optimal provision of public goods, we have to maximize social welfare, which is the weighted sum of the type $J \in \{D, R\}$'s utility levels. The utility of a consumer J is given by:

$$w^{iJ} = W\left(b + g_2\right) + H\left(g_1^J\right) + H\left(g_2^J\right) + \left(\sigma_1^i + \delta_1\right) \cdot K_1^D + \left(\sigma_2^i + \delta_2\right) K_2^D$$

with $H' > 0$, and $H'' < 0$. Therefore, social welfare can be written as

$$d \cdot w^D + (1 - d) \cdot w^R = W\left(b + g_2\right) + d \cdot \left[H\left(g_1^D\right) + H\left(g_2^D\right)\right] + \ldots$$
$$\ldots + (1 - d) \cdot \left[H\left(g_1^R\right) + H\left(g_2^R\right)\right] + \delta_1 K_1^D + \delta_2 K_2^D$$

as the average of σ_t^i is zero.

In both periods, the optimal public good provision is defined by:

$$-\frac{\partial W}{\partial b} = d \cdot H'\left(g_1^D\right) = d \cdot H'\left(g_2^D\right) = -\frac{\partial W}{\partial g_2}$$
$$-\frac{\partial W}{\partial b} = (1 - d) \cdot H'\left(g_1^R\right) = (1 - d) \cdot H'\left(g_2^R\right) = -\frac{\partial W}{\partial g_2}$$

with $J = D, R$, and it is optimal to have D in office at time t iff $\delta_t > 0$.

b. Opportunistic politicians seek voters' support. At the beginning of period 2, voter i belonging to group J votes for D instead of R if:

$$\sigma_2^i > -\delta_2 + W\left[b + g_2\left(R\right)\right] - W\left[b + g_2\left(D\right)\right] + H\left(g_2^J\left(R\right)\right) - H\left(g_2^J\left(D\right)\right)$$
$$= K_2^J\left[\mathbf{g_2}\left(R\right), \mathbf{g_2}\left(D\right); \delta_2\right], \qquad (13.1)$$

where $g_2^J\left(P\right)$ is the level of public goods supplied to group J by party P and $\mathbf{g_2}\left(P\right) = \left\{g_2^D\left(P\right), g_2^R\left(P\right)\right\}$ is vector of public goods supplied by party P in period 2. It follows from (13.1) that party D's vote share is

$$\pi_2^D\left[K_2^D\left[\bullet\right], K_2^R\left[\bullet\right]\right] = 1 - d \cdot F_\sigma\left(K_2^D\left[\cdot; \delta_2\right]\right) - (1 - d) \cdot F_\sigma\left(K_2^R\left[\cdot; \delta_2\right]\right), \quad (13.2)$$

where F_σ denotes the C.D.F. of σ. The vote share of party R is simply $\pi_2^R\left[\bullet\right] = 1 - \pi_2^D\left[K_2^D\left[\bullet\right], K_2^R\left[\bullet\right]\right]$, and the two parties maximize their vote share. For instance, the first order condition for the maximization of π_2^D with respect to g_2^D is:

$$\frac{\partial \pi_2^D\left[\bullet\right]}{\partial g_2^D\left(D\right)} = f_\sigma\left(\cdot; \delta_2\right)\left(W_{g_2}\left[\cdot\right] + d \cdot H_g\left[g_2^D\left(D\right)\right]\right) = 0. \qquad (13.3)$$

As R solves the same problem, it supplies the same quantities. Rewriting the first order conditions yields (for both parties):

$$W_{g_2}\left[b + g_2\right] = -d \cdot H_g\left[g_2^D\right] \qquad (13.4)$$
$$W_{g_2}\left[b + g_2\right] = -(1 - d) \cdot H_g\left[g_2^R\right]. \qquad (13.5)$$

Therefore, the period-two supply of public good is efficient and is not influenced by f_σ nor δ_2.

Nothing would change if the parties were instead to maximize their probability of being elected: the probability that D is elected in the second period is $p_D = \Pr_\delta \left(\pi_2^D [.] \geq .5 \right)$, and the first order condition becomes

$$\frac{dp_D}{dg_2^R(D)} = E_\delta \left[\frac{\partial p_D}{\partial \pi_2^D(.;\delta)} \frac{\partial \pi_2^D(.;\delta)}{\partial g_2^R(D)} \right] = 0.$$

As $\partial p_D / \partial \pi_2^D(\cdot;\delta)$ is always strictly positive, this condition boils down to the same as (13.5).

c. We just showed that $\mathbf{g_2}(D) = \mathbf{g_2}(R)$. Therefore, nor the first-period allocation of public goods, nor total indebtedness can affect reelection probabilities. In addition, as d is constant over time, voters fully internalize the second-period effect of a first-period debt increase. These two elements put together imply that parties solve a problem that is basically the same as in the first period, and therefore spending will be identical to that in the second period. Formally, voter i belonging to group J votes for D in the first period iff

$$W(g(D)) + H\left(g_1^J(D)\right) + H\left(g_2^J[b(D)]\right) + \left(\sigma^i + \delta_1\right) > ...$$
$$... > W(g(R)) + H\left(g_1^J(R)\right) + H\left(g_2^J[b(R)]\right)$$

where $g(P) = g_1^D + g_1^R + g_2^D + g_2^R$ is the sum of all spendings related to the platform of party P. Applying the same steps as in (13.2) and (13.3), we see that the result is the same as in (13.4) and (13.5).

d. First, note that if d varies over time, whereas voters maintain constant preferences, it must be that new voters enter in the second period. Implicitly, we are assuming a population change. For this reason, the results in question (c) do not hold anymore, as we show below.

Let us define the following: d_t is the share of D voters, $g_t = g_t^D + g_t^R$, and we summarize $g_2^J(b)$ as $\bar{g}_2^J$ and $\partial H\left(g_t^J\right) / \partial g_t^J$ as $H_{g_t^J}$. Under this notation, (13.4) and (13.5) become

$$W_{g_2} = -d_2 \cdot H_{g_2^D} \tag{13.6}$$
$$W_{g_2} = -(1 - d_2) \cdot H_{g_2^R}. \tag{13.7}$$

In the first period, we have:

$$W_b = -W_{g_2}\frac{\partial \bar{g}_2}{\partial b} - d_1 \cdot \left[H_{g_1^D} + H_{g_2^D}\frac{\partial \bar{g}_2^D}{\partial b} \right] - (1 - d_1) \cdot H_{g_2^R}\frac{\partial \bar{g}_2^R}{\partial b} \tag{13.8}$$

where $H_{g_2^D} = W_{g_2}/d_2 = W_d/d_2 \neq W_d/d_1$.

Therefore, substituting (13.6) and (13.7) into (13.8), and noting that $\frac{\partial \bar{g}_2}{\partial b} = \frac{\partial \bar{g}_2^D}{\partial b} + \frac{\partial \bar{g}_2^R}{\partial b}$, one can see that the optimal public spending in the first period is given by:

$$W_b = -d_1 \cdot H_{g_1^D} + (d_2 - d_1) \cdot \left(H_{g_2^D}\frac{\partial \bar{g}_2^D}{\partial b} - H_{g_2^R}\frac{\partial \bar{g}_2^R}{\partial b} \right). \tag{13.9}$$

Similarly, the supply of public goods to group R is characterized by

$$W_b = -(1-d_1) \cdot H_{g_1^R} + (d_2 - d_1) \cdot \left(H_{g_2^D} \frac{\partial \bar{g}_2^D}{\partial b} - H_{g_2^R} \frac{\partial \bar{g}_2^R}{\partial b} \right). \tag{13.10}$$

Optimality requires $-\frac{\partial W}{\partial b} = d_1 \cdot H'\left(g^D\right) = (1-d_1) \cdot H'\left(g^R\right)$. To achieve optimality, from (13.9) and (13.10), we see that we need either $d_2 = d_1$ or $d_2 = \frac{1}{2}$ (the latter condition implies $H_{g_2^D} \frac{\partial g_2^D}{\partial b} = H_{g_2^R} \frac{\partial g_2^R}{\partial b}$).

13.2 Population structure's influence on dynamic inconsistency

This problem uses the same framework as problem 13.1 but illustrates how changes in population structure affect parties' preferences.

a. Consider the case in which $d = .5$, and suppose that the σ^i are distributed according to a uniform distribution $\mathcal{U}\left[-\frac{1}{2\phi^J}; \frac{1}{2\phi^J}\right]$, where parameters ϕ^J differ among groups $J \in \{D, R\}$. Show that equilibrium spending will be suboptimal and biased towards the group with the highest ϕ^J, both in the first and the second period.

b. Consider the case in which $d = .5$, and suppose that the values of the ϕ^J parameters vary between the first and the second period. Show that first-period spending can be too high or too low compared to the case in which ϕ^J is constant over time.

c. Consider the case in which $\phi^D = \phi^R$ but the value of d changes between the first and the second period because voters change their preferences. Show that in such a case, equilibrium spending is always optimal in both periods. Compare the results with those in problem 13.1d and comment.

Answer

a. If the random variables σ^{iJ} are distributed uniformly, with $\phi^D \neq \phi^R$, and if $\delta = \frac{1}{2}$, then equation (13.2) in problem 13.1 should be rewritten as:

$$\pi_D^2 (g_2; \delta) = \frac{1}{2} - \frac{\phi^D}{2} \cdot K_2^D (g_2; \delta) - \frac{\phi^R}{2} \cdot K_2^R (g_2; \delta) \tag{13.11}$$

where $g_2 = \left\{ g_2^D(D), g_2^R(D), g_2^D(R), g_2^R(R) \right\}$.

Taking the first order condition with respect to g_2^J:

$$\frac{\partial \pi_D^2 (g_2; \delta_2)}{\partial g_2^J} = \frac{\phi^D + \phi^R}{2} W_{g_2} + \frac{\phi^J}{2} \cdot H_{g_2^J}\left(g_2^J\right) = 0$$

$$\text{or: } -W_{g_2} = \frac{\phi^J}{\phi^D + \phi^R} \cdot H_{g_2^J}\left(g_2^J\right). \tag{13.12}$$

Therefore, group J receives more spending than group K if $\phi^J > \phi^K$. In contrast to this, the answer to question (a) in problem 13.1 shows that the optimal supply to the two groups depends solely on their share in the population, and not on the distribution of the σ^i's.

In other words, the opportunistic politician, instead of maximizing the social welfare function, maximizes another Benthamite social welfare function where each group is weighted by its "cohesion", ϕ^J. More homogenous groups are able to extract a larger share of public goods because, for parties, they are easier to buy out.

The first–period problem is identical and yields the same equilibrium provision of public goods (see also the answer to question (b) in this problem for a complete derivation).

b. Let us denote by ϕ_t^J the value that ϕ^J takes at time t. By (13.12), the second period provision of public goods to group J is determined by

$$-W_{g2} = \frac{\phi_2^J}{\phi_2^D + \phi_2^R} \cdot H_{g_2^J}\left(g_2^J\right). \tag{13.13}$$

In the first period, the vote share of party D is:

$$\pi_D^1\left(\mathbf{g}; \delta_1\right) = \frac{1}{2} - \frac{\phi_1^D}{2} \cdot K_1^D\left(\mathbf{g}_1; \delta_1\right) - \frac{\phi_1^R}{2} \cdot K_1^R\left(\mathbf{g}_1; \delta_1\right)$$

where $\mathbf{g}_1$ is the vector of public good provisions in period 1. As a reminder:

$$\begin{aligned} K_1^J\left(\mathbf{g}_1; \delta_1\right) &= W\left[b\left(R\right) + g_2\left(b\left(R\right)\right)\right] - W\left[b\left(D\right) + g_2\left(b\left(D\right)\right)\right] + \dots \\ &\quad \dots + H\left[g_1^J\left(R\right)\right] - H\left[g_1^J\left(D\right)\right] + \dots \\ &\quad \dots + H\left[g_2^J\left(b\left(R\right)\right)\right] - H\left[g_2^J\left(b\left(D\right)\right)\right] - \delta_1 \end{aligned}$$

where we are explicitly writing that the second-period provision of public goods depends on the amount of debt left by the first-period incumbent, that we denote by $b\left(P\right)$. Differentiating $\pi_D^1\left(\mathbf{g}; \delta_1\right)$ with respect to g_1^D, we find the first order condition:

$$\frac{\phi_1^D + \phi_1^R}{2}\left(-W_b - W_{g2} \cdot \frac{dg_2}{db}\right) - \frac{\phi_1^D}{2}\left(H_{g_1^D} + H_{g_2^D}\frac{dg_2^D}{db}\right) - \frac{\phi_1^R}{2} \cdot H_{g_2^R}\frac{dg_2^R}{db} = 0.$$

Isolating W_b yields:

$$W_b = -W_{g2} \cdot \frac{dg_2}{db} - \frac{\phi_1^D}{\phi_1^D + \phi_1^R}\left(H_{g_1^D} + H_{g_2^D}\frac{dg_2^D}{db}\right) - \frac{\phi_1^R}{\phi_1^D + \phi_1^R} \cdot H_{g_2^R}\frac{dg_2^R}{db}$$

and by (13.13) this becomes

$$W_b = -\frac{\phi_1^D}{\phi_1^D + \phi_1^R}H_{g_1^D} + \frac{\phi_2^D \phi_1^R - \phi_1^D \phi_2^R}{(\phi_2^D + \phi_2^R)(\phi_1^D + \phi_1^R)}\left(H_{g_2^D}\frac{dg_2^D}{db} - H_{g_2^R}\frac{dg_2^R}{db}\right),$$

and a similar result holds for g_1^R.

Therefore, if the value of the ϕ^J's does not vary over time, we find $W_b = -\phi_1^D/\left(\phi_1^D + \phi_1^R\right) \cdot H_{g_1^D}$, which is the result we obtained in question (a).

Instead, if these values vary over time, political groups know that their share in total spending can increase or decrease over time. If a group knows that its power will be lower in the second period, it asks for more spending in the first period, thereby crowding out second-period spending on the other group.

c. There are different ways to specify this problem but the answer remains the same, independently of the specification. Let us assume that each voter knows that, with probability d_2, she will have type D in the second period. With probability $(1 - d_2)$, she will have type R. In this case, the utility of an agent with type D, measured as of period 1, is given by

$$
\begin{aligned}
w^{iD} \;=\;& W\left(b + g_2\right) + H\left(g_1^D\right) + d_2 H\left(g_2^D\right) + (1 - d_2) H\left(g_2^R\right) + \ldots \\
& \ldots + \left(\sigma_1^i + \delta_1\right) \cdot K_1^D + \left(\sigma_2^i + \delta_2\right) K_2^D
\end{aligned}
$$

and a similar equation holds for type R's.

Maximizing the first-period probability to be elected hence requires:

$$
\begin{aligned}
W_b + W_{g_2}\tfrac{dg_2}{db} + d_1\left(H_{g_1^D} + d_2 H_{g_2^D}\tfrac{dg_2^D}{db} + (1 - d_2) H_{g_2^R}\tfrac{dg_2^R}{db}\right) + \ldots \\
\ldots + (1 - d_1)\left(d_2 H_{g_2^D}\tfrac{dg_2^D}{db} + (1 - d_2) H_{g_2^R}\tfrac{dg_2^R}{db}\right) = 0
\end{aligned}
$$

By (13.6) and (13.7), this simplifies to:

$$
W_b = -d_1 H_{g_1^D}
$$

Similarly, by differentiating with respect to g_1^R, and applying the same developments:

$$
W_b = -\left(1 - d_1\right) H_{g_1^R}
$$

Additional notes

What do we learn from these 2 problems? We have shown that population changes can indeed generate inefficient spending levels in the first period, even when parties are purely opportunistic. But sometimes they may not. What is the main difference between this last specification and the other ones? In the case of problem 13.1, the share of the groups changes over time, but preferences remain constant. Similarly, in question (b) in problem 13.2, the political power of the two groups changes over time, but preferences remain the same. In question (c) in problem 13.2, instead, we see that if changes in population structure reflect changes in preferences, then voters dislike sub-optimal spending in the first period. Voters want overspending only if they know that their influence on policy will drop. They want underspending if they know that their influence will increase. But if their preferences change in line with population's average preferences, they just want the optimal level of spending.

13.3   When there is overindebtedness

Consider the same framework as in the two previous problems.

a. Suppose that the ϕ parameters are given and equal to .5. Determine the conditions about the shape of H that ensures that a change in d generates an excessive debt level in the first period.

b. Assume now that $d = .5$. Characterize the conditions about the shape of H that ensures that a change in ϕ^J generates an excessive debt level in the first period.

Answer

a. In problem 13.1, we saw that changes in d generate suboptimal spending in the first period. The first order conditions were:

$$W_b = -d_1 \cdot H_{g_1^D} + (d_2 - d_1) \cdot \left(H_{g_2^D} \frac{\partial \bar{g}_2^D}{\partial b} - H_{g_2^R} \frac{\partial \bar{g}_2^R}{\partial b} \right) \tag{13.9}$$

$$W_b = -(1 - d_1) \cdot H_{g_1^R} + (d_2 - d_1) \cdot \left(H_{g_2^D} \frac{\partial \bar{g}_2^D}{\partial b} - H_{g_2^R} \frac{\partial \bar{g}_2^R}{\partial b} \right). \tag{13.10}$$

However, these equations do not tell us whether b is inefficiently large or inefficiently small. If the second term in (13.9) or (13.10) is negative, there is overspending (remember that $W_b < 0$ and $W_{bb} < 0$). Conversely, if that term is positive, there is underspending.

As we want to derive the condition for over- or underspending, we have to focus on the sign of this second term. What makes it larger or smaller than 0? Let us take the conditions that determine second–period spending:

$$W_{g_2} + d_2 \cdot H_{g_2^D} = 0 \tag{13.14}$$

$$W_{g_2} + (1 - d_2) \cdot H_{g_2^R} = 0 \tag{13.15}$$

and differentiate them with respect to b:

$$W_{bb} \cdot \left(1 + \frac{\partial \bar{g}_2^D}{\partial b} + \frac{\partial \bar{g}_2^R}{\partial b} \right) + d_2 \cdot H'' \left(\bar{g}_2^D \right) \frac{\partial \bar{g}_2^D}{\partial b} = 0$$

$$W_{bb} \cdot \left(1 + \frac{\partial \bar{g}_2^D}{\partial b} + \frac{\partial \bar{g}_2^R}{\partial b} \right) + (1 - d_2) \cdot H'' \left(\bar{g}_2^R \right) \frac{\partial \bar{g}_2^R}{\partial b} = 0$$

Solving them jointly, we obtain:

$$\frac{\partial \bar{g}_2^D}{\partial b} = (1 - d_2) \cdot \Delta \cdot H'' \left(\bar{g}_2^R \right)$$

$$\frac{\partial \bar{g}_2^D}{\partial b} = d_2 \cdot \Delta \cdot H'' \left(\bar{g}_2^D \right)$$

where $\Delta = \dfrac{-W_{bb}}{W_{bb} \left(d_2 H'' \left(\bar{g}_2^D \right) + (1 - d_2) H'' \left(\bar{g}_2^R \right) \right) + d_2 \cdot (1 - d_2) H'' \left(\bar{g}_2^D \right) H'' \left(\bar{g}_2^R \right)} > 0$

and H'' is the second derivative of H.

Inserting this result into the second term of (13.9), considering $d_2 > d_1$, and simplifying, there is overspending in the first period if and only if

$$(1 - d_2) \cdot H'\left(\bar{g}_2^D\right) \cdot H''\left(\bar{g}_2^R\right) < d_2 \cdot H'\left(\bar{g}_2^R\right) \cdot H''\left(\bar{g}_2^D\right).$$

To further simplify this condition, we can use (13.14) and (13.15):

$$(1 - d_2) \cdot \frac{-W_{g_2}}{d_2} \cdot H''\left(\bar{g}_2^R\right) \quad < \quad d_2 \cdot \frac{-W_{g_2}}{1 - d_2} \cdot H''\left(\bar{g}_2^D\right)$$

$$\left(\frac{1 - d_2}{d_2}\right)^2 H''\left(\bar{g}_2^R\right) \quad < \quad H''\left(\bar{g}_2^D\right). \tag{13.16}$$

Now, we have two cases to consider: d_2 larger or smaller than $1/2$.

Case 1: $d_2 > 1/2$. This implies $\bar{g}_2^D > \bar{g}_2^R$ and $\left(\frac{1-d_2}{d_2}\right)^2 < 1$. Hence, by (13.16), we need to have $H''\left(\bar{g}_2^R\right) < H''\left(\bar{g}_2^D\right)$ or $H''\left(\bar{g}_2^D\right)$ not too small compared to $H''\left(\bar{g}_2^R\right)$. As $\bar{g}_2^D > \bar{g}_2^R$, this implies that the third derivative of H must be either positive or not too negative.

Case 2: $d_2 < 1/2$. This implies $\bar{g}_2^D < \bar{g}_2^R$ and $\left(\frac{1-d_2}{d_2}\right)^2 > 1$. Hence, by (13.16), we need to have $H''\left(\bar{g}_2^R\right) << H''\left(\bar{g}_2^D\right)$ or, in other words, $H''\left(\bar{g}_2^D\right)$ sufficiently larger than $H''\left(\bar{g}_2^R\right)$. As $\bar{g}_2^D < \bar{g}_2^R$, this implies that the third derivative of H must be sufficiently negative.

The conditions on the third derivative are reversed if we consider the case $d_1 > d_2$.

b. This case is identical to the previous one. For $t = 1, 2$, let $d_t = \phi_t^D / \left(\phi_t^D + \phi_t^R\right)$, and hence $(1 - d_t) = \phi_t^R / \left(\phi_t^D + \phi_t^R\right)$. Running through the same developments as for question (a), we find the same results. To conclude, for a given shape of the function $H(\cdot)$, only two parameters determine whether there is overspending or not. These parameters are the relative political powers of the two groups in periods 1 and 2 respectively, i.e. d_1 and d_2.

13.4 Endogenous (in)efficiency of the tax system

This problem draws on Cukierman, Edwards and Tabellini 1992. Assume a world in which there is neither public debt nor labor. At each period t, consumers have an endowment $e_t = 1$ that can be taxed. The *tax system*, however, can be inefficient. It is indexed by the parameter θ_{t-1}, which measures the rate of inefficiency: in equilibrium, $g_t = \tau_t = (1 - \theta_{t-1}) \cdot \tau_t^n$, where τ_t^n is the *nominal* tax rate at time t. Thus $c_t = 1 - \tau_t^n$. At time t, the government selects the time t values of the tax rate, government spending, and tax system inefficiency but knows that this inefficiency will affect tax proceeds only at $t + 1$. Tax revenues can be spent on two different types of public goods, g_t^J, $J \in \{D, R\}$, entering the utility of group J agents only:

$$w^J = c_1 + c_2 + H\left(g_1^J\right) + H\left(g_2^J\right).$$

As in section 13.3.1, the probability of party R's being in office in period 2 is defined by $p_R \in [0, 1]$. A tax reform consists of lowering θ_t to zero, which can be done at no cost.

a. Derive the optimal tax system, that is, the one maximizing $\sum_J w^J$ with respect to θ.

b. Derive the equilibrium spending in period 2, given the inherited efficiency of the tax system.

c. Show that the equilibrium efficiency of the tax system in period 2 will be suboptimally low if there is too low a probability that the party is reelected.

d. Show that the equilibrium efficiency of the tax system in period 2 increases if political polarization decreases. To this end, use the utility function

$$w^J = W\left(\tau_1^n, \tau_2^n\right) + H\left(\min\left[\tfrac{g_1^J}{\alpha}, \tfrac{g_1^K}{1-\alpha}\right]\right) + H\left(\min\left[\tfrac{g_2^J}{\alpha}, \tfrac{g_2^K}{1-\alpha}\right]\right)$$

with $J, K \in \{D, R\}$, $K \neq J$, and $\alpha \in [1/2, 1)$, where "polarization" is measured by the distance between α and $\frac{1}{2}$.

Answer

a. At the optimum, the tax system should be fully efficient: $\theta_1^* = 0$. To show this, we derive the equilibrium public good provision given θ_1 and then verify that the optimal value of the latter is zero.

The optimal provision of public goods in period 2 can be found by maximizing the social utility function

$$\max_{g_2^D, g_2^R} w^D + w^R = 2W\left(\tau_1^n + \tau_2^n\right) + H\left(g_2^D\right) + H\left(g_2^R\right)$$

$$\text{s.t. } g_2 = (1 - \theta_1)\,\tau_2^n,$$

where $W\left(\tau_1^n + \tau_2^n\right) = 2 - \tau_1^n - \tau_2^n$. Substituting for the constraint obtains

$$\max_{g_2^D, g_2^R} w^D + w^R = 2\left[2 - \tau_1^n - \frac{g_2}{1 - \theta_1}\right] + H\left(g_2^D\right) + H\left(g_2^R\right),$$

which yields the first order condition:

$$H'\left(g_2^D\right) = H'\left(g_2^R\right) = -2W_{g_2} = \frac{2}{1-\theta_1} \tag{13.17}$$

And, therefore, by the envelope theorem:

$$\frac{d\left(w^D + w^R\right)}{d\theta_1} = \frac{\partial W\left(\tau_1^n + \tau_2^n\right)}{\partial\theta_1} = -\frac{g_2}{\left(1-\theta_1\right)^2} < 0$$

which shows that the optimal value for θ_1 is zero. Note also that, by (13.17), g_2 is decreasing in θ_1.

b. As shown in section 13.2, equilibrium government spending will be biased towards one of the public goods only: if party $P \in \{D,R\}$ is in office in period 2, it maximizes

$$w^J = \left[2 - \tau_1^n - \frac{g_2}{1-\theta_1}\right] + H\left(g_2^J\right), \text{ with } J = P.$$

From the first order condition, in equilibrium we obtain:

$$H'\left(g_2^J\right) = \frac{1}{1-\theta_1} \tag{13.18}$$

$$\text{and } g_2^K = 0, \text{ with } K \in \{D,R\}, \ K \neq P$$

Let us denote by $\bar{g}_2\left(\theta_1\right)$ the equilibrium value of $g_2 = g_2^D + g_2^R$. By (13.18), $\bar{g}_2$ is independent of the identity of the party in office and is decreasing in θ_1.

We can also derive the behavior of the equilibrium tax rate as a function of θ_1. As $\bar{\tau}_2^n\left(\theta_1\right) = \bar{g}_2\left(\theta_1\right) / \left(1-\theta_1\right)$, we have

$$\frac{\partial\bar{\tau}_2^n\left(\theta_1\right)}{\partial\theta_1} = \frac{d\bar{g}_2\left(\theta_1\right)/d\theta_1}{1-\theta_1} + \frac{\bar{g}_2\left(\theta_1\right)}{\left(1-\theta_1\right)^2} \tag{13.19}$$

Differentiating (13.18) and inserting the resulting value of $d\bar{g}_2\left(\theta_1\right)/d\theta_1$, we obtain

$$\frac{\partial\bar{\tau}_2^n\left(\theta_1\right)}{\partial\theta_1} = \frac{\left[H''\left(\bar{g}_2\right)\cdot\left(1-\theta_1\right)\right]^{-1} + \bar{g}_2}{\left(1-\theta_1\right)^2}$$

which ensures that $\lim_{\theta_1 \to 1} \frac{\partial\tau_{2D}^n\left(\theta_1\right)}{\partial\theta_1} = -\infty$. In other words, and as $c_2 = 1 - \tau_2^n$, c_2 will be close to one if θ_1 is close to one (no taxes nor public spending in equilibrium).

c. Now, we can derive the equilibrium degree of efficiency that a party in office would choose in the first period. Let us analyze the behavior of party R when in office at time 1. Party R maximizes

$$Ew^R = \left[c_1 + \bar{c}_2\left(\theta_1\right)\right] + H\left(\bar{g}_1\left(\theta_1\right)\right) + p_R \cdot H\left(\bar{g}_2\left(\theta_1\right)\right) \tag{13.20}$$

where $\bar{g}_1\left(\theta_1\right)$ denotes the equilibrium value of g_1 and $\bar{c}_2\left(\theta_1\right)$ denotes the equilibrium level of private consumption left to the voters, for a given value of θ_1. In the second period, R–consumers benefit from public good spending only with probability p_R, while they are taxed with probability 1. This explains the last term in (13.20).

Taking the first order condition with respect to θ_1 yields:

$$\frac{dEw^R}{d\theta_1} = \frac{dc_2(\theta_1)}{d\theta_1} + p_R \cdot H'\left(\bar{g}_2\left(\theta_1\right)\right) \cdot \frac{d\bar{g}_2(\theta_1)}{d\theta_1} = 0 \qquad (13.21)$$

where, by (13.18), $H'(\bar{g}_2) = (1 - \theta_1)^{-1}$. From the budget constraint, we also have $\bar{c}_2 = 1 - \frac{\bar{g}_2}{1-\theta_1}$ and therefore $\frac{d\bar{c}_2}{d\theta_1} = -\frac{d\bar{g}_2/d\theta_1}{1-\theta_1} - \frac{\bar{g}_2}{(1-\theta_1)^2}$. Substituting these equalities into (13.21), we find:

$$(1 - p_R)\frac{d\bar{g}_2}{d\theta_1} - \frac{\bar{g}_2}{1 - \theta_1} = 0. \qquad (13.22)$$

Therefore, for $p_R = 1$, increasing θ_1 is always welfare decreasing. For that reason, the party will set $\theta_1 = 0$. If $p_R = 0$ instead, the first order condition becomes $(1 - \theta_1) = \bar{g}_2/\frac{d\bar{g}_2}{d\theta_1}$. But $\frac{d\bar{g}_2}{d\theta_1} < 0$. In other terms, the party would like to set $\theta_1 > 1$. As θ_1 must be between 0 and 1, R sets $\theta_1 = 1$ if it were in office.

The same reasoning applies for party D: if p_R is too high, D sets θ_1 larger than zero. We can then deduce that, if the probability of reelection is too low, the party chooses an inefficient tax system.

d. Let us denote by $\bar{g}_2^J(P)$ the equilibrium supply of g_2^J when party P is in office in the second period. The utility of a voter in group J is given by

$$w^J = W\left(\tau_1^n, \tau_2^n\right) + H\left(\min\left[\frac{g_1^J}{\alpha}, \frac{g_1^K}{1-\alpha}\right]\right) + H\left(\min\left[\frac{g_2^J}{\alpha}, \frac{g_2^K}{1-\alpha}\right]\right).$$

Maximizing w^R with respect to g_2^R and g_2^D, we find the equilibrium spending of party R: $\bar{g}_2^R(R) = \alpha\bar{g}_2$; $\bar{g}_2^D(R) = (1 - \alpha)\bar{g}_2$ and $H'(\bar{g}_2) = \frac{1}{1-\theta_1}$.

Similarly, for party D, we find: $\bar{g}_2^R(D) = (1 - \alpha)\bar{g}_2$; $\bar{g}_2^D(D) = \alpha\bar{g}_2$ and $H'(\bar{g}_2) = \frac{1}{1-\theta_1}$.

Therefore, $\bar{g}_2$ is independent of both the identity of the party in office and α. In addition, if $\alpha = 1/2$, the *allocation* of spending is also independent of the party. Hence, in this case, the expected utility of J is independent of P. As of period one, the expected utility of R becomes

$$[1 - \bar{\tau}_1^n - \bar{\tau}_2^n] + H\left(\bar{g}_1^R(R)\right) + p_R \cdot H[\bar{g}_2] + (1 - p_R) \cdot H\left[\frac{(1-\alpha)}{\alpha}\bar{g}_2\right]. \qquad (13.23)$$

The first order condition with respect to θ_1 is then given by:

$$-\frac{d\bar{\tau}_2^n}{d\theta_1} + \left\{p_R \cdot H'[\bar{g}_2] + (1 - p_R)\frac{(1-\alpha)}{\alpha} \cdot H'\left[\frac{(1-\alpha)}{\alpha}\bar{g}_2\right]\right\} \cdot \frac{d\bar{g}_2}{d\theta_1} = 0$$

or, substituting for the budget constraint and the above-mentioned equilibrium supplies:

$$(1 - p_R)\frac{d\bar{g}_2}{d\theta_1} + \frac{\bar{g}_2}{1 - \theta_1} - \left\{(1 - p_R)(1 - \theta_1)\frac{(1-\alpha)}{\alpha} \cdot H'\left[\frac{(1-\alpha)}{\alpha}\bar{g}_2\right] \cdot \frac{d\bar{g}_2}{d\theta_1}\right\} = 0.$$

The term in curly brackets is equal to zero when $\alpha = 1$. In this case, there is pure polarization and we are back to equation (13.22).

If $\alpha = \frac{1}{2}$, this term is equal to $-(1 - p_R)\frac{d\bar{g}_2}{d\theta_1}$, and it cancels out with the first term. In this case, $\theta_1 = 0$ in equilibrium, that is we obtain a fully efficient tax system.

For intermediate values of α, the term in curly brackets is strictly positive, implying that $\frac{\bar{g}_2}{1-\theta_1}$ must be smaller than under full polarization. In other term, for any value of p_R, θ_1 will be smaller if polarization (α) decreases.

Additional notes

This problem is a simplified version of the model by Cukierman, Edwards and Tabellini (AER, 1992). In that paper, the authors allow for two types of taxes: income taxes and seignorage. The more inefficient the tax system, the more the government will have to rely on inflation to finance its spending. Both theoretically and empirically, they show that political instability and political polarization generate higher inflation rates and more inefficient tax systems. In particular, the threat of violent changes in governments (coups) tends to generate even higher inflation rates, as they reveal instability *and* polarization at the same time.

13.5   Voting on the budget deficit: Consequences of a balanced budget rule

This problem is based on Tabellini and Alesina 1990 and Peletier, Dur and Swank 1999. Consider a group of heterogeneous agents in the following two-period model. The group is endowed with one unit of output in each period t and decides, by majority rule, on the consumption of two public goods, g_t and f_t, for $t = \{1, 2\}$. At the beginning of period 1, the group can borrow or lend to the rest of the world at zero interest, and the debt, denoted by b, must be repaid in full at the end of the second period. Agent i's preferences are given by

$$w^i = E\left\{\sum_{t=1}^{2} \alpha^i H(g_t) + (1 - \alpha^i)H(f_t)\right\},$$

where $H(\cdot)$ is strictly increasing and concave and α^i identifies voter i. We assume that the parameter α^i is distributed on $(0, 1)$, and we denote its median value in period t by α_t^m. In other words, the identity of the median voter can change over time.

a. Determine the provision of public goods in the second period. Suppose that the median voter at date 1 is identified by any α_1^m in $(0, 1)$. What is the level of debt issued in period 1 when the median voter at date 1 is certain to be the median voter at date 2? Suppose now that $\alpha_2^m = 1$ with probability π and $\alpha_2^m = 0$ with probability $1 - \pi$. Show that the amount of debt issued in period 1 is positive. How does the level of debt vary with the difference between α_1^m and the expected value of α_2^m?

b. Suppose that b is chosen before the composition of public spending in period 1 is known, i.e. at a time when the median voters in both periods 1 and 2 are uncertain. Furthermore, assume that both α_1^m and α_2^m are drawn from the same prior distribution. Show that a balanced budget rule is ex ante efficient. Discuss.

Now consider the following variation of the model. At each date, the group can also invest an amount i_t in a stock of public capital, k. Furthermore, this investment remains productive for two periods, that is $k_1 = i_1$ and $k_2 = i_1 + i_2$. Agent i's preferences are modified in the following way:

$$w^i = E\left\{\sum_{t=1}^{2}\alpha^i H(g_t) + (1-\alpha^i)H(f_t) + V(k_t)\right\},$$

where $V(\cdot)$ is strictly increasing and concave.

c. What investment is selected in period 2 when $\alpha_1^m = 1$ and $\alpha_2^m = 0$? Suppose that $\alpha_2^m = 1$ with probability π and $\alpha_2^m = 0$ with probability $1 - \pi$. Characterize the levels of both investment and debt chosen in period 1 when $\alpha_1^m = 1$. Discuss your results in cases $\pi = 1$ and $\pi < 1$.

d. What is the level of investment when a balanced budget rule is imposed? Compare your findings with the results obtained in question (b) and discuss.

Answer

a. The constraint faced by agents in period 2 is $g_2 + f_2 + b \leq 1$. Let $g_2^*(\alpha_2^m, b)$ and $f_2^*(\alpha_2^m, b)$ be the provisions of public goods that are preferred by the median voter. Note that individual preferences satisfy the intermediate preferences property so that the preferred policy of the median agent is selected under majority rule. Suppose that $\alpha_2^m \in (0,1)$. Then the provision of public good g_2 satisfies:

$$\alpha_2^m H_g(g_2) - (1-\alpha_2^m)H_f(1-b-g_2) = 0 \tag{13.24}$$

Suppose now that the median voter in the second period is indexed by $\alpha_2^m = 1$. Then, he sets $g_2^*(1,b) = 1 - b$, and $f_2^*(1,b) = 0$. By contrast, if $\alpha_2^m(0) = 0$, then $g_2^*(0,b) = 0$ and $f_2^*(0,b) = 1 - b$.

In period 1, there is uncertainty about the identity of the median voter in the second period. The intertemporal constraint faced by agents at that period is $f_1 + g_1 - b \leq 1$. Basically, the most preferred policy of the median voter at that time solves:

$$\max_{g_1,b} \quad \alpha_1^m H(g_1) + (1-\alpha_1^m)H(1-g_1+b)$$

$$+ E\left[\alpha_1^m H(g(\alpha_2^m,b)) + (1-\alpha_1^m)H(f(\alpha_2^m,b))\right]$$

where $E[\cdot]$ denotes expectations. Suppose that $\alpha_1^m \in (0,1)$. Then, the first-order solution with respect to g_1 is:

$$\alpha_1^m H_g(g_1) - (1-\alpha_1^m)H_g(1-g_1+b) = 0 \tag{13.25}$$

Let $g_1^*(\alpha_1^m, b)$ and $f_1^*(\alpha_1^m, b)$ be the provisions of public goods that are preferred by the median voter. If $\alpha_1^m = 1$ (respectively, $\alpha_1^m = 0$), we get a corner solution. Formally $f_1^*(1, b) = 0$ and $g_1^*(1, b) = 1 + b$ (respectively, $f_1^*(0, b) = 1 + b$ and $g_1^*(0, b) = 0$). The first-order condition with respect to b is:

$$(1 - \alpha_1^m)H_g(1 - g_1^*(\alpha_1^m, b) + b) + E[\alpha_m^1 H_g(g_2^*(\alpha_2^m, b))\frac{\partial g_2^*}{\partial b} +$$
$$(1 - \alpha_1^m)H_g(f_2^*(\alpha_2^m, b))\frac{\partial f_2^*}{\partial b}] = 0 \qquad (13.26)$$

Suppose first that the median voter at time 1 is certain to be the median voter at date 2. Then, combining (13.26) and (13.24), we see that the equilibrium value of b satisfies:

$$H_g(f_1^*(\alpha_1^m)) = H_g(f_2^*(\alpha_1^m)) \qquad (13.27)$$

In other words, $f_1^*(\alpha_1^m) = f_2^*(\alpha_1^m)$. Moreover, given (13.27), (13.24) and (13.25), we must have $g_1^*(\alpha_1^m, b) = g_2^*(\alpha_1^m, b)$. Then, $b = 0$ is the only solution to the problem.

Suppose now that $\alpha_2^m = 1$ with probability π and $\alpha_2^m = 0$ with probability $1 - \pi$. Then, (13.26) can be rewritten as:

$$(1 - \alpha_1^m)H_g(1 - g_1^*(\alpha_1^m, b) + b) - \tilde{\alpha}H_g(1 - b) = 0 \qquad (13.28)$$

where $\tilde{\alpha} = \alpha_1^m \pi + (1 - \alpha_1^m)(1 - \pi)$. Note that the utility is concave in b. Moreover, in $b = 0$, we get $(1 - \alpha_1^m)H_g(1 - g_1^*(\alpha_1^m, 0)) - \tilde{\alpha}H_g(1) > 0$. Therefore, $b > 0$ in equilibrium. Besides, let $b^*(\pi)$ be the equilibrium debt. We have $\frac{db^*}{d\pi} = \frac{db^*}{d\tilde{\alpha}}\frac{d\tilde{\alpha}}{d\pi} = \frac{db^*}{d\tilde{\alpha}}(2\alpha_1^m - 1)$. From (13.28), we find $\frac{db^*}{d\tilde{\alpha}} < 0$. This implies that b^* is increasing in the difference between α_1^m and α_2^m.

b. The optimal level of debt for each agent is obtained by solving the following program:

$$\max_b \quad E\{\alpha^i[H(g_1^*(\alpha_1^m, b)) + H(g_2^*(\alpha_2^m, b))] + (1 - \alpha^i)[H(f_1^*(\alpha_1^m, b)) + H(f_2^*(\alpha_2^m, b))]\}$$

Suppose that α_1^m and α_2^m are drawn from the same distribution. Then, the derivative of the previous expression is 0 for all α^i, when evaluated in $b = 0$. In other words, $b = 0$ satisfies the first order condition of the program. Therefore, a balanced budget rule is ex ante efficient.

c. The budget constraints are in periods 1 and 2 respectively $g_1 + f_1 + i_1 = 1 + b$ and $g_2 + f_2 + i_2 = 1 - b$. Consider the last period. As before, $f_2^*(1, b) = 0$ and $g_2^*(0, b) = 0$. Besides, investment satisfies:

$$H_g(1 - b - i_2) = V_k(i_1 + i_2) + V_k(i_2)$$

This expression defines the investment in period 2 as a function of b and i_1. We denote it by $i_2^*(i_1, b)$. Using the same reasoning as in question (a), we can derive the optimal decision at date 2. Formally, we have:

$$H_g(1 + b - i_1) - H_g(1 - b - i_2^*(i_1, b))[\pi - (1 - \pi)\frac{\partial i_2^*}{\partial b}] = 0$$

$$-H_g(1 + b - i_1) + H_g(1 - b - i_2^*(i_1, b))[1 - \pi]\frac{\partial i_2^*}{\partial i_1} + V_k(k_1) + V_k(k_2) = 0$$

If $\pi = 1$, i.e. if the current and future majorities share the same preferences for sure, the level of investment is the same at each period. We call it i^*. As before, $b = 0$ in equilibrium.

Conversely, if $\pi < 1$, we have $i_1 > i_2$. Besides, $1 + b - i_1 > 1 - b - i_2$, and therefore $b > \frac{i_1 - i_2}{2} > 0$. As a consequence, the results are qualitatively the same as in the previous question.

d. Suppose that a balanced budget rule is imposed. Differentiating the utility of a given agent with respect to i_1 and computing it at $b = 0$ and $i_1 = i_2 = i^*$ yields:

$$\frac{\partial w^i}{\partial i_1}\bigg|_{b=0, i_1=i_2=i^*} = (1 - \pi)\frac{\partial i_2^*}{i_1}H_g(1 - i_2^*(i^*, 0)) < 0$$

This implies that the equilibrium investment level is smaller than i^*. In other words, a balanced budget rule induces under-investment. In order to reach the ex ante efficient state, an additional rule must be imposed on the level of investment.

Chapter 14

Growth

14.1 Public debt, political instability and growth

Consider the following model of public debt, political instability and growth. There are two periods, with elections held at the start of the second period. The electorate consists of two groups of voters, R and D. Each group has infinitely many voters and is normalized to have size $1/2$. Two public goods, g_t^D and g_t^R, can be provided in each period t, each specific to one group. The incumbent politician in the first period cares about maximizing the utility of group D. In the second period, he is re-elected with exogenous probability p. With probability $(1-p)$, he is replaced by a politician who cares about maximizing group R's welfare.

The structure of the game is the following. In the first period, the incumbent chooses public spending, g_1^D and g_1^R, and public debt, b, so that the budget constraint is given by

$$\bar{I} + g_1^D + g_1^R + b = \bar{t},$$

where lump–sum taxes, $\bar{t}$, and public investment, $\bar{I}$, are exogenously fixed. Voters buy public debt, which yields a return R_b. Voters also invest in capital to gain a return R_k. Both R_b and R_k are determined endogenously in the model.

In the second period, the office holder sets proportional taxes on capital, τ, and public goods, g_2^D and g_2^R, so that his budget constraint is satisfied: $g_2^D + g_2^R = \tau A(\bar{I})k - R_b b$, where $A(\bar{I})$ is the return on capital net of taxes, τ. Thus, proportional taxes are the government's only source of revenue in period 2. Moreover, the government is constrained to pay a return R_b to voters holding debt. Voters' utility is given by

$$u^j = U(c_1) + H(g_1^j) + c_2 + H(g_2^j).$$

Finally, voters budget constraints for the two periods are given by $c_1 = e - \bar{t} - k - b$ and $c_2 = (1 - \tau)A(\bar{I})k + Rb$, where e is the voter's endowment, k the voter's investment in capital, and b his public debt holding.

a. Write the equilibrium conditions for investment in both capital and public debt to be positive. Compute the voters' capital investment decision as a function of second–period taxes, $k(\tau)$. Show that this function is decreasing in τ.

b. Calculate the second–period office holder's tax decision as a function of first–period debt, $\tau(b)$. Show that taxes are increasing in debt.

c. Write the expressions for the first–period debt decision.

d. Discuss the effect of political instability on the equilibrium level of public debt in this model.

Answer

a. Voters should be indifferent between investing in capital or in debt. Thus,

$$R \equiv R_b = R_k = (1 - \tau)A(\bar{I}).$$

Moreover, to move income from period to period we have the condition:

$$U_c(c_1) = (1 - \tau)A(\bar{I}).$$

From this, we have: $k(\tau) = e - \bar{t} - b - U_c^{-1}((1 - \tau)A(\bar{I}))$, which is clearly decreasing in τ.

b. How is τ chosen in second period? Well suppose politician j is in power. He faces the following problem:

$$\max_{\substack{\tau \geq 0 \\ g_2^j \geq 0}} c_2 + H(g_2^j) = \max_{\substack{\tau \geq 0 \\ \frac{\tau}{(1-\tau)} k \geq b}} (1 - \tau)A(\bar{I})k + Rb + H(\tau A(\bar{I})k - Rb)$$

with a first order condition given by: $1 = H_g(\tau A(\bar{I})k - Rb)$. From this, we have

$$\tau(b) = \frac{H_g^{-1}(1) + Rb}{A(\bar{I})k}.$$

Obviously, $\tau'(b) > 0$.

c. Now, how is b chosen in the first period? The first period incumbent faces the following problem:

$$\max \quad U(c_1) + H(g_1^D) + p(c_2 + H(g_2^D)) + (1 - p)(c_2)$$
$$\text{s.t. } b \geq 0; \ \bar{I} + g_1^j + b = \bar{t}; \ g_2^D \geq 0$$

or:
$$\max \quad U(c_1) + H(g_1^D) + c_2 + pH(g_2^D)$$
$$\text{s.t. } b \geq 0; \ \bar{I} + g_1^j + b = \bar{t}; \ g_2^D \geq 0$$

where $H(0) = 0$.

Considering the way c_1, c_2, g_1^D, and g_2^D are determined, we can also write the objective function as

$$U\left[e - \bar{t} - b - k(\tau(b))\right] + H\left[\bar{t} + b - \bar{I}\right] + (1 - \tau(b)) \cdot A(\bar{I}) \cdot k(\tau(b)) + \dots$$
$$\dots + pH\left[A(\bar{I})\{\tau(b) \cdot (k(\tau(b)) + b) - b\}\right]$$

Taking the first order condition with respect to b, we find:

$$-U_c\left[e - \bar{t} - b - k(\tau(b))\right] \cdot (1 + k_\tau(\tau(b)) \cdot \tau_b(b)) + \dots$$
$$\dots + H_g\left[\bar{t} + b - \bar{I}\right] - \tau_b(b) \cdot \left[A(\bar{I}) \cdot \{k(\tau(b)) + k_\tau(\tau(b)) \cdot (1 - \tau(b))\}\right] + \dots$$
$$\dots + pH_g\left[A(\bar{I})\{\tau_b(b) \cdot [k(\tau(b)) + b + \tau(b) \cdot k_\tau(\tau(b))] + \tau(b) - 1\}\right] = 0$$

d. In this model, political instability affects the first period choice of debt. Let us consider two extreme situations. In the first $p = 1$. In this case there is full political stability. The party in power must fully internalize the second year choice of the public good, that is affected by the current debt decision, and the second year consumption.

In the case where $p = 0$. There is no political stability at all. Now the first period party chooses debt having in mind only the effect of this choice on the consumption in the second period. Therefore the solution of this case will yield a different level of debt. To determine which way the effect goes one must make further assumptions on the functional forms of the primitives in the model.

14.2 Inequality and growth-human capital

Consider the following model of the connection between inequality and growth. There are two periods, 1 and 2. Voters live one period and have one child. There are infinitely many voters and population size is normalized to one. Voters care about their own consumption, c_{i1}, and are also altruistic in that they care about the child's human capital, h_{i2},

$$U(c_{i1}, h_{i2}) = c^\alpha h^{1-\alpha}, \ 0 < \alpha < 1.$$

The human capital of the child, h_{i2}, is transferred from the parents' human capital, h_{i1}, and through education g_1,

$$h_{i2} = (1 - z)\delta h_{i1} + g_1,$$

where $(1 - z)$ is the amount of time parents devote to transferring human capital to children and $\delta \geq 1$ is the productivity of this transfer. Initial human capital levels are given by a distribution $F(\cdot)$ on $[0, 1]$, with a median level which is smaller than the expected level, $h_{m1} < \bar{h}_1$.

The production function in the economy is given by

$$Y_t = H_t$$
$$H_t = z \int_0^1 h_{it} dF \equiv z\bar{h}_t.$$

The income of individual i is zh_{it}. Education is produced by the production function $g_t = \delta h'_t$, where h'_t is the amount of human capital devoted to public education. Thus the productivity of public and private education are both equal to δ. Public education is financed by a proportional tax, τ_1, decided upon by majority rule in period 1.

a. Show that preferences over taxes derived from the above model imply the existence of a Condorcet winner.

b. Calculate the equilibrium tax rate and show that it is decreasing in $h_{it}/\bar{h}_t$.

c. Write the expression for the growth rate and show that it is increasing in the income inequality of the population.

Answer

a. The voters problem is given by:

$$\max_{\substack{\tau_t \geq 0 \\ s.t.\ g_t = \delta z \tau_t \bar{h}_t}} (zh_{it}(1-\tau_t))^\alpha ((1-z)\delta h_{it} + g_t)^{1-\alpha}.$$

The first order condition is:

$$\frac{\alpha}{1-\alpha} \frac{h_{it}}{\delta \bar{h}_t} = \frac{(z\frac{h_{it}}{\bar{h}_t}(1-\tau_t))}{((1-z)\delta\frac{h_{it}}{\bar{h}_t} + \delta z\tau_t)}.$$

Note that voters have single peaked preferences as the right–hand side of the first order condition is monotonously decreasing in τ_t. Thus majority rule will lead to the implementation of the median voter's ideal point $\tau_t(h_{mt}/\bar{h}_t)$.

b. Now we can compute $\tau_t(h_{it}/\bar{h}_t)$,

$$\tau_t\left(\frac{h_{it}}{\bar{h}_t}\right) = \frac{z - \frac{\alpha}{1-\alpha}(1-z)\delta\frac{h_{it}}{\bar{h}_t}}{z + \frac{\alpha}{1-\alpha}\delta z}.$$

Obviously, $\tau_t(h_{it}/\bar{h}_t)$ is decreasing in $h_{it}/\bar{h}_t$.

c. The growth rate is given by:

$$\frac{\bar{h}_{t+1}}{\bar{h}_t} = \delta((1-z) + \tau_t^*(\frac{h_{mt}}{\bar{h}_t})z).$$

which is increasing in the tax rate. The tax rate is decreasing in $\frac{h_{it}}{\bar{h}_t}$ and $h_{mt} < \bar{h}_t$ and thus inequality increases growth.

14.3 Unions and taxation

The following problem is adopted from Daveri and Tabellini 1997. Consider a two-period overlapping-generations model with a constant population. Individuals have utility on consumption when young and old, c_y and c_o, given by

$$U = \sqrt{c_y} + \sqrt{c_o}.$$

Only young can work. They can be employed, earning $w(1 - \tau^l)$ or unemployed, earning a subsidy of s. τ^l is the labor income tax rate, which is also exogenously given. Old individuals earn a return $(1 + (1 - \tau^k)r)$ on their investments in capital when young. τ^k is the tax rate on capital which is exogenously given. Let l stand for the fraction of employed individuals. We can write the government budget constraint as

$$\tau^k r k + \tau^l w l = g + (1 - l)s,$$

where k is the average holding of capital by current old and g the exogenously determined public spending per capita. Average capital per worker evolves according to

$$k = lk^E + (1 - l)k^U,$$

where subscripts E and U stand for employed and unemployed respectively.

Production takes place in a large number of identical firms with production functions $y = Akl^{1-\alpha}$. Firms are competitive in hiring workers and acquiring capital.

a. Given w, τ^k and τ^l calculate the demand function for workers and the rate of return on capital.

b. Suppose labor unions set wages (unions are assumed to be large enough to set wages but small enough as to not affect fiscal policy). A proportion λ of the labor force are members in labor unions. First employed individuals become members and then the $\lambda - l$ of the unemployed also become members. Thus, assume wages are set by the maximization of

$$\frac{l(k, w)}{\lambda} w(1 - \tau^l) + \frac{\lambda - l(k, w)}{\lambda} s.$$

Compute the equilibrium wage.

c. Show that in this model employment and growth are positively correlated. What is the explanation for this relation?

Answer

a. First, let us compute the investment decisions of voter i,

$$\max U = \sqrt{(y^i - k^i)} + \sqrt{(k^i(1 + (1 - \tau^k)r))}$$

The first order condition is given by:

$$k^i = y^i \frac{(1 + (1 - \tau^k)r))}{1 + (1 + (1 - \tau^k)r))} \equiv y^i F((1 - \tau^k)r).$$

Note that investment (and $F(\cdot)$) is increasing in the return.

In equilibrium, marginal productivity is equalized to factor prices so that

$$w = \frac{dAkl^{1-\alpha}}{dl} = (1 - \alpha)Akl^{-\alpha}$$

which implies:

$$l(k, w) = (\frac{(1-\alpha)Ak}{w})^{\frac{1}{\alpha}},$$

and

$$r = \frac{dAkl^{1-\alpha}}{dk} = Al^{1-\alpha}.$$

b. The wage is given by the maximization of:

$$\frac{l(k, w)}{\lambda}w(1 - \tau^l) + \frac{\lambda - l(k, w)}{\lambda}s.$$

The first order condition is therefore:

$$w(1 - \tau^l) + \frac{l(k, w)}{\frac{dl(k, w)}{dw}}(1 - \tau^l) = s.$$

Which can be simplified to:

$$w = \frac{s}{(1 - \alpha)(1 - \tau^l)}.$$

c. New capital is given by:

$$k^{new} = lk^E + (1 - l)k^U,$$

where

$$k^E = w(1 - \tau^l)F((1 - \tau^k)r) \quad \text{and} \quad k^U = sF((1 - \tau^k)r)$$

thus,

$$k^{new} = F((1 - \tau^k)r)(lw(1 - \tau^l) + (1 - l)s),$$

and the growth rate is given by

$$\frac{k^{new}}{k^{stock}} = \frac{F((1 - \tau^k)r)(lw(1 - \tau^l) + (1 - l)s)}{k}$$

$$= \frac{F((1 - \tau^k)Al^{1-\alpha})(l\frac{s}{(1-\alpha)} + (1 - l)s)}{k}.$$

This is increasing in l.

14.4 Growth and the common-pool problem

The following problem demonstrates the effect of the common pool problem on growth. Suppose that there are two groups, D and R, each with an infinite number of voters and of size 1. The utility of voters in group j is given by

$$u^j = U(c_1) + c_2 + H(g_2^j).$$

There are two periods. In the first-period voters must decide how much to invest in capital and how much to consume. The budget constraint for voter i is given by

$$e = c_{i1} + k_i,$$

where e is the initial endowment, c_{i1} the first-period consumption and k_i their investment in capital. The return on capital is assumed to be fixed and equal to $R > 1$.

In the second period both groups simultaneously choose g^j and a proportional tax, τ on capital earnings finances spending. If groups demands are not compatible with total capital earnings, then no public good is produced. Thus taxes are given by

$$\tau 2kR = \begin{cases} g^D + g^R & \text{if } g^D + g^R \leq 2kR \\ 0 & \text{if } g^D + g^R > 2kR \end{cases}.$$

Throughout assume that R is large enough so that you get interior solutions.

a. Solve for the choice of g^D and g^R in the second period, given the choices in the first period.

b. Solve for the investment choice in the first period given the choice in the second period.

c. Write the expression for the growth rate in this model.

d. Show the growth rate would increase if the groups were to coordinate in the second period.

Answer

a. In the second period, resources are given by $2kR\tau$. Given a choice g^{-j} by group $-j$, group j faces the following problem:

$$\max_{\tau} \ kR(1 - \tau) + H(2kR\tau - g^{-j})$$

The first order conditions are given by

$$H_g(2kR\tau - g^{-j}) = \frac{1}{2}, \ \forall j$$

Let $\tilde{g}$ be such that $H_g(\tilde{g}) = \frac{1}{2}$. Thus we have $2kR\tau - g^{-j} = \tilde{g}$ and setting $g^{-j} = g^j$ we get

$$\tilde{\tau} = \frac{\tilde{g}}{kR}.$$

b. Investment, given τ in the second period, is given by the maximization of

$$\max_{k} U(e - k) + Rk(1 - \tau) + H(\tilde{g}).$$

Note that as voters are infinitely small they do not take account of their possible effect on the choice of tax. The first order condition states

$$U_c(e - k) = R(1 - \tau) \Rightarrow k(\tau) = e - U_c^{-1}(R(1 - \tau)).$$

Thus, as in the text, investment is decreasing in taxes.

c. The growth rate is given by

$$\tilde{\gamma} = \frac{Rk(\tilde{\tau})}{e}.$$

d. If groups coordinate they solve

$$\max_{\tau} 2kR(1 - \tau) + H(kR\tau) + H(kR\tau)$$

Now the first order condition is

$$1 = H_g(kR\tau).$$

Setting g^* be such that $g^* = kR\tau$, we have that equilibrium tax is given by

$$\tau^* = \frac{g^*}{kR} < \frac{\tilde{g}}{kR} = \tilde{\tau}.$$

Thus the growth rate of this equilibrium is higher than the common pool equilibrium as

$$\gamma^* = \frac{Rk(\tau^*)}{e} > \frac{Rk(\tilde{\tau})}{e} = \tilde{\gamma}.$$

14.5   Inequality and growth: a specific functional form for $A(I)$

Consider a two-period economy inhabited by a continuum of heterogenous agents. Everyone has the same quasi-linear preferences over private consumption in periods 1 and 2 and over government (per capita) consumption in period 2. Government consumption is endogenous and denoted by g. Consumer $i's$ utility is:

$$u^i = U(c_1^i) + c_2^i + H(g).$$

The consumer's budget constraints are

$$
\begin{aligned}
c_1^i &= e^i - t - k^i \\
c_2^i &= (1 - \tau_K)A(I)k^i,
\end{aligned}
$$

where k^i is private investment, t and τ_K lump sum and capital taxes, respectively, and the gross return to private capital is given by

$$A(I) = \begin{cases} \alpha & \text{if } I \geq \bar{I}, \text{ where } \alpha > 1 \\ 0 & \text{otherwise.} \end{cases}$$

The government can commit to policy instruments before private capital accumulation. Finally, e^i is the endowment of agent i. Agent's endowments are distributed in the population with mean e and a distribution function for the idiosyncratic part $\mathfrak{F}(e^i - e)$. To proxy empirical income distributions, assume that $\mathfrak{F}$ is skewed to the right: the median value of $e^i - e$, labeled $e^m - e$ and defined by $\mathfrak{F}(e^m - e) = \frac{1}{2}$, is negative. Assuming a balanced budget in every period, the government budget constraint in per capita terms is: $I = t$ and $g = \tau_K A(I)\bar{k}$, where $\bar{k}$ denotes per capita (average) capital.

a. Characterize the equilibrium in the model.

b. Show that compared to the symmetric distribution case ($e^m = e$) this equilibrium involves higher taxes and a lower growth rate.

Answer

a. Now public investment will be either $\bar{I}$ or zero. Voters saving behavior will be given by

$$k(\tau_K, \bar{I}, e^i) = e - \bar{I} - U_c^{-1}(\alpha(1 - \tau_K)) + (e^i - e) \equiv K(\tau_K, \bar{I}) + (e^i - e),$$

where the common investment function satisfies $K_\tau < 0$. We express the utility from private consumption as an indirect utility function defined over the policy variables:

$$
\begin{aligned}
W^i(\tau_K, \bar{I}, e^i) &\equiv Max \quad [U(c_1^i) + c_2^i] \hspace{3cm} (14.1) \\
&= U(e - \bar{I} - K(\tau_K, \bar{I})) + (1 - \tau_K)\alpha K(\tau_K, \bar{I}) + \alpha(1 - \tau_K)(e^i - e) \\
&= W(\tau_K, \bar{I}) + \alpha(1 - \tau_K)(e^i - e).
\end{aligned}
$$

By the envelope theorem, the direct welfare cost of the capital tax $W_\tau = -\alpha K$ is negative. For $I = 0$ we have

$$W^i(\tau_K, 0, e^i) \equiv Max \quad [U(c_1^i) + c_2^i] = U(e^i)$$

The equilibrium will be determined by the preferred policy of the median voter. The conditions for this policy are given by

$$W^i(\tau_K, \bar{I}, e^i) \geq W^i(\tau_K, 0, e^i) \Leftrightarrow I = \bar{I}$$

$$W_\tau + H_g\alpha(K + \tau_k K_\tau) - \alpha(e^m - e) = 0.$$

Now if $(e^m - e) < 0$ this means that the third term in the second equation is negative. Thus evaluated at the optimal tax rate in the symmetric case, the median voter in the asymmetric distribution would like to increase taxes.

Part V

Monetary politics

Chapter 15

Credibility of monetary policy

15.1 Reputation with state-dependent incentives

Consider the following model of monetary policy with reputation: the government controls inflation directly, and his instantaneous loss function is $L\left(\pi_t, x_t\right) = \frac{1}{2}\left(\pi_t^2 + \lambda \cdot x_t^2\right)$, where $x_t = \theta_t + \pi_t - \pi_t^e$, and π_t denotes inflation, π_t^e expected inflation, and x_t the level of employment. θ_t is random and i.i.d. The intertemporal loss is $\sum_{t=0}^{\infty} \beta^t \cdot L\left(\pi_t, x_t\right)$. The government's reputation affects expected inflation and depends on past behavior: $\pi_t^e = \pi^C$ if $\pi_{t-1} = \pi^C$ and $\pi_t^e = \pi^D$ otherwise, where π^C denotes the optimal policy under commitment and π^D under discretion, respectively.

a. Compute the equilibrium policy under commitment and discretion, respectively.

b. Compute the optimal deviation for a government that is expected to play π^C. What are the benefits and the cost of such a deviation? For what values of θ is it optimal for the government to stick to the commitment rule?

Answer

a. Note first that we restricted uncertainty to θ_t. In this way, there is never any surprise for the wage setters: all the uncertainty is resolved before they form their expectations. As a consequence, $\pi_t = \pi_t^e$, $\forall t$, and there cannot be output surprises in equilibrium. Under commitment, the central bank (CB henceforth) takes then x_t as exogenous. In this case, the loss function can be summarized by:

$$L\left(\pi_t, x_t\right) = \frac{\pi_t^2}{2} + \frac{\lambda}{2}\theta_t^2 \qquad (15.1)$$

The first order condition for the minimization of (15.1) with respect to π_t is therefore $\pi_t^C = 0$, leading to an optimal loss $L\left(0, \theta_t\right) = \frac{\lambda}{2}\theta_t^2$ under commitment.

Under discretion, however, the CB does not take this "no surprise" constraint into account. When the CB sets inflation, expectations have already been formed and the temptation to generate an inflationary surprise remains. To see this, let us rewrite the loss function without commitment:

$$L\left(\pi_t, x_t\right) = \frac{\pi_t^2}{2} + \frac{\lambda}{2}\left(\theta_t + \pi_t - \pi_t^e\right)^2 \tag{15.2}$$

which gives $\frac{\partial L(\pi_t, x_t)}{\partial \pi_t} = \pi_t + \lambda \cdot \left(\theta_t + \pi_t - \pi_t^e\right) = 0$ as a first order condition. Rearranging the terms yields:

$$\pi_t = \frac{-\lambda}{1+\lambda}\left(\theta_t - \pi_t^e\right). \tag{15.3}$$

Wage setters being rational, they set expectations to $\pi_t^e = \mathsf{E}\left[\pi_t | \theta_t\right]$. Substituting this into (15.3) yields: $\pi_t^D = -\lambda\theta_t$. As a result, the equilibrium loss under discretion becomes:

$$L\left(-\lambda\theta_t, \theta_t\right) = \frac{\left(\lambda\theta_t\right)^2}{2} + \frac{\lambda}{2}\theta_t^2 = (1+\lambda)\cdot\frac{\lambda}{2}\theta_t^2 \tag{15.4}$$

which is always larger than under commitment.

To summarize: $\pi^C = 0$ and $\pi_t^D = -\lambda\theta_t$.

b. If the government is expected to play π^C, then $\pi_t^e = 0$. (15.3) shows that the CB will set $\pi_t = \frac{-\lambda\theta_t}{1+\lambda}$ if it deviates. The benefit (B) of such a deviation is given by the difference between the loss without the deviation $(\frac{\lambda}{2}\theta_t^2)$ and that with the new inflation rate:

$$B = \frac{\lambda}{2}\theta_t^2 - L\left(\frac{-\lambda\theta_t}{1+\lambda}, \frac{\theta_t}{1+\lambda}\right) = \frac{\lambda^2}{2}\frac{\theta_t^2}{1+\lambda}$$

There is also a cost, C, to this deviation. Indeed, in $t + 1$, expected inflation will be $(-\lambda\theta_{t+1})$, yielding the loss derived in (15.4) instead of $\frac{\lambda}{2}\theta_{t+1}^2$, the loss that would prevail under commitment:

$$C = \frac{\beta}{2}\cdot\mathsf{E}_t\left[(1+\lambda)\cdot\lambda\theta_{t+1}^2 - \lambda\theta_{t+1}^2\right] = \beta\frac{\lambda^2}{2}\mathsf{E}_t\left[\theta_{t+1}^2\right] = \beta\frac{\lambda^2}{2}\left[(\mathsf{E}\theta)^2 + \sigma_\theta^2\right]$$

where σ_θ^2 denotes the variance of θ and $\mathsf{E}\theta$ its mean. Therefore, the government sticks to the commitment rule as long as B is smaller than C, i.e. if:

$$\theta_t^2 < (1+\lambda)\cdot\beta\cdot\mathsf{E}_t\left[\theta_{t+1}^2\right]$$

where the left-hand side depends on the actual realization of θ_t while the right-hand side depends on the expected distribution of the same variable.

15.2 Optimal punishment rules

This problem is based on Persson and Tabellini 1990, chapter 3. Consider a model with reputation, in which the punishment rule is more stringent than in section 15.4:

$$\pi_0^e = 0$$

$$\pi_t^e = \begin{cases} 0 & \text{if } \pi_v = \pi_v^e, \ \nu = t-1, ..., t-T \\ \kappa \cdot \lambda, \text{with } \kappa \geq 1 & \text{otherwise} \end{cases}$$

The instantaneous loss function is given by $L(\pi_t, x_t) = \frac{\pi_t^2}{2} - \lambda \cdot x_t$, and the intertemporal loss function by $\sum_{t=0}^{\infty} \beta^t \cdot L(\pi_t, x_t)$, with $\beta < 1$. As usual, $x_t = \theta_t - \pi_t^e + \pi_t$, where π_t denotes inflation, π_t^e expected inflation, and x_t the level of employment.

a. In the absence of punishment, what would be the deviation when $\pi_t^e = 0$? What would be the deviation if $\pi_t^e = \kappa\lambda$?

b. Assume the government is forced to bear the punishment after a deviation, that is, it is forced to set $\pi_{t+v} = \kappa\lambda$ for $v = 1, 2, ..., T$ after deviating from π_t^e. What are the cost and benefits of deviating at time t, depending on history (that is, if $\pi_t^e = 0$ or if $\pi_t^e = \kappa\lambda$)?

c. Assume the government is not forced to bear this punishment, but π_t^e still follows the same rule. Would it be rational to expect $\pi_t^e = \kappa\lambda$ after a deviation in $t-1$ for any value of κ and T? How does the incentive to deviate from high inflation ($\kappa\lambda$) evolve with κ and T?

d. Draw the graph of equilibrium inflation after a deviation as a function of κ when the government is not forced to bear the punishment after a deviation. If we impose the rational expectations condition $\pi_t^e(\kappa) = \mathsf{E}_{t-1}[\pi_t|\kappa]$ after a deviation, how does the incentive to deviate from zero inflation evolve with κ and T?

Answer

a. If the government deviates, it minimizes the instantaneous loss function at time t. When $\pi_t^e = 0$, the first order condition is given by:

$$\frac{\partial L_t(\pi_t, x_t)}{\partial \pi_t} \equiv \pi_t - \lambda = 0 \tag{15.5}$$

which yields $\pi_t = \lambda$. If the government deviated the period before, then $\pi_t^e = \kappa\lambda$. In this case, the instantaneous loss function becomes $L(\pi_t, x_t) = \frac{\pi_t^2}{2} - \lambda \cdot (\theta_t + \pi_t - \kappa\lambda)$ but the first order condition remains unchanged, and inflation is still equal to λ after a deviation.

b. If the government is forced to bear the punishment, and $\pi_t^e = 0$, the cost of a deviation is given by:

$$
\begin{aligned}
C &= \sum_{s=t+1}^{t+T} \beta^{s-t} \cdot \left[L_t \left(\kappa\lambda, \theta_t \right) - L_t \left(0, \theta_t \right) \right] \\
&= \sum_{s=t+1}^{t+T} \beta^{s-t} \cdot \left[\frac{(\kappa\lambda)^2}{2} - 0 \right] = \beta \frac{1 - \beta^T}{1 - \beta} \frac{(\kappa\lambda)^2}{2}
\end{aligned}
\tag{15.6}
$$

(note that the term λx_t does not enter in the cost of a deviation, because there cannot be any inflation surprise, either under the zero inflation rule or after a deviation). The benefit of this deviation, instead, is the instantaneous benefit of creating a one-off inflation surprise:

$$
B = L_t \left(0, \theta_t \right) - L_t \left(\lambda, \theta_t + \lambda \right) = -\frac{\lambda^2}{2} + \lambda^2 = \frac{\lambda^2}{2}.
\tag{15.7}
$$

As in problem 15.1, the government is tempted to deviate if $B \geq C$. However, C is monotonically increasing in both T and κ. Therefore, at first glance, it seems that a tougher punishment rule prevents deviations more efficiently. However, this needs not be the case. To see this, we now compute the cost and benefit of deviating from the punishment equilibrium.

Assume the government deviated in $t - 1$, so that $\pi_t^e = \kappa\lambda$. In this case, setting inflation to λ instead of $\kappa\lambda$ (remember that λ is the preferred inflation rate also after a deviation) only lengthens the punishment by one period: in $t + T + 1$, inflation expectations will be $\kappa\lambda$ instead of 0. The cost of this deviation is then:

$$
C_\kappa = \beta^T \cdot \left[L_t \left(\kappa\lambda, \theta_t \right) - L_t \left(0, \theta_t \right) \right] = \beta^T \cdot \frac{(\kappa\lambda)^2}{2},
\tag{15.8}
$$

while its benefit is given by the instantaneous change in π_t and L_t:

$$
\begin{aligned}
B_\kappa &= L_t \left(\kappa\lambda, \theta_t \right) - L_t \left(\lambda, \theta_t - (\kappa - 1)\lambda \right) = \frac{(\kappa\lambda)^2 - \lambda^2}{2} - (\kappa - 1)\lambda^2 \\
&= \frac{\kappa^2 - 2\kappa + 1}{2}\lambda^2.
\end{aligned}
\tag{15.9}
$$

c. $\pi_t^e = \kappa\lambda$ needs not be the rationally expected inflation rate, even after a deviation. Why not? Because the policymaker may be tempted to deviate from $\kappa\lambda$. The net benefit of such a deviation is:

$$
\begin{aligned}
B_\kappa - C_\kappa &= \frac{\kappa^2 - 2\kappa + 1}{2}\lambda^2 - \beta^T \cdot \frac{(\kappa\lambda)^2}{2} \\
&= \left[1 + \left(1 - \beta^T \right) \kappa^2 - 2\kappa \right] \cdot \frac{\lambda^2}{2}
\end{aligned}
$$

which is strictly increasing in T (note that if $T = \infty$, $B_\kappa - C_\kappa$ is non-negative for any value of $\kappa \geq 1$), and one can check that $B_\kappa - C_\kappa$ is positive for any value of

$\kappa > \kappa_0 = \frac{1+\sqrt{\beta^T}}{1-\beta^T}$. If the temptation to deviate from high inflation is non negative (i.e. if $B_\kappa - C_\kappa \geq 0$, or if $\kappa > \kappa_0$), the government sets $\pi_t = \lambda$ after deviating from 0-inflation. In this case, $\pi_t^e = \lambda$, and we are back to the case where $\kappa = 1$, as in section 15.4 in the textbook.

d.

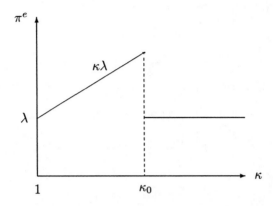

The temptation to deviate when $\pi_t^e = 0$ is then determined by:

$$B - C = \begin{cases} \frac{\lambda^2}{2} - \beta \frac{1-\beta^T}{1-\beta} \frac{(\kappa\lambda)^2}{2}, & \text{if } \kappa < \kappa_0 \\ \frac{\lambda^2}{2} - \beta \frac{1-\beta^T}{1-\beta} \frac{\lambda^2}{2}, & \text{if } \kappa \geq \kappa_0 \end{cases}$$

The highest credible value of κ is then the one that sets $B_\kappa - C_\kappa = 0$. The optimal value of κ is therefore κ_0 if it allows to prevent a deviation from $\pi_t = 0$, and it is 1 otherwise.

15.3 Reputation with incomplete information

This problem is based on Persson and Tabellini 1990, chapter 4. Consider a policy-maker i with a policy preference $L^i(\pi_t, x_t) = \frac{\pi_t^2}{2} - \lambda^i x_t$, where $x_t = \theta_t - \pi_t^e + \pi_t$, and λ^i represents the policymaker's type. The world lasts for two periods, and therefore the intertemporal loss is given by $\sum_{t=1}^{2} \beta^{t-1} \cdot L^i(\pi_t, x_t)$. The actual value of λ^i, however, is private information to the policymaker and hence unknown to the other economic agents. With probability p, the policymaker has a preference $\lambda^i = \lambda^D$ and with probability $(1-p)$, $\lambda^i = \lambda^R$, with $0 = \lambda^R < \lambda^D$. At the start of the first period, economic agents know only the values of λ^D, λ^R, and p. At the beginning of the second period, they update their beliefs through Bayesian updating, using first–period inflation as an additional piece of information. Note that policymakers cannot precommit to a given inflation rate.

a. Compute the most desired rate of inflation for each type of policymaker.

b. Show that the type D policymaker may want to mimic the behavior of the type R whereas the opposite is never true.

c. Compute the conditions under which a separating, a semi-separating, or a pooling equilibrium exists.   Assume   that   the   updating   of   beliefs   is   such   that $q = \Pr(i = D | \pi > \pi_R) = 1$, where q is the posterior probability that the policy-maker has type D.

Answer

a.   To find the preferred inflation rate, we take the first order condition for the minimization of L with respect to π_t:

$$\frac{\partial L}{\partial \pi_t} \equiv \beta^{t-1} \cdot \left(\pi_t - \lambda^i\right) = 0$$

$$\pi_t = \lambda^i, \; i \in \{D, R\}$$

b. Let us denote by q the posterior belief that the policymaker has type D (q has yet to be computed).   In this case, the expected rate of inflation is $\pi^e = (1 - q) \cdot 0 + q \cdot \lambda^D = q \cdot \lambda^D$, and the second–period loss function is given by:

$$L_2^R (\pi_2, x_2) = \frac{\pi_2^2}{2} \text{ for an } R\text{-type, and}$$

$$L_2^D (\pi_2, x_2) = \frac{\pi_2^2}{2} - \lambda^D \cdot (\theta_2 - \pi_2^e + \pi_2) \text{ for a } D\text{-type.}$$

This shows that the type R policymaker does not care about expectations, whereas type D does. Therefore, it may be in the interest of a type D not to set $\pi_1 = \lambda^D$, and instead to mimic the behavior of the type R, in order to alter posterior beliefs. If she manages to do so, π_2^e would be reduced, and therefore output increased. Conversely, as type R does not care about expectations, she does not either value the behavior of type D. For a type R, it is a dominant strategy to set $\pi_1 = 0$.

c. Separating equilibria exist if, for a type D, the first-period cost of setting $\pi_1 = 0$ is larger than the discounted second-period benefit of altering beliefs. To check when such an equilibrium exists, first consider the loss of a type D who sets $\pi_t = \lambda^D$ in both periods. Expected inflation in the first period is $\pi_1^e = p\lambda^D$, as there is a probability p that the policymaker has type D. But if type D sets inflation to λ^D in the first period, then $q = 1$ through Bayesian updating, and $\pi_2^e = \lambda^D$. For a type D, the intertemporal loss in a separating equilibrium is then given by:

$$L_{separ}^D = \lambda^D \cdot \left[\frac{\lambda^D}{2} - \left(\theta_1 + (1 - p) \lambda^D\right) + \beta \cdot \left(\frac{\lambda^D}{2} - \theta_2 \right) \right].$$

To see whether or not the separating equilibrium is sustainable, we need to compute the benefit of a deviation. If a type D is expected to set inflation to λ^D but deviates and sets it equal to zero, q will be equal to 0 instead of 1. As a result, the intertemporal loss with a deviation from the separating equilibrium is:

$$L_{nosepar}^D = \lambda^D \cdot \left[-\left(\theta_1 - p\lambda^D\right) + \beta \cdot \left(\frac{\lambda^D}{2} - \left(\theta_2 + \lambda^D\right)\right) \right].$$

That is, she would be creating a fall of activity in the first period, but would be able to create a complete surprise in the second period, and increase output by λ^D. The benefit of the deviation is given by the difference between the two losses. After simplification, this yields:

$$B_{separ} = L_{separ}^D - L_{nosepar}^D = \left(\lambda^D\right)^2 \cdot \left(\beta - \frac{1}{2}\right)$$

that is, the separating equilibrium is sustainable for values of $\beta \leq \frac{1}{2}$.

We can apply the same methodology to compute when pooling equilibria exist. In a pooling equilibrium, the two types set the same inflation rate (zero in this case). Given Bayesian updating, economic agents know that observing 0 inflation in the first period is not informative about the type of the policymaker, and therefore $q = p$. Knowing this, we can compute the loss of the type D when she plays the pooling equilibrium and when she deviates, respectively:

$$L_{pool}^D = \lambda^D \cdot \left[-\left(\theta_1 - p\lambda^D\right) + \beta \cdot \left(\frac{\lambda^D}{2} - \left(\theta_2 + (1-p)\lambda^D\right)\right) \right]$$

$$L_{nopool}^D = \lambda^D \cdot \left[\left(\frac{\lambda^D}{2} - \left(\theta_1 + (1-p)\lambda^D\right)\right) + \beta \cdot \left(\frac{\lambda^D}{2} - \theta_2\right) \right].$$

Therefore, the temptation to deviate is given by:

$$B_{pool} = L_{pool}^D - L_{nopool}^D$$
$$= \left(\lambda^D\right)^2 \cdot \left(\frac{1}{2} - (1-p)\beta\right)$$

which shows that a pooling equilibrium is sustainable only for values of $\beta \geq \left[2\left(1-p\right)\right]^{-1}$.

Semi-separating equilibria arise when a type D is indifferent between setting inflation low (zero) or high (λ^D). When this is the case, she plays "low" with a probability that we denote by l, and "high" with probability $(1-l)$, and $0 < l < 1$. For a given l, the updating of beliefs after observing zero inflation is given by:

$$q_0^{semi} = \Pr\left(i = D | \pi_1 = 0\right) = \frac{p \cdot l}{1 - p \cdot (1-l)}$$

where *semi* stands for semi-separating and the subscript denotes the observed inflation rate. Conversely, observing $\pi_1 = \lambda^D$ allows the agents to learn the type with certainty: $q_{\lambda^D}^{semi} = 1$. There exists a semi-separating equilibrium if there is a value of l that makes the D-type indifferent between setting inflation low or high. In other words, it exists if the following equality can hold for some value of $l \in (0,1)$:

$$\left(\lambda^D\right)^2 \left[p + \beta \cdot \left(\tfrac{1}{2} - \tfrac{1-p}{1-p(1-l)}\right)\right] = \left(\lambda^D\right)^2 \left[\tfrac{1}{2} - (1-p) + \tfrac{\beta}{2}\right]$$

where the left-hand side represents the loss from low inflation in the first period, the right-hand side represents the loss from setting inflation to λ^D, and we already simplified the θ_t's away. Simplifying further and isolating l shows that a semi-separating equilibrium exists if:

$$0 < l = \frac{(2\beta - 1)\,(1 - p)}{p} < 1$$

or:

$$\frac{1}{2} < \beta < \frac{1}{2\,(1-p)}$$

Therefore, for values of β lower than $\frac{1}{2}$, only separating equilibria are sustainable. For values of β strictly between $\frac{1}{2}$ and $\frac{1}{2(1-p)}$, only semi-separating equilibria exist, and for values of $\beta \geq \frac{1}{2(1-p)}$, only pooling equilibria exist. The intuition for this result is relatively straightforward: the trade-off is between a (small) inflation surprise at time 1 and a (larger) inflation surprise at time 2. If the future is strongly valued (β large), the short-run cost of mimicking R in the first period is small compared to the benefit of the stronger inflation surprise in the second period. For small values of β, a D-policymaker prefers to enjoy the short-run benefit to the strongly discounted second-period benefit.

15.4   The inflation and stabilization biases

This problem is inspired by Clarida, Gali, and Gertler (1999). Consider an economy in which output depends on realized and prospective inflation: $x_t = \pi_t - E_t\left[\pi_{t+1}\right] - \varepsilon_t$, with $\varepsilon_t = \rho \cdot \varepsilon_{t-1} + \hat{\varepsilon}_t$ and $E_t\left[\hat{\varepsilon}_{t+1}\right] = 0$. The instantaneous loss function is $L\left(\pi_t, x_t\right) = \frac{1}{2}\left(\pi_t^2 + \lambda \cdot x_t^2\right)$, and the intertemporal loss is given by $E_t\left\{\sum_{v=0}^{\infty} \beta^v \cdot L\left(\pi_{t+v}, x_{t+v}\right)\right\}$.

a. Compute the first-order condition linking equilibrium inflation and output under discretion.

b. Use this first-order condition to compute the rational expectations equilibrium for inflation one period ahead (employ the Phillips curve to do this). Using this result, compute equilibrium output and inflation under discretion as a function of ε_t.

c.   Show that if the policymaker instead has a loss function of the shape $\frac{1}{2}E_t\left\{\sum_{\nu=0}^{\infty} \beta^\nu \cdot \left[\pi_{t+\nu}^2 + \lambda \cdot (x_{t+\nu} - \bar{x})^2\right]\right\}$, $\bar{x} > 0$, an inflation bias appears. That is, equilibrium inflation increases, whereas equilibrium output remains unaffected.

d. Compute the optimal inflation and output levels under commitment when x_t^C belongs to the class $x_t^C = -\psi \cdot \varepsilon_t$ (in other words, compute the optimal ψ under commitment. Set also $E_t[\pi_{t+\infty}] = 0$). Show that under commitment, output tends to vary more and inflation to vary less than under discretion, that is, that discretion generates a stabilization bias.

Answer

a. The intertemporal loss function can be separated into a contemporaneous and a future loss function. Formally, we denote by $\mathcal{L}_t$ the sum of current and future discounted losses:

$$\mathcal{L}_t = \frac{1}{2}\left(\pi_t^2 + \lambda \cdot x_t^2\right) + \mathcal{F}_t,$$

where $\mathcal{F}_t = \sum_{v=1}^{\infty} \beta^v \cdot L\left(\pi_{t+v}, x_{t+v}\right)$ stands for "future losses". Similarly, in the Phillips curve we can separate the variables under the current control of the policymaker on the one hand and those variables that depend on future actions or external circumstances (shocks):

$$x_t = \pi_t - E_t[\pi_{t+1}] - \rho \cdot \varepsilon_{t-1} - \hat{\varepsilon}_t = \pi_t - \mathcal{E}_t, \tag{15.10}$$

where $\mathcal{E}_t$ denotes variables that are external to today's controls of the policymaker. Rewriting the optimization problem in this way, we can see that the first order condition is perfectly standard:

$$\frac{d\mathcal{L}_t}{d\pi_t} = \pi_t^D + \lambda x_t = 0,$$

resulting in the following inflation under discretion:

$$\pi_t^D = -\lambda x_t = -\lambda\left(\pi_t^D - \mathcal{E}_t\right) = \frac{\lambda}{1+\lambda}\mathcal{E}_t. \tag{15.11}$$

Let us compare this first order condition with equation (15.14) in the textbook. Here, by assumption, $\bar{\pi} = \bar{x} = \theta = 0$. Therefore, the only difference is the value of $\mathcal{E}_t$, which here is equal to $E_t[\pi_{t+1}^D] + \varepsilon_t$ instead of ε_t in the textbook. This difference arises from the forward-lookingness assumption. Economic agents take *future* inflation into account, instead of the expectation of *current* inflation. This difference, together with the auto-correlation of the error term, determines equilibrium policy, as we show below.

b. Let us plug (15.11) into the expected Phillips curve for period $t+1$:

$$E_t[\pi_{t+1}^D] = E_t\left[x_{t+1} + \pi_{t+2}^D + \rho\varepsilon_t + \hat{\varepsilon}_{t+1}\right] = E_t\left[\frac{-\pi_{t+1}^D}{\lambda} + \pi_{t+2}^D + \rho\varepsilon_t\right]$$

$$= \frac{\lambda}{1+\lambda}\left\{\rho\varepsilon_t + E_t[\pi_{t+2}^D]\right\},$$

where $E_t[\pi_{t+2}^D]$ remains unknown.

From the Phillips curve, however, we know that $\mathsf{E}_t\left[\pi_{t+2}^D\right] = \mathsf{E}_t\left[x_{t+2} + \pi_{t+3}^D + \rho^2\varepsilon_t\right]$. By recursion, we find:

$$\mathsf{E}_t\left[\pi_{t+1}^D\right] = \frac{\lambda\rho}{1+\lambda}\cdot\left\{\sum_{v=0}^{\infty}\left(\frac{\lambda\rho}{1+\lambda}\right)^v\varepsilon_t\right\} = \frac{\lambda\rho}{1+(1-\rho)\lambda}\varepsilon_t. \qquad (15.12)$$

Substituting (15.12) into (15.11), we find: $\quad\pi_t^D = \frac{\lambda}{1+(1-\rho)\lambda}\varepsilon_t$ and $x_t^D = \frac{-1}{1+(1-\rho)\lambda}\varepsilon_t$.

Here again, we can compare this result with equation (15.14) in the textbook to see that, without autocorrelation, π_t^D would be the same as in (15.14). With autocorrelation, however, the current value of ε_t tells something about the likely value of ε_{t+1}. This affects inflation expectations and induces a stronger reaction by the CB to avoid output contraction (or expansion if $\varepsilon_t < 0$). In question (d), we are also showing that this reaction is too strong: there is a stabilization bias under discretion.

c. With this alternative utility function, the first order condition becomes:

$$\pi_t^D = -\lambda\left(x_t - \bar{x}\right) = -\lambda\left(\pi_t^D - \mathcal{E}_t - \bar{x}\right) = \frac{\lambda}{1+\lambda}\left(\mathcal{E}_t + \bar{x}\right). \qquad (15.13)$$

Following the same steps as in (b), we plug (15.13) into the Phillips curve:

$$\begin{aligned}\mathsf{E}_t\left[\pi_{t+1}^D\right] &= \mathsf{E}_t\left[\frac{-\pi_{t+1}^D}{\lambda} + \bar{x} + \pi_{t+2}^D + \rho\varepsilon_t\right] \\ &= \frac{\lambda}{1+\lambda}\left\{\bar{x} + \rho\varepsilon_t + \mathsf{E}_t\left[\pi_{t+2}^D\right]\right\}\end{aligned}$$

and by recursion, we find: $\pi_t^D = \lambda\bar{x} + \frac{\lambda}{1+(1-\rho)\lambda}\varepsilon_t$, and $x_t^D = \frac{-1}{1+(1-\rho)\lambda}\varepsilon_t$. Therefore, inflation is higher (there is an inflation bias), but output remains the same as in question (b) (there is no extra stabilization bias).

d. Under commitment, one should minimize the expected intertemporal loss function. Restricting ourselves to the policy class $x_t^C = -\psi\varepsilon_t$, we can rewrite the Phillips curve as

$$\pi_t = (1 - \psi)\,\varepsilon_t + \mathsf{E}_t\left[\pi_{t+1}\right].$$

By recursion again:

$$\begin{aligned}\pi_t &= (1 - \psi)\,\varepsilon_t + \sum_{i=1}^{\infty}(1 - \psi)\cdot\mathsf{E}_t\left[\varepsilon_{t+i}\right] + \mathsf{E}_t\left[\pi_{t+\infty}\right] \\ &= \frac{1-\psi}{1-\rho}\varepsilon_t = \frac{1}{1-\rho}\left[\varepsilon_t + x_t^C\right]. \qquad (15.14)\end{aligned}$$

Let us now minimize the expected intertemporal loss function, using (15.14) to substitute for the inflation rate at each period:

$$\min_{\psi} \mathsf{E}_0 \left[\sum_{i=0}^{\infty} \frac{\beta^i}{2} \cdot \left\{ \left(\frac{1-\psi}{1-\rho} \varepsilon_i \right)^2 + \lambda \left(-\psi \varepsilon_i \right)^2 \right\} \right]$$

$$\min_{\psi} \left\{ \left(\frac{1-\psi}{1-\rho} \right)^2 + \lambda \psi^2 \right\} \cdot \mathsf{E}_0 \left[\sum_{i=0}^{\infty} \frac{\beta^i \cdot \varepsilon_i^2}{2} \right]$$

$$\min_{\psi} \left\{ \left(\frac{1-\psi}{1-\rho} \right)^2 + \lambda \psi^2 \right\} \cdot \frac{\sigma_\varepsilon^2}{1-\beta}$$

where σ_ε^2 is the variance of $\hat{\varepsilon}$. Taking the first order condition and solving for ψ, we find:

$$\psi = \left(1 + \lambda \left(1 - \rho \right)^2 \right)^{-1}$$

This implies that the policy under commitment is:

$$\pi_t^C = \frac{1-\psi}{1-\rho} \varepsilon_t = \frac{\lambda \left(1 - \rho \right)}{1 + \lambda \left(1 - \rho \right)^2} \varepsilon_t. \tag{15.15}$$

To show that there is a stabilization bias under discretion, we have to compare π_t^C with π_t^D:

$$\frac{\pi_t^C}{\pi_t^D} = \frac{1 - \rho + \lambda \left(1 - \rho \right)^2}{1 + \lambda \left(1 - \rho \right)^2} < 1,$$

which proves that the reaction under discretion is always larger than under commitment. Under discretion, the CB puts too much weight on output stabilization.

15.5 Monetary policy with employment persistence

This problem draws on L. Svensson (1997a). Consider a world with infinite horizon, in which the instantaneous loss function is quadratic: $L\left(\pi_t, x_t; \bar{\pi}, \bar{x}, \lambda \right) = \frac{1}{2} \left[\left(\pi_t - \bar{\pi} \right)^2 + \lambda \cdot \left(x_t - \bar{x} \right)^2 \right]$. Employment evolves in the same way as in section 15.5: $x_t = \theta_t + \pi_t - \pi_t^e - \varepsilon_t$, where $\theta_t = \rho \cdot x_{t-1}$ (we are setting the natural employment rate to zero for simplicity), and $\mathsf{E}_{t-1} \left[\varepsilon_t \right] = 0$. Consumers are rational and set expected inflation to $\pi_t^e = \mathsf{E}_{t-1} \left[\pi_t | x_{t-1} \right]$. Policy can be conditioned on x_{t-1} and ε_t. It follows that under a policy rule $\pi_t = \Psi \left(x_{t-1}, \varepsilon_t \right)$, and following the notation of chapter 11, the value function is given by $W\left(x_{t-1}; \Psi \right) = -\mathsf{E}_{t-1} \left[L \left(\pi_t, x_t; \bar{\pi}, \bar{x}, \lambda \right) - \beta \cdot W \left(x_t; \Psi \right) \right]$, where β is the discount rate.

a. Compute the first-order conditions for the maximization of $W^C \left(x_t; \Psi^C \right)$ (the value function under commitment) with respect to both π_t and π_t^e subject to the rational expectations condition, $\pi_t^e = \mathsf{E}_{t-1} \left[\pi_t \right]$. [Hint: You must obtain a condition that depends on $W_x^C \left(x_t; \Psi \right)$, where the subscript denotes a partial derivative].

b. The shape of $W(x; \Psi)$ depends on the policy rule the government chooses (see chapter 11). Still, as the loss function is quadratic, we know two things. First, the shape of the welfare function will be $W^C(x) = \omega_0^C + \omega_1^C \cdot x + \frac{\omega_2^C}{2} \cdot x^2$, where the parameters ω_i^C depend on the equilibrium policy rule. Second, the policy rule will be linear: $\pi_t^C = \psi^C + \psi_x^C \cdot x_{t-1} + \psi_\varepsilon^C \cdot \varepsilon_t$. By substituting for $W^C(x)$ and x_t in the first-order condition, show that the equilibrium policy rule is of the type $\pi_t = \bar{\pi} + \psi_\varepsilon^C \cdot \varepsilon_t$. [Hint: Compute ψ_x^C and ψ_ε^C as a function of the parameters ω_i^C]

c. Compute the value of the parameters ω_i^C [Hint: Use the method of undetermined coefficients[1]]. Compare this rule with the one derived in section 15.2, and comment on the differences.

d. Suppose that the government cannot commit to a policy rule. Without computing the actual value of the new ω_i^D in the value function under discretion, show that there is an inflation bias when $\bar{x} > 0$ and that π^D generally depends on employment, x, in contrast to π^C.

e. Consider the particular case in which $\bar{x} = 0$, $\rho = 0.1$, $\lambda = 1$, and $\beta = 1$ to compute the commitment and the discretionary policy. Is there an inflation bias? Is there a stabilization bias?

Answer

a. We are dropping the superscripts C to simplify notation. The optimization problem can be written as:

$$\min_{\pi_t, \pi_t^e} -W(x_{t-1}; \Psi) = \mathsf{E}_{t-1}\left\{\frac{1}{2}\left[(\pi_t - \bar{\pi})^2 + \lambda \cdot (x_t - \bar{x})^2\right] - \beta \cdot W(x_t; \Psi)\right\}$$

$$\text{s.t. } \pi_t^e = \mathsf{E}_{t-1}[\pi_t] \; ; \quad x_t = \rho \cdot x_{t-1} + \pi_t - \pi_t^e - \varepsilon_t.$$

After substituting for the second constraint (the Phillips curve), the optimization problem results in the following two first order conditions:

$$-\frac{\partial W(.)}{\partial \pi_t} = (\pi_t - \bar{\pi}) + \lambda \cdot (x_t - \bar{x}) - \beta \cdot W_x(x_t; \Psi) = \Omega_t \quad (15.16)$$

$$-\frac{\partial W(.)}{\partial \pi_t^e} = -\mathsf{E}_{t-1}\{\lambda \cdot (x_t - \bar{x}) - \beta \cdot W_x(x_t; \Psi)\} = -\Omega_t \quad (15.17)$$

where Ω_t is the Lagrange multiplier to the rational expectations condition at date t. Note an important difference between (15.17) and (15.16). When inflation is set, all relevant information is revealed. Equation (15.16) reflects this by the absence of the expectational operator. Inflation will be set in a way that the derivative of W with respect to π_t is always equal to the shadow value of the constraint. By

---

[1]To this end, substitute for π_t^C, the resulting evolution of employment (x_t as a function of x_{t-1} and ε_t), and the quadratic guess of the value function in the original W^C. Then, identifying the appropriate terms with $\omega_2^C/2$ and ω_1^C, compute the exact value function W^C (computing ω_0 is not important).

contrast, expectations are formed before ε_t is revealed, which explains the presence of the expectations operator in (15.17). Substituting (15.17) into (15.16) yields:

$$(\pi_t - \bar{\pi}) + \lambda \cdot (x_t - \bar{x}) - \beta \cdot W_x (x_t; \Psi) = \ldots$$
$$\ldots = \mathsf{E}_{t-1} \{\lambda \cdot (x_t - \bar{x}) - \beta \cdot W_x (x_t; \Psi)\} \tag{15.18}$$

b. When expectations are formed, the value of θ_t is already revealed. Therefore, $\mathsf{E}_{t-1}[\pi_t] = \psi^C + \psi_x^C \cdot x_t$. By taking the expectations of (15.18), we thus find $\psi^C = \bar{\pi}$ and $\psi_x^C = 0$.

It remains to compute ψ_ε^C. As $W(.)$ is quadratic, $W_x (x_t; \Psi) = \omega_1 + \omega_2 \cdot x_t$. Substituting this and the values of ψ^C and ψ_x^C into the Phillips curve, we obtain:

$$x_t = \rho \cdot x_{t-1} - \left(1 - \psi_\varepsilon^C\right) \cdot \varepsilon_t,$$

which leads to the further simplification of (15.18):

$$\psi_\varepsilon^C \cdot \varepsilon_t + \lambda \cdot (x_t - \bar{x}) - \beta \cdot [\omega_1 + \omega_2 \cdot x_t] = \lambda \cdot (\rho \cdot x_{t-1} - \bar{x}) - \beta \cdot [\omega_1 + \omega_2 \cdot \rho \cdot x_{t-1}]$$

Substituting now for the equilibrium value of x_t and simplifying again yields

$$\psi_\varepsilon^C - \lambda \cdot \left(1 - \psi_\varepsilon^C\right) + \beta \cdot \left[\omega_2 \cdot \left(1 - \psi_\varepsilon^C\right)\right] = 0$$

$$\psi_\varepsilon^C = \frac{\lambda - \beta\omega_2}{1 + \lambda - \beta\omega_2} \tag{15.19}$$

c. Now that we have computed the optimal policy rule in function of ω_2, we can evaluate the optimal policy in function of the parameters of the model. We can rewrite the value function, incorporating in it the results we already obtained:

$$-W \left(x_{t-1}; \Psi^C\right) = \mathsf{E}_{t-1} \left\{ \tfrac{1}{2} \left[\left(\psi_\varepsilon^C \varepsilon_t\right)^2 + \lambda \left(\rho x_{t-1} - \left(1 - \psi_\varepsilon^C\right)\varepsilon_t - \bar{x}\right)^2\right] + \ldots \right.$$
$$\left. \ldots - \beta \left[\omega_0^C + \omega_1^C \left(\rho x_{t-1} - \left(1 - \psi_\varepsilon^C\right)\varepsilon_t\right) + \tfrac{\omega_2^C}{2} \left(\rho x_{t-1} - \left(1 - \psi_\varepsilon^C\right)\varepsilon_t\right)^2\right]\right\}$$

Substituting for the value of ψ_ε^C found in (15.19), expanding the expression and taking expectations yields:

$$-W (x_{t-1}; \Psi) = \tilde{\omega}_0 - (\beta \rho \omega_1 + \lambda \rho \bar{x}) \cdot x_{t-1} - \left(\frac{\beta\rho^2\omega_2 - \lambda\rho^2}{2}\right) \cdot x_{t-1}^2$$

where $\tilde{\omega}_0$ is a (very complex) expression that depends on most parameters of the model. As it is just a constant, computing it is of little interest. Given the definition of ω_1 and ω_2, we know that, under commitment, the values of those parameters must satisfy:

$$-\left(\beta \rho \omega_1^C + \lambda \rho \bar{x}\right) = -\omega_1^C$$
$$\text{and} \quad -\left(\frac{\beta\rho^2\omega_2^C - \lambda\rho^2}{2}\right) = -\frac{\omega_2^C}{2}.$$

Isolating ω_1^C and ω_2^C, we find:

$$\omega_1^C = \frac{\lambda\rho\bar{x}}{1-\beta\rho}$$

$$\omega_2^C = -\frac{\lambda\rho^2}{1-\beta\rho^2}$$

Finally, substituting for ω_2^C into ψ_ε^C yields:

$$\psi_\varepsilon^C = \frac{\lambda + \beta\frac{\lambda\rho^2}{1-\beta\rho^2}}{1+\lambda+\beta\frac{\lambda\rho^2}{1-\beta\rho^2}} = \frac{\lambda}{1+\lambda-\beta\rho^2}$$

d. Under discretion, the policymaker takes into account the effect of inflation on employment but not on inflation expectations, as those are given. The first order condition then becomes:

$$-\frac{\partial W^D\left(x_{t-1}\right)}{\partial\pi_t} = \pi_t - \bar{\pi} + \lambda\left(x_t - \bar{x}\right) - \beta\frac{\partial W^D\left(x_t\right)}{\partial\pi_t} = 0$$

Substituting for employment and the quadratic guess for the value function yields:

$$\pi_t - \bar{\pi} + \lambda\left(\rho x_{t-1} + \pi_t - \pi_t^e - \varepsilon_t - \bar{x}\right) + ...$$
$$... - \beta\cdot\left[\omega_1^D + \omega_2^D\cdot\left(\rho\cdot x_{t-1} + \pi_t - \pi_t^e - \varepsilon_t\right)\right] = 0$$

Taking expectations as of $t-1$ and introducing the rational expectations condition ($\pi_t^e = \mathsf{E}_{t-1}\left[\pi_t\right]$) allows us to compute the value of the policy coefficients other than ψ_ε:

$$\mathsf{E}_{t-1}\left[\pi_t\right] - \bar{\pi} + \lambda\left(\rho x_{t-1} - \bar{x}\right) - \beta\cdot\left[\omega_1^D + \omega_2^D\cdot\left(\rho\cdot x_{t-1}\right)\right] = 0$$
$$\pi_t^e = \mathsf{E}_{t-1}\left[\pi_t\right] = \left(\bar{\pi} + \lambda\bar{x} + \beta\omega_1^D\right) + \left(\beta\omega_2^D - \lambda\right)\rho x_{t-1}$$

meaning that $\psi^D = \bar{\pi} + \lambda\bar{x} + \beta\omega_1^D$ and $\psi_x^D = \left(\beta\omega_2^D - \lambda\right)\rho$.

Now, if we substitute for π_t^e into the first order condition, and simplify, we also find the coefficient ψ_ε:

$$\psi_\varepsilon^D + \lambda\left(\psi_\varepsilon^D - 1\right) - \beta\cdot\omega_2^D\cdot\left(\psi_\varepsilon^D - 1\right) = 0$$

$$\psi_\varepsilon^D = \frac{\lambda - \beta\omega_2^D}{1+\lambda-\beta\omega_2^D}$$

Admittedly, this last value is of little interest, as we cannot directly compare ψ_ε^D with ψ_ε^C if we do not derive ω_2^D. Deriving the latter however is much more complex than under commitment, because the existence of Ψ^D is not always warranted, as L. Svensson (1997) shows. In that paper, the author computes these existence conditions and shows that the inflation bias is systematic for $\bar{x} > 0$, that inflation reacts negatively to the employment level and that there is a stabilization bias. This proof, however, requires lengthy computations, and this is why we omit it in this problem. Question (e) focuses instead on a set of parameters where these existence conditions are satisfied.

e. When $\bar{x} = 0$, $\rho = 0.1$, $\lambda = 1$ and $\beta = 1$, the problem simplifies down to:

$$\min_{\pi_t, \pi_t^e} -W(x_{t-1}; \Psi) = \mathsf{E}_{t-1}\left\{\frac{1}{2}\left[(\pi_t - \bar{\pi})^2 + x_t^2\right] - W(x_t; \Psi)\right\}$$

$$x_t = \frac{x_{t-1}}{10} + \pi_t - \pi_t^e - \varepsilon_t$$

The problem under commitment has already been analyzed. It is then enough to substitute for our parameter values in order to find the optimal policy under commitment:

$$\psi_\varepsilon^C = \frac{\lambda}{1 + \lambda - \beta\rho^2} = \frac{1}{2 - .01} = .502513$$

Under discretion, the problem still needs to be solved. Under the selected set of parameters, we already know that:

$$\pi_t^D = \left(\bar{\pi} + \omega_1^D\right) + \left(\omega_2^D - 1\right)\frac{x_{t-1}}{10} + \frac{1 - \omega_2^D}{2 - \omega_2^D}\varepsilon_t$$

$$x_t = \frac{x_{t-1}}{10} + \frac{1 - \omega_2^D - \left(2 - \omega_2^D\right)}{2 - \omega_2^D} \cdot \varepsilon_t = \frac{x_{t-1}}{10} - \frac{1}{2 - \omega_2^D} \cdot \varepsilon_t$$

We can thus exploit this information to rewrite the value function:

$$-W^D(x_{t-1}; \Psi) = \mathsf{E}_{t-1}\left\{\frac{1}{2}\left[\left(\omega_1^D + \left(\omega_2^D - 1\right)\frac{x_{t-1}}{10} + \frac{1 - \omega_2^D}{2 - \omega_2^D}\varepsilon_t\right)^2 + \dots\right.\right.$$

$$\left.\left. \dots + \left(\frac{x_{t-1}}{10} - \frac{\varepsilon_t}{2 - \omega_2^D}\right)^2\right] - \left(\omega_0^D + \omega_1^D x_t + \frac{\omega_2^D}{2}x_t^2\right)\right\}$$

$$= \tilde{\omega}_0^D - \frac{2 - \omega_2^D}{10}\omega_1^D \cdot x_{t-1} + \frac{\left(1 - \omega_2^D\right)\left(2 - \omega_2^D\right)}{200} \cdot x_{t-1}^2$$

where $\tilde{\omega}_0^D$ is a lengthy expression containing most parameters of the model. We use again the method of undetermined coefficients to solve for ω_1^D and ω_2^D:

$$-\frac{2 - \omega_2^D}{10}\omega_1^D = \omega_1^D \implies \omega_1^D = 0$$

$$\frac{\left(1 - \omega_2^D\right)\left(2 - \omega_2^D\right)}{200} = -\frac{\omega_2^D}{2} \implies \omega_2^D = -\frac{97 \pm \sqrt{9401}}{2} = \begin{cases} -96.9794 \\ -0.02062 \end{cases}$$

As ω_2^D has two roots, we substitute for both of them into ψ_ε^D:

$$\psi_\varepsilon^D = \frac{1 - \omega_2^D}{2 - \omega_2^D} \in \{0.505103, 0.989897\}$$

But we know that variability of monetary policy is disliked (actually, in this case, Svensson (1997) even shows that the larger value is destabilizing for the economy), and hence that the lower value of ψ_ε^D will be the optimal discretionary policy.

Therefore, $\psi_\varepsilon^D = 0.505103 > \psi_\varepsilon^C = 0.502513$. Here the discrepancy is small because ρ is small, but one could show that it is increasing in ρ. To summarize, the discretionary policy is

$$\pi_t^D = \bar{\pi} - 0.102062 \cdot x_{t-1} + 0.505103 \cdot \varepsilon_t$$

There is no inflation bias under this parameter constellation (this is because $\bar{x} = 0$), but inflation will be countercyclical (it reacts negatively to x_{t-1}) and there is a stabilization bias (the reaction to supply shocks is larger than under commitment).

15.6   Inflation and default

This problem draws on Jahjah (1999). Consider an economy in which the control over inflation and over the government budget are in different hands. Inflation is set by the central bank and taxes by the government. The central bank can commit to a given inflation rate but is interested in both monetary and financial stability. Here, the risk of the government defaulting on its debt represents financial instability. The central bank's loss function is given by $L^B = \frac{\pi^2}{2} - \lambda \cdot (1 - \delta)$, where $\delta \in [0, 1]$ is the government's default rate.

The government's revenue consists of taxes, τ, and seignorage revenue (see below). At date 1, the government should repay its debt, together with the interest on it: $(1 + R) D_0$. But the government may decide to default on its debt partly or entirely and shrink this expense to $(1 + R) \cdot (1 - \delta) \cdot D_0$.

The timing is as follows. At time $t = 0$, the central bank first commits to some rule over the inflation rate. Expectations are formed. The government borrows some debt D_0. At $t = 1$, the central bank implements the inflation rate, and at $t = 2$, the government chooses the default and tax rates. Payoffs are realized.

a. Assuming that money demand is defined by $M_t = P_t$, where M stands for the money base and P for the price level, and knowing that the seignorage revenue of the government is given by $\frac{M_1 - M_0}{P_1}$, compute the seignorage as a function of $m_0 = \frac{M_0}{P_0}$ and π. Write down the government's budget constraint as a function of R, D_0, δ, π, τ, and m_0. How does the repayment rate depend on the tax rate?

b. If the government's loss function is given by $L^G = \frac{\tau^2}{2} - \gamma \cdot (1 - \delta)$, what will be the tax rate and the default rate as a function of the initial debt level and the inflation rate?

c. What is the optimal inflation rate in this situation?

d. If lenders demand a fixed real return, $(1 + R) = \frac{1 + \pi^e}{1 - \delta^e}$, and if the central bank commits to zero inflation, would the resulting default rate always be zero in equilibrium? Why, or why not?

Answer

a. This first question only relates to "accounting" computations, as there is no optimization yet in the hands of the government. It is rather straightforward to find the following two results: 1) Seignorage can be written as $\frac{\pi}{1+\pi}m_0$. 2) As the revenue of the government is given by $\tau + \frac{\pi}{1+\pi}m_0$ and there is no other spending than repaying the debt, the budget constraint becomes: $(1+R)\cdot(1-\delta)\cdot D_0 = \tau + \frac{\pi}{1+\pi}m_0$.

Given these results, we can look at the relation between taxes and the repayment rate: from the budget constraint, and if there is an interior solution, we find ($\tilde{\delta}$ denotes the prevailing default rate if the solution is interior, i.e. if $\tilde{\delta} \in (0,1)$):

$$1 - \tilde{\delta} = \frac{\tau + \frac{\pi}{1+\pi}m_0}{(1+R)\,D_0} \tag{15.20}$$

$$\frac{\partial\left(1-\tilde{\delta}\right)}{\partial\tau} = \frac{1}{(1+R)\,D_0}$$

Taking corner solutions into account:

$$1 - \delta = 1 \text{ if } \tau \geq \bar{\tau} = (1+R)\,D_0 - \frac{\pi m_0}{1+\pi}$$

$$= 1 - \tilde{\delta} \text{ otherwise}$$

Note that we are not considering disinflation ($\pi < 0$).

b. In contrast to question (a), we are here looking at the *equilibrium* behavior of the government, instead of looking at its budget constraint. The budget constraint and our previous calculations, however, prove necessary to compute the government's trade-off between taxes and default. Substituting for the equilibrium level of default in the loss function, and taking the first order condition with respect to the tax rate, we find:

$$\tilde{\tau} = \gamma \cdot \frac{\partial\left(1-\tilde{\delta}\right)}{\partial\tau} = \frac{\gamma}{(1+R)\,D_0}$$

$$\tau = \begin{cases} \bar{\tau} \text{ if } \tilde{\tau} \geq \bar{\tau} \\ \tilde{\tau} \text{ otherwise} \end{cases}$$

Therefore, if $\frac{\gamma}{(1+R)D_0} > (1+R)\,D_0 - \frac{\pi m_0}{1+\pi}$, default is nil, or $\delta = 0$. This is equivalent to:

$$(1+R)\,D_0 < \frac{\frac{\pi m_0}{1+\pi} + \sqrt{\left(\frac{\pi m_0}{1+\pi}\right)^2 + 4\gamma}}{2} \Rightarrow \delta = 0 \tag{15.21}$$

For higher indebtedness levels, however,

$$1 - \delta^* = \frac{\frac{\gamma}{(1+R)D_0} + \frac{\pi}{1+\pi}m_0}{(1+R)\,D_0} \tag{15.22}$$

$$\frac{\partial\left(1-\delta^*\right)}{\partial\pi} = \frac{m_0}{(1+\pi)^2}\frac{1}{(1+R)\,D_0} > 0.$$

That is, higher debt implies lower reimbursement (a larger default rate), but this can be mitigated by a higher inflation rate. Interestingly, improved financial stability may require a high enough inflation rate. In other words, improving the commitment of the CB to lower inflation may destabilize the financial system and lower the ranking of the government's debt. This is one of the findings in Jahjah (1999): in Europe, the creation of the European Central Bank improved commitment on inflation. But as a result, it induced a fall in the credibility of some governments. This motivates the reduction of debt levels across Europe through the stability pact.

c. The CB takes the equilibrium behavior of the government into account to set the inflation rate. That is, it takes equations (15.21) and (15.22) as the determinants to the equilibrium default rate. The CB, however, knows that it can improve financial stability by increasing inflation. Two cases must be considered.

Case 1. $(1 + R) D_0 < \sqrt{\gamma}$.
In this case, even with $\pi = 0$, there is no default. Therefore, the CB sets inflation to 0 and there is no default. To achieve such a result, however, it is necessary to reduce both the interest rate and the debt level in the country.

Case 2. $(1 + R) D_0 > \sqrt{\gamma}$.
In this case, setting inflation to 0 induces the government to default. To reduce default, the central bank would have to increase inflation. Does it do so? The answer is yes: with $\pi = 0$, the marginal cost of inflation is zero, whereas the marginal cost of default is equal to λ. It follows directly that the optimal rate of inflation must be positive. By how much? For strictly positive default rates, the behavior of the government is given by (15.22). In equilibrium, the CB thus sets inflation to the level that satisfies the following equality:

$$\pi_\delta = \lambda \frac{\partial (1 - \delta^*)}{\partial \pi} = \frac{\lambda}{(1 + \pi_\delta)^2} \frac{m_0}{(1 + R) D_0}.$$

However, by setting inflation to

$$\pi_0 = \frac{\chi}{[D_0 (1 + R)]^2 - \chi}, \quad \text{where } \chi = [D_0 (1 + R)]^4 - \gamma,$$

the CB is able to reduce the default rate to zero (π_0 is obtained by binding the inequality in (15.21) and solving for π). The resulting optimal inflation rate is thus the minimum between these two rates:

$$\pi^* = \min \{\pi_0, \pi_\delta\}.$$

d. Given the behavior of the investors and $\pi = 0$, we find: $1 + R = (1 - \delta^e)^{-1}$. By (15.21), there is no default as long as $D_0 < \sqrt{\gamma}$. Above that debt level, the default rate will be determined by (15.22). Solving for $\delta^e = \delta$ yields:

$$(1 - \delta^*) = \frac{D_0^2}{\gamma}.$$

Clearly, if the debt level were higher than $\sqrt{\gamma}$, we would have $(1 - \delta^*) > 1$. In other words, there is never any default in equilibrium. Why is this? By rational expectations, having default in equilibrium increases the interest rate in proportion. The equilibrium total repayment is then constant. Therefore, it is better to stick to a zero default rate.

This result contrasts with Jahjah (1999)'s. In that paper, the author considers different loss functions. The government for instance maximizes consumption, which can increase in inflation. Under this specification, there can be default even in the rational expectations equilibrium. Lenders expect the default rate to be δ, and therefore demand a risk premium. The government borrows and defaults, exactly by this proportion δ.

Refer also to Alesina and Tabellini (1987) "Rules and discretion with noncoordinated monetary and fiscal policies", Economic Inquiry, Vol XXV, pp619-630.

Chapter 16

Electoral cycles

16.1 Timing, moral hazard, adverse selection and the political business cycle

Consider the model of section 16.1, in which output depends on the policymaker's ability, and there is an election every other year. Assume in addition that η_t is uniformly distributed on $\left[-\frac{a}{2}, \frac{a}{2}\right]$, with $a > 0$, and that $\beta = 1$.

a. Assume that η_t is not observed by any agent at date t but only at date $t + 1$. Nevertheless, both x_t and π_t are commonly observed immediately after they are realized (before the election, if there is one). Compute equilibrium inflation in on-election years and in off-elections years. Show that under this timing there is no political business cycle and explain why not.

b. Change the timing and assume that neither η_t nor π_t are observed at date t, but only at date $t + 1$. Only x_t is observed at time t, before the election, if there is one. Compute equilibrium inflation in on–election years and in off–election years. Show that the moral hazard problem of section 16.1 arises.

c. What happens if the incumbent has an informational advantage and is informed about her ability before setting inflation? Show that if the voters' information set is the same as in question (a), equilibrium inflation remains the same as in question (a) and explain why this is so.

d. Finally, what happens if the policymaker has an informational advantage but voters have the same information as in question (b) (that is, they do not observe inflation before the election)? What inflation rate and output level will an incumbent with type η_t choose in on–election years and in off–election years? (Assume that voters reelect the incumbent only if $x_t > \xi$, where ξ has to be determined.)

Answer

a. In off–election years, the incumbent minimizes the social loss function. The first order condition is then given by $\pi_t = \lambda$, as we know from chapter 15 or from section 16.1. Therefore $\pi_t^e = \lambda$ and $x_t = -\varepsilon_t$. If there is an election, the incumbent minimizes instead $(L(\pi_t, x_t) - \Pr_t(R|\pi_t) \cdot R)$, where $\Pr_t(R|\pi_t)$ is the perceived probability to be reelected, and R is the rent from being an incumbent. To compute equilibrium policy, we first have to derive this probability.

A randomly drawn challenger has an expected value of ε equal to 0. An incumbent has an expected quality $E_t[-\varepsilon_{t+1}|\pi_t] = E_t[\eta_t|\pi_t] + 0$, and will be reelected only if $E_t[\eta_t|\pi_t] \geq 0$.

The information set of all players is $\{\eta_{t-1}, x_t, \pi_t\}$, and hence $E_t[\eta_t|\pi_t] = x_t - \pi_t + \pi_t^e - \eta_{t-1} = \eta_t$ (refer to the definition of x_t in section 16.1 of the textbook). As one can see, manipulating x_t has no effect on voters' beliefs: the difference $(x_t - \pi_t)$ would remain constant. It is impossible to fool the voters. Therefore, with this information set,

$$\frac{\partial \Pr_t(R|\pi_t)}{\partial \pi_t} = 0 \text{ and } \pi_t = \lambda$$

also in on-election years. There is no political business cycle, because parties cannot influence voters' beliefs.

b. In off-election years, incentives –and therefore equilibrium inflation– remain unchanged: $\pi_t = \lambda$. When there is an election, however, incentives change. As voters cannot observe π_t, but can only *expect* it to be π_t^e, the expected future ability of the present incumbent is $E_t[\eta_t|\pi_t] = x_t - \eta_{t-1}$. This implies that voters' beliefs can be manipulated:

$$\frac{\partial \Pr_t(R|\pi_t)}{\partial \pi_t} = \frac{\partial \Pr_t(\pi_t - \pi_t^e + \eta_t > 0)}{\partial \pi_t} = \frac{1}{a}, \ \forall \pi_t \in \left[\pi_t^e - \frac{a}{2}, \pi_t^e + \frac{a}{2}\right].$$

Minimizing $(L(\pi_t, x_t) - \Pr_t(R|\pi_t) \cdot R)$ thus leads to the first order condition:

$$\pi_t = \lambda + \frac{R}{a}$$

if an interior solution exists.

However, rational voters anticipate this and set $\pi_t^e = \lambda + \frac{R}{a}$. As a result, output remains unchanged: $x_t = \pi_t - \pi_t^e - \varepsilon_t = -\varepsilon_t$, whereas inflation is systematically higher in on-election years. This is the moral hazard problem described in the main book.

c. If the incumbent is informed about her ability one period before the voters, her incentives to manipulate inflation will depend on the value of η_t. However, if voters observe the triplet $\{\eta_{t-1}, x_t, \pi_t\}$ before voting, their beliefs cannot be manipulated, for the same reason as in question (a). The incentives to manipulate inflation are nil and $\pi_t = \lambda$ both in on– and off–election years.

d. Under this information set, the incumbent knows her ability, whereas voters are not informed either about this ability, nor about the inflation rate. For the sake of clarity, let us present the exact timing of the game:

i. η_t is drawn and the incumbent observes it. η_{t-1} and π_{t-1} are revealed to voters.

ii. The incumbent chooses π_t. x_t is realized and is observed by all agents.

iii. Voters form posteriors on η_t and reelect the incumbent if $E\left[\eta_t | \bullet\right] \geq 0$.

iv. Pay-offs realize.

Solving for the equilibrium of this game requires to work by backward induction. We know that voters reelect the incumbent if $x_t \geq \xi$, where ξ is the reelection strategy. The latter depends on η_{t-1} and on the equilibrium strategy of the incumbent. For a given ξ, the incumbent has two choices. Either, she sets $\pi_t = \lambda$ and does not try and alter her reelection probability, or she increases π_t beyond that level to increase $\Pr_t(R|\pi_t)$.

In the former case, the incumbent's loss is:

$$L\left(\lambda, x_t\right) = \frac{\lambda^2}{2} - \lambda\left(\lambda - \pi_t^e - \varepsilon_t\right) - K$$

where K is the (unmanipulated) reelection probability times R. In the second case, output is increased to ξ and the loss becomes:

$$L\left(\pi_t, \xi\right) = \frac{\left(\xi + \pi_t^e + \varepsilon_t\right)^2}{2} - \lambda \cdot \xi - R.$$

and the incumbent is reelected with probability 1 under this output level. The benefit of increasing inflation to ξ is therefore:

$$
\begin{aligned}
B &= L\left(\lambda, x_t\right) - L\left(\pi_t, \xi\right) \\
&= (R - K) + \lambda \cdot \left(\xi + \pi_t^e - \frac{\lambda}{2} + \varepsilon_t\right) - \frac{\left(\xi + \pi_t^e + \varepsilon_t\right)^2}{2}.
\end{aligned}
$$

Now, we can solve for the optimal reelection strategy. Voters do not want to reelect incumbents with $\eta_t < 0$. Therefore, B must be negative for types $\eta_t < 0$ and $B \geq 0$ for types $\eta_t \geq 0$. This is achieved by setting:

$$\xi = \eta_{t-1} + \lambda - \pi_t^e \pm \sqrt{2R}$$

Substituting these two potential values of ξ in B yields:

$$B = -\frac{\eta_t^2 \pm 2\eta_t\sqrt{2R}}{2}$$

By checking the behavior of these two possible values solutions around $\eta_t = 0$, one sees that only one of them induces the correct behavior on the side of incumbents:

$$B = \frac{-\eta_t^2 + 2\eta_t\sqrt{2R}}{2} = \eta_t \cdot \left(\sqrt{2R} - \frac{\eta_t}{2}\right)$$

In this case, incumbents with $\eta_t < 0$ set $\pi_t = \lambda$, and output is shrunk because of their lack of ability. Incumbents with ability $0 \leq \eta_t \leq \sqrt{2R}$ set inflation to $\lambda + \sqrt{2R} - \eta_t$, and output is ξ. Those with $\eta_t \geq \sqrt{2R}$ set $\pi_t = \lambda$ and generate an output level larger than ξ.

What do we learn from this problem? First, that there is a noticeable difference between the political business cycle arising from moral hazard and from adverse selection. With moral hazard, inflation cycles whereas output remains the same as under full information. This happens because the incumbent has no informational advantage over voters and therefore inflation manipulation is a pure waste. It creates no additional information. Under adverse selection, the incumbent owns relevant information. The reelection strategy of the voters serves then as a tool to discriminate between "good" and "bad" incumbents. Moreover, as the incumbent's behavior depends on her ability, output will also be affected by the reelection strategy. The second lesson of this problem is that the informational advantage of the incumbent is not enough to generate a political business cycle. In questions (a) and (c), voters own so much information that inflation manipulation becomes redundant. Even if voters cannot observe the ability of the incumbent, they must own sufficiently little information about the current state of the economy for the political business cycle to arise.

16.2   Partisan political competition and the strategic use of inflation

This problem is based on Jonsson 1997. Let the loss function of an agent J be given by $\sum_{t=1}^{2} \frac{\beta^{t-1}}{2} \cdot \left(\pi_t^2 + \lambda \left(x_t - \bar{x}^J \right)^2 \right)$, where $x_0 = 0$ and $x_t = \rho x_{t-1} + \pi_t - \pi_t^e$, $t = 1, 2$. Notation is the same as in previous problems. Two citizen-candidates, D and R, compete to control policy. Their preferences have the same shape as those of any other agent, with a bliss output level denoted by x^D and x^R respectively.

a. Compute the equilibrium level of inflation and output if party P is the decision-maker for the two periods (and this is common knowledge).

b. Assume now that either party D or party R is in power in the first period (and that this is common knowledge at time 0). At date 2, however, either can be elected, each with probability 1/2. Suppose also that $\bar{x}^R = -\bar{x}^D$ and $\bar{x}^D > 0$. If inflation expectations are formed before the election, what will be the equilibrium level of inflation and output in each period? Solve for each type $P = D, R$ being in office in the first and/or the second period.

c. Consider a simplified probabilistic voting model in which the probability that D is elected in the second period is given by some exogenously defined function $p(x_1)$ where p is symmetric around $\frac{1}{2}$ such that $p(x_1) = \frac{1}{2} - p(-x_1)$, $p_x > 0$, for all x_1 and $p_{xx} < 0$ for $x_1 > 0$. Show that endogenous election probabilities add another incentive to manipulate first-period output. Does this reinforce the first-period (dis)inflation bias? (Maintain the same assumptions as in question (b) about the preferences of D and R.)

Answer

a. Note first that $\frac{\partial x_1}{\partial \pi_1} = 1$. Taking this into account, we can write the optimization program and find the first order condition with respect to both π_2 and π_1 for an agent with preferences $\bar{x}_J$:

$$\min_{\pi_1, \pi_2} \sum_{t=1}^{2} \frac{\beta^{t-1}}{2} \cdot \left(\pi_t^2 + \lambda \left(x_t - \bar{x}^J \right)^2 \right) \tag{16.1}$$

$$\Rightarrow \frac{\partial L}{\partial \pi_2} = \beta \cdot \left[\pi_2 + \lambda \cdot \left(x_2 - \bar{x}^J \right) \right] = 0 \tag{16.2}$$

$$\Rightarrow \frac{\partial L}{\partial \pi_1} = \pi_1 + \lambda \left(x_1 - \bar{x}^J \right) + \beta \left[\pi_2 \frac{\partial \pi_2}{\partial x_1} + \lambda \left(x_2 - \bar{x}^J \right) \frac{\partial x_2}{\partial x_1} \right] = 0 \tag{16.3}$$

To find the equilibrium level of inflation in (16.2), we use 2 pieces of information. First, by the definition of the Phillips curve, there is no uncertainty, and therefore $\pi_2 = \pi_2^e$ in equilibrium. Second, we can replace x_2 by the value defined in the Phillips curve. Doing this, we find:

$$
\begin{aligned}
\pi_2 \left(J \right) &= \lambda \left(\bar{x}^J - x_2 \right) = \frac{\lambda}{1+\lambda} \left(\bar{x}^J - \rho x_1 + \pi_2^e \right) \tag{16.4} \\
&= \lambda \left(\bar{x}^J - \rho x_1 \right),
\end{aligned}
$$

and therefore $x_2 \left(J \right) = \rho x_1$.

Substituting for these values of π_2 and x_2 in (16.3) yields:

$$
\begin{aligned}
\pi_1 \left(J \right) &= \lambda \left(\bar{x}^J - x_1 \right) + 2\beta \cdot \lambda \cdot \left(\bar{x}^J - \rho x_1 \right) \cdot \rho \\
&= \lambda \left(\bar{x}^J - \rho x_0 - \pi_1 + \pi_1^e \right) + 2\beta \cdot \lambda \cdot \left(\bar{x}^J - \rho x_1 \right) \cdot \rho
\end{aligned}
$$

but, again, $\pi_1 \left(J \right) = \pi_1^e$, and therefore $x_1 \left(J \right) = \rho x_0 = 0$. This implies:

$$
\begin{aligned}
\pi_1 \left(J \right) &= \left(1 + 2\beta\rho \right) \cdot \lambda \bar{x}^J \\
\pi_2 \left(J \right) &= \lambda \bar{x}^J \\
x_1 \left(J \right) &= x_2 \left(J \right) = 0
\end{aligned}
$$

b. To solve this problem, we must work by backward induction. By (16.4):

$$
\begin{aligned}
\pi_2 \left(D \right) &= \tfrac{\lambda}{1+\lambda} \cdot \left(\bar{x}^D - \rho x_1 + \pi_2^e \right) = \tfrac{\lambda}{1+\lambda} \cdot \bar{x}^D - \lambda \rho x_1 \tag{16.5} \\
\pi_2 \left(R \right) &= \tfrac{\lambda}{1+\lambda} \cdot \left(\bar{x}^R - \rho x_1 + \pi_2^e \right) = \tfrac{\lambda}{1+\lambda} \cdot \bar{x}^R - \lambda \rho x_1 \tag{16.6}
\end{aligned}
$$

where the second equality in each line results from $\pi_2^e = -\lambda \rho x_1$. Why does this hold? By assumption, each party is elected with probability one half and $\bar{x}^D = -\bar{x}^R$. Therefore, $\pi_2^e = \frac{\lambda}{1+\lambda} \cdot \left(\frac{\bar{x}^D + \bar{x}^R}{2} - \rho x_1 + \pi_2^e \right) = -\lambda \rho x_1$. It follows that:

$$x_2 \left(J \right) = \tfrac{\lambda}{1+\lambda} \cdot \bar{x}^J + \rho x_1, \ J \in \{D, R\}$$

Now that we solved for the behavior of the parties and of the economy in the second period, we can turn to the first period problem. Because of the uncertainty prevailing about the identity of the policymaker at time 2, incentives differ from those in question (a). If the incumbent at time 1 is denoted by $I \in \{D, R\}$, the optimization problem writes as:

$$\min_{\pi_1} \frac{1}{2}\left[\pi_1^2 + \lambda\left(x_1 - \bar{x}^I\right)^2\right] + \ldots$$

$$\ldots + \frac{\beta}{2}\mathsf{E}_{D,R}\left\{\left[\frac{\lambda}{1+\lambda}\bar{x}^J - \lambda\rho x_1\right]^2 + \lambda\left(\rho x_1 + \frac{\lambda\bar{x}^J}{1+\lambda} - \bar{x}^I\right)^2\right\}.$$

Taking the first order condition with respect to π_1 and simplifying for the expectations operator yields:

$$\pi_1 + \lambda\left(x_1 - \bar{x}^I\right) + \beta \cdot \left[\lambda^2\rho^2 x_1 + \lambda\rho^2 x_1 - \lambda\rho\bar{x}^I\right] = 0.$$

But, by rational expectations $x_0 = 0$, and $x_1 = 0$ in equilibrium, and hence:

$$
\begin{aligned}
\pi_1(I) &= (1 + \beta\rho) \cdot \lambda\bar{x}^I \\
x_1(I) &= 0
\end{aligned}
$$

$$
\begin{aligned}
\pi_2(J) &= \tfrac{\lambda}{1+\lambda} \cdot \bar{x}^J \\
x_2(J) &= \tfrac{\lambda}{1+\lambda} \cdot \bar{x}^J
\end{aligned}
$$

So, as we can see, uncertainty about the second-period incumbent mitigates the desire to manipulate inflation in the first period. In the second period, this uncertainty also enables the policymaker to manipulate output, generating lower inflation variability, and higher output volatility.

c. With endogenous reelection probabilities, the optimization problem becomes more complex. Let us use some extra notation: $L_1(\pi_1, x_1; I)$ is the first period loss incurred by an agent with type I.

$L_2^J(I, p(x_1)) = L_2(\pi_2(J), x_2(J); I, p(x_1))$ is the second-period loss incurred by an agent with type I when second-period policy is set by type J, and the election probability is $p(x_1)$. With this notation, the intertemporal loss of an incumbent I can be written as:

$$L_1(\pi_1, x_1; I) + \beta \cdot \left[p(x_1) \cdot L_2^D(I, p(x_1)) + (1 - p(x_1)) \cdot L_2^R(I, p(x_1))\right]$$

The first order condition with respect to π_1 is then:

$$
\begin{aligned}
\frac{\partial L_1(\cdot; I)}{\partial \pi_1} + \beta \cdot &\left\{p(x_1) \cdot \frac{dL_2^D(I, p(x_1))}{dx_1} + (1 - p(x_1)) \cdot \frac{dL_2^R(I, p(x_1))}{dx_1}\right\} + \ldots \\
&\ldots + \beta \cdot p_x(x_1) \cdot \left[L_2^D(I, p(x_1)) - L_2^R(I, p(x_1))\right] = 0
\end{aligned} \tag{16.7}
$$

The first two terms in this derivative represent the trade-off we already studied in question (b). The third one, however, is new and results from the possibility to influence reelection probabilities. There is an additional incentive to manipulate first-period output.

How is the inflation bias affected by endogenous probabilities? To evaluate this, we have to expand each term in (16.7). The first term appeared under the same shape in parts (a) and (b). The third term is clearly positive for $I = R$ and negative for $I = D$. Below, we denote this third term by K^J.

The second term is more intricate to analyze, as second period losses are altered. Indeed, when $p(x_1)$ is different from $\frac{1}{2}$, π_2^e in (16.2) and (16.3) is different from $-\lambda \rho x_1$. Instead, we now have:

$$\pi_2^e = \lambda \cdot \left((2p - 1)\, \bar{x}^D - \rho x_1 \right),$$

and therefore:

$$\pi_2(D) = \frac{\lambda \bar{x}^D}{1+\lambda} \left[(2p - 1)\, \lambda + 1 \right] - \lambda \rho x_1 \tag{16.8}$$

$$\pi_2(R) = \frac{\lambda \bar{x}^D}{1+\lambda} \left[(2p - 1)\, \lambda - 1 \right] - \lambda \rho x_1, \tag{16.9}$$

$$\frac{d\pi_2(D)}{dx_1} = \frac{d\pi_2(R)}{dx_1} = 2\frac{\lambda \bar{x}^D}{1+\lambda} p_x(x_1) - \lambda \rho. \tag{16.10}$$

In terms of output, this translates to:

$$x_2(D) = \rho x_1 + \frac{\lambda \bar{x}^D}{1+\lambda}; \qquad x_2(R) = \rho x_1 - \frac{\lambda \bar{x}^D}{1+\lambda},$$

$$\frac{dx_2(D)}{dx_1} = \frac{dx_2(R)}{dx_1} = \rho.$$

Compared to the case with exogenous election probabilities, the reaction of x_2 with respect to x_1 is unchanged (and remember that $\frac{\partial x_1}{\partial \pi_1} = 1$), whereas the reaction of π_2 is larger than before (and it is negative when p is exogenous).

In equilibrium, still, there is no possible surprise in the first period, and $\pi_1^e = \pi_1$, $x_1 = 0$. This implies that $p(0) = \frac{1}{2}$ in equilibrium and hence that second-period equilibrium inflation rates are the same as in question (b). Exploiting this result, after some algebra, we can show that the first order condition with respect to π_1 yields:

$$\pi_1(J) = \lambda(1 + \beta\rho)\, \bar{x}^J - K^J$$

where K^J is the third term in (16.7). The first-period bias is reinforced by the endogeneity of the election probability, either upwards for D or downwards for R.

16.3   Monetary policy in majoritarian elections

Assume that two parties (A and B) compete to have the right to set monetary policy. The population is composed of three districts J of size $S^J > 0$, $\sum_{J=1}^{3} S^J = 1$. Preferences in district J are described by the loss function $L^J(\pi, x) = \frac{\pi^2}{2} - \lambda^J \cdot x$, with $0 = \lambda^1 < \lambda^2 < \lambda^3$. The two parties have ideological preferences $\lambda^A = \lambda^1 = 0$ and $\lambda^B = \lambda^3$. The elections are assumed to be majoritarian, that is a party must collect at least 50% of the votes in at least two districts to win the elections. There is uncertainty about the political support for each party: elector i in district J votes for A instead of B if $L^J(\pi_A, x_A) - \delta - \sigma^i \leq L^J(\pi_B, x_B)$, where δ is a nation-wide preference component uniformly distributed over $\left[-\frac{1}{2\psi}, \frac{1}{2\psi}\right]$, and σ^i is an individual preference component that has a (uniform) distribution which is district-specific: $\sigma^i \sim \mathcal{U}\left[-\frac{1}{2\phi^J}, \frac{1}{2\phi^J}\right]$, with $\phi^2 > \phi^1 = \phi^3$. Employment, x, depends only on expected and realized inflation: $x = \pi - \pi^e$. Inflation expectations are formed before the result of the elections is revealed.

Political competition works as follows: after expectations are formed, parties simultaneously announce an inflation rate. This announcement is binding. After the announcement, voters observe their political preferences for each party (σ^i and δ) and decide for which party to vote. The winning party then implements the promised policy for one period.

a. What is the target district for political competition?

b. Compute the first order conditions for the announced inflation rate. Show that platforms partially converge in equilibrium. Why are they converging here, whereas in section 16.2 they are not?

Answer

a. The target is district 2 only: the share of votes going to party A in district J is:

$$
\begin{aligned}
s_A^J(\pi_A, \pi_B) &= 1 - F^J\left[L^J(\pi_A, x_A) - L^J(\pi_B, x_B) - \delta\right] \\
&= 1 - F^J\left[(\pi_A - \pi_B)\left(\tfrac{\pi_A + \pi_B}{2} - \lambda^J\right) - \delta\right] \\
&= \tfrac{1}{2} - \phi^J \cdot \left\{(\pi_A - \pi_B)\left(\tfrac{\pi_A + \pi_B}{2} - \lambda^J\right) - \delta\right\}
\end{aligned}
$$

Let us consider first the case where $(\pi_A - \pi_B) < 0$. By assumption, $\phi^2 > \phi^1$ and $\lambda^2 > \lambda^1 = 0$. Under these conditions, if $s_A^2(\pi_A, \pi_B) \geq \frac{1}{2}$, $s_A^1(\pi_A, \pi_B)$ is automatically larger than $\frac{1}{2}$ also. Conversely, $s_A^2(\pi_A, \pi_B) < \frac{1}{2}$ if and only if $\left[(\pi_A - \pi_B)\left(\frac{\pi_A + \pi_B}{2} - \lambda^2\right) - \delta\right] > 0$. This requires $\left(\frac{\pi_A + \pi_B}{2} - \lambda^2\right)$ sufficiently below zero. As $\lambda^3 > \lambda^2$, it follows immediately that s_A^3 will be lower than a half.

For the other case, where $(\pi_A - \pi_B) > 0$, the political advantage of each party in each district is reversed, but the reasoning still applies. Therefore, political competition focuses on district 2: winning a majority in district 2 ensures to obtain a majority in at least one other district.

b. Denoting by $\Pr(\pi_A)$ the probability that platform A is implemented, the expected loss of party A and B are respectively given by:

$$EL_A(\pi_A, \pi_B) = \Pr(\pi_A) \cdot \frac{\pi_A^2}{2} + [1 - \Pr(\pi_A)] \cdot \frac{\pi_B^2}{2}$$

$$EL_B(\pi_A, \pi_B) = \Pr(\pi_A) \cdot \frac{\pi_A^2}{2} + [1 - \Pr(\pi_A)] \cdot \frac{\pi_B^2}{2} + \ldots$$

$$\ldots - \lambda^B (\Pr(\pi_A)\pi_A + [1 - \Pr(\pi_A)]\pi_B - \pi^e)$$

where $\pi^e = \Pr(\pi_A) \cdot \pi_A + [1 - \Pr(\pi_A)] \cdot \pi_B$. The first order condition for A yields:

$$\frac{\partial \Pr(\pi_A)}{\partial \pi_A} \frac{\pi_A^2 - \pi_B^2}{2} + \Pr(\pi_A) \cdot \pi_A = 0 \tag{16.11}$$

and for B:

$$\frac{\partial \Pr(\pi_A)}{\partial \pi_B} \frac{(\pi_A - \pi_B)(\pi_A + \pi_B - 2\lambda^B)}{2} + [1 - \Pr(\pi_A)] \cdot \left(\pi_B - \lambda^B\right) = 0 \tag{16.12}$$

We could solve the system of equations (16.11) and (16.12), but the solution is barely tractable. Instead, we determine the behavior of the election probability. As the probability to win is entirely defined by the share of votes received in district 2, we can focus on that district only:

$$s_A^2 = \frac{1}{2} - \phi^2 \cdot \left\{ (\pi_A - \pi_B)\left(\frac{\pi_A + \pi_B}{2} - \lambda^2\right) - \delta \right\}$$

The latter is larger than $\frac{1}{2}$ if and only if

$$\delta \geq (\pi_A - \pi_B)\left(\frac{\pi_A + \pi_B}{2} - \lambda^2\right)$$

which happens with probability:

$$\Pr(\pi_A) = 1 - F_\delta\left[(\pi_A - \pi_B)\left(\frac{\pi_A + \pi_B}{2} - \lambda^2\right)\right]$$

$$= \frac{1}{2} - \psi \cdot (\pi_A - \pi_B) \cdot \left(\frac{\pi_A + \pi_B}{2} - \lambda^2\right)$$

Therefore,

$$\frac{\partial \Pr(\pi_A)}{\partial \pi_A} = -\psi \cdot \left(\pi_A - \lambda^2\right) \tag{16.13}$$

$$\text{and} \quad \frac{\partial \Pr(\pi_A)}{\partial \pi_B} = \psi \cdot \left(\pi_B - \lambda^2\right). \tag{16.14}$$

Plugging (16.13) into (16.11), we see that the solution entails $\frac{\partial \Pr(\pi_A)}{\partial \pi_A} > 0$ and $\left(\pi_A^2 - \pi_B^2\right) < 0$, which implies $\pi_A > 0$, that is party A increases inflation to gain votes in district 2. Similarly, using (16.14) into (16.12), we find that the solution entails $\frac{\partial \Pr(\pi_A)}{\partial \pi_B} > 0$, and $\pi_B < \lambda^B$.

These results and the value of the two derivatives shows that partial convergence occurs: $\lambda^A < \pi_A < \lambda^2 < \pi_B < \lambda^B$. The intuition for this result is straightforward: absent electoral competition, $\pi_A = 0$ and $\pi_B = \lambda_B$. But each party can deviate from these levels in the direction of the inflation rate most desired by the voters in the target district. This increases the probability to be elected and has only second order costs in terms of suboptimal inflation.

Convergence however is only partial. Full convergence is not optimal, because returning to one's preferred inflation rate can only lower one's loss. For instance, if $\pi_B = \lambda^2$, then choosing $\pi_A < \lambda^2$, implies that inflation will be at most λ^2. But with some probability, it will be lower. Instead, choosing $\pi_A = \lambda^2$ means that inflation would never be lower than λ^2. $\pi_A < \lambda^2$ is then preferred by party A.

The difference between this model and the one in section 16.2 is that parties are able to commit to some inflation policy. The commitment happens after expectations are formed (we are thus in the discretionary case of chapter 15.3), but is binding for the policy implemented after the election. Announcing different platforms therefore influences voters' behavior, which forces parties to moderate their platforms.

16.4   Monetary policy in proportional elections

Consider a country made up of three districts of equal size: $S_1 = S_2 = S_3 = \frac{1}{3}$. The loss functions and the population are in all other respects identical to those of the previous problem. The political system, however, may be different.

a. Would this country gain by choosing a proportional representation system instead of a majoritarian system? Discuss intuitively why inflation would be higher or lower under each electoral system.

b. Assume proportional elections (a party wins if it gets more than 50% of total votes) and that each district has the ability to secede from this "monetary union". After a secession, only politicians from the local district can run in the election, and therefore monetary policy is set at the local (district) level. Which of the districts (1, 2, and/or 3) would gain from this secession? Under what condition would all the three districts agree to build together such a monetary union? Draw a parallel with the location of the European Central Bank.

Answer

a. In this setup, as the three districts are of equal size, parties need to rely on two districts at least, whatever the electoral system. As we showed in the previous problem, under the majoritarian system, only district 2 matters to select policy. Under the proportional representation system, however, the preferences of the three districts matter. As shown in chapter 3, the districts are weighted by their "cohesion" parameter ϕ^J. Policy will then depend on the three values of λ^J.

Consider the case where $\phi^3 = \phi^2$ and λ^3 is *very* large. The political weight of the three districts will then be equal under proportional representation. But as λ^3 is very large, equilibrium (and expected) inflation increases. Because of this, output will remain 0 on average, but losses will be higher than under the majoritarian system.

Consider the complementary case where $\lambda^3 = \lambda^2$ and $\phi^3 = \phi^2$. Under the majoritarian system, only λ^2 matters. Under proportional representation, however, the preferences of district 1 will also influence policy. This drives inflation down and increases welfare.

Therefore, depending on the parameters, either system may generate lower losses in equilibrium.

b. Clearly, district 1 would benefit from secession: by doing so, it reproduces the commitment solution of a zero inflation policy. Therefore, $\pi = \pi^e = 0$ and the expected loss is minimized. If district 1 secedes, we have then a country made up of districts 2 and 3 only. In that country, inflation is a weighted average of λ^2 and λ^3. But then, district 2 has an incentive to secede and have $\pi = \lambda^2$. District 2 benefits from the union only inasmuch as the latter brings in some extra commitment to lower inflation. Inflation is reduced only thanks to the presence of district 1, whereas it is increased by the presence of district 3.

The three districts agree on forming a union together only if the inflation policy is delegated to district 1 (in chapter 17, we see that this amounts to electing a conservative central banker). This is exactly what happened with the European Central Bank: Germany's main concern with the European Monetary Union was some other countries's bad reputation (historically, Italy or Spain, for instance, used to have high inflation). Germany's principal demand was then to have the European Central Bank located in Germany, so that German's influence would be stronger on inflation policy.

Chapter 17

Institutions and incentives

17.1 Escape clauses within a simple rule

This problem is based on Persson and Tabellini 1990, chapter 2. Consider an economy in which the loss function is $L(\pi, x) = \frac{1}{2}\left[\pi^2 + \lambda \cdot (x - \bar{x})^2\right]$, with $\bar{x} > 0$ and $x = \pi - \pi^e - \varepsilon$, where $\mathsf{E}[\varepsilon] = 0$ and $f(-\varepsilon) = f(\varepsilon)$. As usual, expectations are set before the realization of ε, whereas inflation is chosen afterward.

a. Consider a simple rule in which the central bank is constrained to set inflation at $\pi^S = \bar{\pi}$. What are the levels of inflation, output and the expected loss as a function of $\bar{\pi}$? Compute the optimal value of $\bar{\pi}$. Under which condition is this simple rule preferred to discretion?

b. Consider a simple rule with an escape clause: if the shock ε belongs to $[-\bar{\varepsilon}, \bar{\varepsilon}]$, the central bank must set $\pi = \bar{\pi}$. This happens with probability $(1-q)$. Otherwise, if $\varepsilon \notin [-\bar{\varepsilon}, \bar{\varepsilon}]$ (which happens with probability q), the central bank can set inflation to π^E. Compute this value of π^E as a function of $\bar{\pi}$ and ε. Compute the optimal value of $\bar{\pi}$ given q. Consider the optimal value of $\bar{\pi}$ and demonstrate that the optimal value of q is strictly between 0 and 1 if σ_ε^2 is not too small.

c. Assume that a penalty c is imposed on the policymaker if he deviates from zero inflation. Assume also that $\lambda = 1$ and that ε is uniformly distributed over $[-\bar{\varepsilon}, \bar{\varepsilon}]$, where $\bar{\varepsilon}$ is close to zero. Show that for some values of c, there are multiple equilibria: if economic agents believe either that $\mathsf{E}[\pi] = 0$ or that $\mathsf{E}[\pi] = \bar{x}$, their expectations will be correct (i.e., equilibrium inflation is a self-fulfilling prophecy).

Answer

a. Inflation is given and equal to $\bar{\pi}$. Clearly, this implies $\pi^e = \bar{\pi}$ and $x^S = -\varepsilon$. The expected loss is then

$$EL^S = \frac{1}{2}\mathsf{E}_\varepsilon\left[\bar{\pi}^2 + \lambda\left(-\varepsilon - \bar{x}\right)^2\right] = \frac{\bar{\pi}^2 + \lambda\bar{x}^2}{2} + \frac{\lambda}{2}\sigma_\varepsilon^2$$

where σ_ε^2 is the variance of ε. Hence, setting $\bar{\pi} = 0$ minimizes this expected loss. Under discretion, the equilibrium levels of inflation and output are respectively:

$$\pi^D = \lambda\bar{x} + \frac{\lambda}{1+\lambda}\varepsilon \quad \text{and} \quad x^D = -\frac{\varepsilon}{1+\lambda}.$$

This generates the following expected loss:

$$\begin{aligned}
EL^D &= \frac{1}{2}\mathsf{E}_\varepsilon\left[\left(\lambda\bar{x} + \tfrac{\lambda}{1+\lambda}\varepsilon\right)^2 + \lambda\left(-\tfrac{\varepsilon}{1+\lambda} - \bar{x}\right)^2\right] \\
&= \frac{\lambda}{2}\cdot\left[(1+\lambda)\,\bar{x}^2 + \tfrac{\sigma_\varepsilon^2}{1+\lambda}\right].
\end{aligned}$$

Therefore, $EL^D < EL^S$ holds only if the variance of ε is sufficiently large.

b. For values of ε that do not belong to $[-\bar{\varepsilon}, \bar{\varepsilon}]$, minimizing the loss requires:

$$\pi^E(\varepsilon) = \frac{\lambda}{1+\lambda}\left(\pi^e + \varepsilon + \bar{x}\right),$$

where expected inflation will be $\pi^e = (1-q)\bar{\pi} + \frac{q\lambda}{1+\lambda(1-q)}\left((1-q)\bar{\pi} + \bar{x}\right)$. This implies:

$$\pi^E(\varepsilon) = \frac{\lambda}{1+\lambda}\left(\frac{\lambda(1-q)\bar{\pi}}{1+\lambda(1-q)} + \varepsilon\right) + \frac{\lambda\bar{x}}{1+\lambda(1-q)}.$$

For $q < 1$, $\pi^E(\varepsilon)$ is increasing in $\bar{\pi}$. Moreover, $\bar{\pi}$ does not affect output. Quite intuitively, the expected loss is then increasing in $\bar{\pi}$ (we are omitting these computations here), and the optimal $\bar{\pi}$ is 0. Under this value, the expected loss can be written as

$$\begin{aligned}
EL^E(q) &= \frac{1-q(\bar{\varepsilon})}{2}\cdot\lambda\left[(\pi^e + \bar{x})^2 + \sigma_N^2(\bar{\varepsilon})\right] + \dots \\
&\quad \dots + \frac{q(\bar{\varepsilon})}{2}\cdot\left[\chi^2 + \left(\tfrac{\lambda}{1+\lambda}\right)^2\sigma_E^2(\bar{\varepsilon}) + \lambda\left((\chi/\lambda)^2 + \tfrac{\sigma_E^2(\bar{\varepsilon})}{(1+\lambda)^2}\right)\right]
\end{aligned}$$

where $\chi = \frac{\lambda\bar{x}}{1+\lambda(1-q)}$, $\sigma_N^2(\bar{\varepsilon})$ is the variance of the distribution of ε conditional on $\varepsilon < \bar{\varepsilon}$ ("Normal" times), and $\sigma_E^2(\bar{\varepsilon})$ is the variance of the distribution of ε conditional on $\varepsilon > \bar{\varepsilon}$ ("Exceptional" times). Finally, $q(\bar{\varepsilon})$ is the probability to use the escape clause, and $\pi^e = \frac{q\lambda\bar{x}}{1+\lambda(1-q)}$.

If $\bar{\varepsilon} \to \infty$, then $q(\bar{\varepsilon}) \to 0$, and the loss becomes that of the simple rule without escape clause. Computing the derivative of $\mathsf{E}L^E(q)$ with respect to q at that point yields

$$\frac{d\mathsf{E}L^E(0)}{dq} = -\frac{\lambda}{2}\left(\frac{x^2\lambda}{1+\lambda} + \sigma_\varepsilon^2\right) + \frac{d\sigma_N^2}{dq} < 0,$$

as $d\sigma_N^2/dq < 0$. It is thus always better to increase q above 0, that is to renege on the simple rule.

If $\bar{\varepsilon} \to 0$, then $q(\bar{\varepsilon}) \to 1$ and the loss becomes the same one as under discretion. Computing the derivative of $\mathsf{E}L^E(q)$ with respect to q at that point yields

$$\frac{d\mathsf{E}L^E(1)}{dq} = \frac{\lambda}{2}\left(\frac{\sigma_\varepsilon^2}{1+\lambda} - \lambda(1+\lambda)\bar{x}^2\right) + \frac{\lambda}{2(1+\lambda)}\frac{d\sigma_E^2}{dq} \gtrless 0.$$

Clearly, if σ_ε^2 is large enough, this derivative is larger than zero, meaning that the loss could be reduced by lowering q below 1.

c. Let us compute the difference between the loss of the policymaker when it follows the rule and deviates, respectively. After simplification, this yields

$$\Delta(\pi^e) = L(0, -\pi^e - \varepsilon) - L(\pi^E, \pi^E - \pi^e - \varepsilon) = \frac{(\pi^e + \varepsilon + \bar{x})^2}{2} - c$$

Let us consider the case in which $\bar{\varepsilon} \to 0$, as we know that the condition we are computing also holds around $\varepsilon = 0$. If economic agents expect the policymaker to always implement the discretionary policy, $\pi^e = \bar{x}$. What is the value of $\Delta(\bar{x})$?

$$\Delta(\pi^e) = 2\bar{x}^2 - c$$

Therefore, if $c < 2\bar{x}^2$, the policymaker would experience a larger loss by following the rule. Consequently, under this condition, expecting inflation to be $\bar{x}$ is enough to induce the policymaker to deviate.

If the policymaker is instead expected to follow the rule with probability one, then $\pi^e = 0$. The value of Δ in this case is:

$$\Delta(0) = \frac{\bar{x}^2}{2} - c.$$

Therefore, if $c > \bar{x}^2/2$, the expectation of zero inflation is enough for the policymaker to follow the rule. To summarize, if

$$c \in \left[\frac{\bar{x}^2}{2}, 2\bar{x}^2\right],$$

inflation is a self-fulfilling prophecy.

17.2 Endogenous credibility of the central bank

Consider two parties, R and D, that alternate in power. Each is elected with probability $1/2$. The decision to delegate responsibility for controlling inflation to a central bank has yet to be made. Delegation will be credible, however, only if both parties prefer delegating to a central bank rather than having a 50% chance of being the one that controls inflation –and a 50% chance of seeing the opponent have that control. Each agent has quadratic preferences $L^i\,[\pi, x] = \pi^2 + \lambda^i \cdot (x - \bar{x})^2$, with $x = \pi - \pi^e - \varepsilon$. There are three types of preferences in the economy: $\lambda^R = 0 < \lambda < \lambda^D = 1$, where λ represents social preferences, λ^R the preferences of the right-wing party and λ^D those of the left-wing party.

a. Assume that $\bar{x} = 0$ and compute the expected loss of having policy made by an agent with type $\lambda^B \in (0, 1)$ for each of the three existing types.

b. Show that both D and R may benefit from delegating to a central bank with preference $\lambda^B \in (0, 1)$, still under the assumption that $\bar{x} = 0$.

c. Consider now the case in which $\bar{x} > 0$. Compare three different equilibria: *i)* Policy is delegated to a central banker with preferences $\lambda^B = \lambda$ who operates under commitment (optimal inflation rate). *ii)* Policy is delegated to a central bank with preferences $\lambda^B \in (0, 1)$ that operates under discretion (suboptimal inflation rate). *iii)* Policy is set randomly by one of the parties (D or R), who operate under discretion. Show that there exist cases where parties can agree to switch from equilibrium *iii)* to *ii)* but not from *iii)* to *i)*.

Answer

a. An agent with type λ^B minimizes her loss under discretion by setting:

$$\pi^D\left(\lambda^B\right) = \frac{\lambda^B \cdot \varepsilon}{1 + \lambda^B}.$$

For any agent with preferences $\lambda^i \in \left\{\lambda^D, \lambda, \lambda^R\right\}$, the ensuing expected loss is

$$EL^{Delegation} = \left[\left(\frac{\lambda^B}{1 + \lambda^B}\right)^2 + \lambda^i \left(\frac{1}{1 + \lambda^B}\right)^2\right] \cdot \sigma_\varepsilon^2.$$

b. If policy is delegated to each party with probability $1/2$, the expected loss of an agent with type $\lambda^i \in \left\{\lambda^D, \lambda^R\right\}$ is given by

$$
\begin{aligned}
EL^D\,(Alt) &= \frac{\sigma_\varepsilon^2}{2}\left[\lambda^i + (1 + \lambda^i)\frac{1}{4}\right] = \frac{\sigma_\varepsilon^2}{2}\left(\frac{1}{4} + \frac{5}{4}\lambda^i\right) \\
&= \frac{\sigma_\varepsilon^2}{8} \text{ for type } \lambda^R, \text{ and} \\
&= \frac{3\sigma_\varepsilon^2}{4} \text{ for type } \lambda^D.
\end{aligned}
$$

In that equation, L^D stands for "loss under discretionary policy" and "*Alt*" stands for alternation.

Therefore, if $\lambda^B < \frac{1+2\sqrt{2}}{7}$, type R prefers delegation to alternation. Similarly, if $\lambda^B \in [3 - 2\sqrt{2}, 3 + 2\sqrt{2}]$, type D prefers delegation to alternation. Therefore, if $\lambda^B \in \left\{3 - 2\sqrt{2}, \frac{1+2\sqrt{2}}{7}\right\}$, both parties prefer delegation.

c. Under the first type of equilibrium, inflation is set to

$$\pi^C = \frac{\lambda \cdot \varepsilon}{1 + \lambda}$$

(see section 15.2 for the intermediate developments). As a result, expected inflation is zero.

Under the second and third types of equilibria, inflation is set to

$$\pi^D \left(\lambda^i\right) = \lambda^i \bar{x} + \frac{\lambda^i \cdot \varepsilon}{1 + \lambda^i}$$

(see section 15.3 for the intermediate developments). The difference between these two equilibria is the following one: under the type-*ii* equilibrium, inflation is always chosen by a fixed type, λ^B. The ensuing expected inflation is then $\pi^e \left(\lambda^B\right) = \lambda^B \bar{x}$. By contrast, under the type-*iii* equilibrium, inflation is set alternatively by D and R. As a result, expected inflation is $\pi^e \left(Alt\right) = \lambda^D \bar{x}/2$.

Let us compute the expected loss under each of the 3 equilibria for an agent with type i:

$$\mathsf{EL}^C = \left[\left(\frac{\lambda}{1 + \lambda}\right)^2 + \lambda^i \cdot \left(\frac{1}{1 + \lambda}\right)^2\right] \sigma_\varepsilon^2 + \lambda^i \bar{x}^2$$

$$\mathsf{EL}^D \left(\lambda^B\right) = \left[\left(\frac{\lambda^B}{1 + \lambda^B}\right)^2 + \lambda^i \cdot \left(\frac{1}{1 + \lambda^B}\right)^2\right] \sigma_\varepsilon^2 + \left[\left(\lambda^B\right)^2 + \lambda^i\right] \cdot \bar{x}^2$$

$$\mathsf{EL}^D \left(Alt\right) = \left(\frac{1}{8} + \frac{5\lambda^i}{8}\right) \sigma_\varepsilon^2 + \left(\frac{1}{2} + \frac{5\lambda^i}{4}\right) \bar{x}^2$$

Can parties agree to switch from equilibrium *iii)* to equilibrium *ii)* but refuse to switch from *iii)* to *i)*? Let us take a numerical example to demonstrate this may happen (analytical solutions exist, but are intractable). Let us take $\lambda = 0.9$, $\lambda^B = 0.2$, $\sigma_\varepsilon = 1$ and $\bar{x} = 0.2$.

Party R's losses are respectively:

$$\begin{array}{ll} i) & \left(\frac{\lambda}{1+\lambda}\right)^2 \sigma_\varepsilon^2 = 0.224 \\[2mm] ii) & \left(\frac{\lambda^B}{1+\lambda^B}\right)^2 \sigma_\varepsilon^2 + \left(\lambda^B \bar{x}\right)^2 = 0.029 \\[2mm] iii) & \frac{1}{8}\sigma_\varepsilon^2 + \frac{1}{2}\bar{x}^2 = 0.145 \end{array}$$

For party D, these losses become

$$i) \qquad \left(\left(\tfrac{\lambda}{1+\lambda} \right)^2 + \left(\tfrac{1}{1+\lambda} \right)^2 \right) \sigma_\varepsilon^2 = 0.501$$

$$ii) \quad \left(\left(\tfrac{\lambda^B}{1+\lambda^B} \right)^2 + \left(\tfrac{1}{1+\lambda^B} \right)^2 \right) \sigma_\varepsilon^2 + \left(\left(\lambda^B \right)^2 + 1 \right) \cdot \bar{x}^2 = 0.764$$

$$iii) \qquad\qquad \tfrac{3}{4}\sigma_\varepsilon^2 + \tfrac{7}{4}\bar{x}^2 = 0.82$$

With this parameter constellation, the preferences of party D and of the population are close (λ is close to 1). Therefore, D would prefer the optimal policy. But party R would find the variance of inflation too high in this case, and would revert to alternation. Instead, electing a central banker with preferences $\lambda^B = 0.2$ is a good compromise for the two parties, and it is even the preferred solution for party R. Note that we assumed $\bar{x}$ to be relatively small in this example. If $\bar{x}$ were too large, the loss of discretion would also be large. This would favor the optimal policy (equilibrium i).

17.3   Political competition and optimal delegation

Consider two parties, D and R, who compete for office. In contrast to the other cases we have analyzed, they compete not on the inflation rate, but on the shape of the contract they offer to the central bank. Their platform is binding, and the elected party has to implement the proposed contract. The central bank acts under discretion and has a preference parameter λ, identical to that of the median voter, whose preferences are given by $\mathsf{E}_{t-1}\left[L\left(\pi_t, x_t\right)\right] = \mathsf{E}_{t-1}\left[\frac{\pi_t^2}{2} + \frac{\lambda}{2}\left(x_t - \bar{x}\right)^2\right]$. The feasible contracts belong to the class $T\left(\pi_t\right) = t_0 + t_1 \cdot \pi_t$ and cannot be made contingent on shocks. Employment is determined as $x_t = \pi_t - \pi_t^e - \varepsilon_t$, with $\mathsf{E}_{t-1}\left[\varepsilon_t\right] = 0$. Once the contract is implemented, the central bank minimizes $L\left(\pi_t, x_t\right) - T\left(\pi_t\right)$.

a. Compute the platform that a purely opportunistic party would propose to maximize its probability of being elected.

b. Compute the platform that purely ideologist parties with preferences λ^D or λ^R would propose to minimize $\mathsf{E}_{t-1}\left[L^i\left(\pi_t, x_t\right)\right] = \mathsf{E}_{t-1}\left[\frac{\pi_t^2}{2} + \frac{\lambda^i}{2}\left(x - \bar{x}\right)^2\right]$. Does the result depend on some uncertainty about the median voter's preferences? Discuss the intuition for your result.

c. What would happen with opportunistic parties if they were unable to commit to implementing the contract and instead had a chance to recover direct control on inflation once elected? Would the parties gain by creating such a commitment device?

Answer

a. Ex-post, the central bank will minimize $L(\pi_t, x_t) - T(\pi_t)$. The first order condition thus yields

$$\pi_t = \frac{\lambda(\pi_t^e + \varepsilon_t + \bar{x}) + t_1}{1 + \lambda}.$$

Consequently:

$$\pi_t^e = \mathsf{E}_{t-1}[\pi_t] = \lambda\bar{x} + t_1$$

Substituting for this into π_t, we get

$$\pi_t = \frac{\lambda\varepsilon_t}{1+\lambda} + \lambda\bar{x} + t_1, \tag{17.1}$$

$$\text{and then} \quad x_t = -\frac{\varepsilon_t}{1+\lambda} \tag{17.2}$$

The winning platform is the one that minimizes the expected loss, i.e. the one that minimizes

$$\mathsf{E}[L(\cdot)] = \frac{\mathsf{E}\left[\frac{\lambda}{1+\lambda} \cdot \varepsilon_t + \lambda\bar{x} + t_1\right]^2}{2} + \frac{\lambda}{2}\mathsf{E}\left[\frac{\varepsilon_t}{1+\lambda}\right]^2 \tag{17.3}$$

Minimizing this loss with respect to t_1, we obtain:

$$\frac{\partial \mathsf{E}[L(\cdot)]}{\partial t_1} = \lambda\bar{x} + t_1 = 0 \quad \text{or} \quad t_1 = -\lambda\bar{x} \tag{17.4}$$

which means that inflation will be $\pi_t = \frac{\lambda\varepsilon_t}{1+\lambda}$ under this platform. If one compares it with the models of chapter 15, one can see that this policy is actually the optimal one, as it generates the same inflation as under commitment.

b. Having solved for question (a), the answer to this question is straightforward: for any preference λ^i, the optimal platform is $t_1 = -\lambda\bar{x}$. To see this, we compute the optimal policy under discretion, which yields a result identical to (17.1) and (17.2). As a result, the loss function of the candidate is given by (17.3), with the appropriate value of λ, and the first order condition remains (17.4).

So, opportunistic and ideologist parties propose the same platforms. Why? Because this contract T implements the socially optimal policy. Of course, ideologist parties would like to change λ^B. But this is not feasible under the constraints we imposed on feasible contracts. As a result, the optimal value of t_1 is independent of λ^i, and uncertainty about λ would not change anything to this result.

c. Without ex ante commitment, the party will always implement the discretionary policy once elected. That is, equilibrium inflation will be $\pi_t = \lambda^i\bar{x} + \frac{\lambda^i\varepsilon_t}{1+\lambda^i}$ and $x_t = -\frac{\varepsilon_t}{1+\lambda^i}$. As we saw in question (a), the party would still gain by committing, as commitment allows to reduce inflation by $\lambda^i\bar{x}$ without affecting output. Hence, the desire for committing to the rule (e.g. by making the central bank more independent) is not a matter of ideology or opportunism. With the appropriate contract, any party, be it opportunistic or ideologically motivated, prefers such a contract to having a direct hand on inflation. Of course, as we saw in chapter 15, they always want to escape from the commitment once elected but this is a matter of time inconsistency, and not of welfare.

17.4 Optimal delegation with persistent output shocks

This problem is inspired by Clarida, Gali, and Gertler (1999). Consider the same economy as in Problem 15.4: the Phillips curve is given by $x_t = \pi_t - \mathsf{E}_t\left[\pi_{t+1}\right] - \varepsilon_t$, with $\varepsilon_t = \rho \cdot \varepsilon_{t-1} + \hat{\varepsilon}_t$ and $\mathsf{E}_{t-1}\left[\hat{\varepsilon}_t\right] = 0$. The intertemporal function is $L = \frac{1}{2}\mathsf{E}_t\left\{\sum_{\nu=0}^{\infty}\beta^{\nu} \cdot \left[\pi_{t+\nu}^2 + \lambda \cdot x_{t+\nu}^2\right]\right\}$. In this framework, we have already defined the optimal policy under commitment and under discretion: $\pi_t^C = \frac{(1-\rho)\lambda}{1+(1-\rho)^2\lambda}\varepsilon_t$, and $\pi_t^D = \lambda^B \cdot x^B + \frac{\lambda^B}{1+(1-\rho)\lambda^B}\varepsilon_t$, where x^B is the central banker's output target.

a. Show that unless x^B is equal to zero, electing a conservative central banker with $\lambda^B < \lambda$ is not enough to reach the optimal policy under commitment.

b. Can an inflation target or a simple linear contract restore the optimal policy under commitment?

c. Nevertheless, the above value of π_t^C is not the globally optimal policy. Because of error autocorrelation, the globally optimal policy must instead yield $x_t = \delta x_{t-1} - \frac{\beta\delta}{\lambda(1-\beta\delta\rho)}\varepsilon_t$, where $\delta = \frac{1-\sqrt{1-4a^2\beta}}{2a\beta}$, $a = \frac{\lambda}{(1+\lambda)\beta+\lambda}$. Equivalently, this yields a globally optimal inflation rate $\pi_t = \frac{1-\delta\beta}{\beta}\lambda x_{t-1} + \frac{\beta\delta}{1-\beta\delta\rho}\varepsilon_t$. Design the contract that would induce the central bank to implement this globally optimal policy.

Answer

a. To achieve the optimal policy with a policymaker that acts under discretion, we would need to remove both the inflation and the stabilization biases. With $x^B > 0$, we need to impose $\lambda^B = 0$ to remove the inflation bias. In this case, however, $\pi^D = 0$, whatever the value of ε. Instead, the multiplier of ε_t is strictly positive under commitment.

b. With a simple linear contract, the central bank minimizes

$$\frac{1}{2}\mathsf{E}_t\left\{\sum_{\nu=0}^{\infty}\beta^{\nu} \cdot \left[\pi_{t+\nu}^2 + \lambda \cdot \left(x_{t+\nu} - x^B\right)^2\right] - 2t_1\pi_{t+\nu}\right\} - t_0.$$

We are solving this minimization problem in the same way as in problem 15.4, and using the same notation. The first order condition is:

$$\frac{d\mathcal{L}_t}{d\pi_t} = \pi_t^D - t_1 + \lambda\left(x_t - x^B\right) = 0 \tag{17.5}$$

In (17.5) already, we can see that the linear contract can remove the inflation bias but not the stabilization bias: by setting $t_1 = -\lambda x^B$, the problem boils down to the same one as in problem 15.4, questions (a) and (b), resulting in the same stabilization bias.

For the sake of verification, we can pursue the resolution and derive the equilibrium inflation policy given the value of t_1. Let us plug this condition into the expected Phillips curve for period $t + 1$:

$$\mathsf{E}_t\left[\pi_{t+1}^D\right] = \frac{\lambda}{1+\lambda}\left\{\frac{t_1}{\lambda} + x^B + \rho\varepsilon_t + \mathsf{E}_t\left[\pi_{t+2}^D\right]\right\}$$

Following the same steps as in problem 15.4, by recursion we find:

$$\mathsf{E}_t\left[\pi_{t+1}^D\right] = t_1 + \lambda x^B + \frac{\lambda\rho}{1+(1-\rho)\lambda}\varepsilon_t.$$

As $x_t = \pi_t - \mathsf{E}_t\left[\pi_{t+1}\right] - \varepsilon_t$, and substituting for $\mathsf{E}_t\left[\pi_{t+1}^D\right]$, (17.5) can be rewritten as

$$\pi_t^D = t_1 + \lambda x^B + \frac{\lambda\varepsilon_t}{1+(1-\rho)\lambda}. \tag{17.6}$$

So, by setting $t_1 = -\lambda x^B$, the linear contract can remove the inflation bias, but not the stabilization bias.

Similarly, an inflation target would modify the loss function in the following way:

$$\frac{1}{2}\mathsf{E}_t\left\{\sum_{\nu=0}^{\infty}\beta^\nu\cdot\left[\left(\pi_{t+\nu} - \bar\pi^B\right)^2 + \lambda\cdot\left(x_{t+\nu} - x^B\right)^2\right] - t_1\pi_{t+\nu}\right\}.$$

But in this case, the first order condition would have the same shape as with the linear contract:

$$\frac{d\mathcal{L}_t}{d\pi_t} = \pi_t^D - \bar\pi^B + \lambda\left(x_t - x^B\right) = 0, \tag{17.7}$$

and the solution would be identical to the simple linear contract.

c. We want to obtain

$$\pi_t^* = \frac{1-\delta\beta}{\beta}\lambda x_{t-1} + \frac{\beta\delta}{1-\beta\delta\rho}\varepsilon_t = \psi_x x_{t-1} + \psi_\varepsilon\varepsilon_t$$

in equilibrium. From (17.5) we also know that:

$$\pi_t^D = t_1\left(x_{t-1}, x_t, \varepsilon_t\right) - \lambda\left(x_t - x^B\right).$$

Therefore, setting

$$t_1\left(x_{t-1}, x_t, \varepsilon_t\right) = \lambda\left(x_t - x^B\right) + \psi_x x_{t-1} + \psi_\varepsilon\varepsilon_t$$

implements the optimal policy.

17.5 Optimal delegation when there is employment persistence

This problem is based on L. Svensson (1997a). Consider the same framework as in problem 15.5: when there is persistence in employment ($x_t = \rho \cdot x_{t-1} + \pi_t - \pi_t^e - \varepsilon_t$) and society has preferences of the shape

$$L(\pi_t, x_t; \bar{\pi}, \bar{x}, \lambda) = \frac{1}{2} \mathsf{E}_0 \left\{ \sum_{t=0}^{\infty} \beta^\nu \cdot \left[(\pi_t - \bar{\pi})^2 + \lambda \cdot (x_t - \bar{x})^2 \right] \right\},$$

the optimal policy under commitment is given by

$$\pi_t^C = \bar{\pi} + \psi_\varepsilon^C \cdot \varepsilon_t = \bar{\pi} + \frac{\lambda}{1+\lambda-\beta\rho^2} \cdot \varepsilon_t.$$

Under discretion, however, one can show that the equilibrium policy of a government sharing the same preferences as society would be

$$\pi_t^D = \bar{\pi} + \frac{\lambda \cdot \bar{x}}{1 - \beta\rho - \beta\psi_x^D} - \psi_x^D \cdot x_{t-1} + \psi_\varepsilon^D \cdot \varepsilon_t,$$

$$\text{where} \quad \psi_x^D = \frac{1 - \beta\rho^2 - \sqrt{(1-\beta\rho^2)^2 - 4\lambda\beta\rho^2}}{2\beta\rho},$$

$$\text{and} \quad \psi_\varepsilon^D = \frac{\lambda + \beta(\psi_x^D)^2}{1 + \lambda - \beta\rho^2 + \beta(\psi_x^D)^2}$$

That is, when it exists, the discretionary policy leads (1) to a systematic inflation bias: $\frac{\lambda\bar{x}}{1-\beta\rho-\beta\psi_x^D}$; (2) to a state-contingent inflation bias: $\psi_x^D \cdot x_{t-1}$, that is, the discretionary outcome is inefficiently sensitive to lagged output; and (3) to a stabilization bias: $\psi_\varepsilon^D > \psi_\varepsilon^R$.

a. Show that electing a conservative central banker generally does not allow the optimal policy under commitment to be reached.

b. Show intuitively that a simple linear contract (which imposes an additional penalty that is linear in the inflation level) can eliminate the systematic inflation bias but cannot alter the third and fourth terms of the reaction function π_t^D (As in problem 15.5, you have to use the intertemporal value function to show this).

c. Show intuitively that imposing an inflation target on the central banker (replacing $\bar{\pi}$ by some other π^B in the loss function) implements the same equilibrium behavior as the simple linear contract.

d. Show intuitively that a more elaborate contract makes it possible to implement the optimal policy under commitment. Consider the case in which the government can appoint a conservative central banker and give her a linear state–contingent inflation target.

Answer

a. By the definition of the solution under discretion (which is defined in the problem), a central bank with a weight λ^B on employment implements a policy:

$$\pi_t^B\left(\lambda^B\right) = \bar{\pi} + \frac{\lambda^B \bar{x}}{1-\beta\rho-\beta \cdot \psi_x^D\left(\lambda^B\right)} + \psi_\varepsilon^D(\lambda^B) \cdot \varepsilon_t - \psi_x^D(\lambda^B) \cdot x_{t-1} \qquad (17.8)$$

where $\psi_x^D(\lambda^B)$ and $\psi_\varepsilon^D(\lambda^B)$ are respectively the values that ψ_x^D and ψ_ε^D take when λ is replaced with λ^B.

As (17.8) shows, one must set λ^B to zero to remove the inflation bias. But in this case, inflation will not either react to supply shocks ($\psi_\varepsilon^D(\lambda^B)$ drops to zero). Selecting a conservative central banker reduces the inflation bias, but at the expense of increased output volatility (Excepted for the particular case in which $\lambda = 0$. But in this case, the discretionary outcome is optimal too). Hence, a conservative central banker never implements the optimal policy.

b. A simple linear contract amounts to setting the loss function of the central bank to

$$L\left(\pi_t, x_t; \bar{\pi}, \bar{x}, \lambda\right) = \frac{1}{2}\left[(\pi_t - \bar{\pi})^2 + \lambda \cdot (x_t - \bar{x})^2\right] + t_1 \cdot (\pi_t - \bar{\pi})$$

(See sections 17.3.1 and 17.3.3 for the presentation of the optimal and the simple contract respectively.)

Following the same steps as in problem 15.5, we can see that the first order condition becomes:

$$-\frac{\partial W^B\left(x_{t-1}; \Psi^B\right)}{\partial \pi_t} = (\pi_t - \bar{\pi} + t_1) + \lambda \cdot (x_t - \bar{x}) - \beta \cdot W_x^B\left(x_t; \Psi^B\right) = 0 \qquad (17.9)$$

where Ψ^B is the equilibrium policy chosen by the Bank and W is the intertemporal value function, of which the exact shape is unknown. By (17.9), increasing t_1 above 0 amounts to shifting the reference inflation level from $\bar{\pi}$ to $\bar{\pi} - t_1$. Now, refer again to the solution under discretion (the one presented in the problem). The constant term in there is $\left(\bar{\pi} + \frac{\lambda\bar{x}}{1-\beta\rho-\beta\psi_x^D}\right)$. With the simple contract, it becomes $\left(\bar{\pi} - t_1 + \frac{\lambda\bar{x}}{1-\beta\rho-\beta\psi_x^D}\right)$. Hence, setting $t_1 = \frac{\lambda\bar{x}}{1-\beta\rho-\beta\psi_x^D}$ removes the inflation bias. Still, even if it shifts the constant term, it does not affect the other parameters, ψ_x^D and ψ_ε^D.

c. To see this, simply replace $\bar{\pi}$ with $\left(\bar{\pi} - \frac{\lambda\bar{x}}{1-\beta\rho-\beta\psi_x^D}\right)$ in the equation for the discretionary policy. The inflation bias has disappeared, but the other terms do not depend on $\bar{\pi}$ and are therefore left unchanged.

d. If the government can appoint a conservative central banker and, in addition, impose her a state-contingent inflation target, the loss function becomes:

$$L\left(\pi_t, x_t; \pi^B, \bar{x}, \lambda\right) = \frac{1}{2}\left[\left(\pi_t - \bar{\pi}^B\left(x_{t-1}\right)\right)^2 + \lambda^B \cdot \left(x_t - \bar{x}\right)^2\right],$$

and the first order condition will be

$$-\frac{\partial W^B\left(x_{t-1}; \Psi^B\right)}{\partial \pi_t} = \left(\pi_t - \bar{\pi}^B\left(x_{t-1}\right)\right) + \lambda^B \cdot \left(x_t - \bar{x}\right) - \beta \cdot W_x^B\left(x_t; \Psi^B\right) = 0.$$

So, the new first order condition allows to set $\pi^B\left(x_{t-1}\right)$ in a way such that the whole inflation bias is removed (the sum of the first three terms in π_t^D can be equalized to $\bar{\pi}$ whatever the value of x_{t-1}). It remains to set λ^B appropriately to obtain $\psi_\varepsilon^D(\lambda^B) = \frac{\lambda}{1+\lambda-\beta\rho^2}$, the value of ψ_ε that is reached under commitment.

Some additional comments

This problem and problem 15.5 follow the article by Lars Svensson (1997) "Optimal Inflation Targets, 'Conservative' Central Banks, and Linear Inflation Contracts". In that article, Svensson uses a slightly more general specification, but we managed in these two problems to reproduce his main insights and results. There is however one of his results that we did not reproduce. Namely, he shows that a linear state-contingent inflation target allows to achieve the commitment solution, even without electing a conservative central banker. At first glance, this may seem surprising. We showed that the constant inflation target and the simple linear contract are formally equivalent one to the other. Why then is the linear state-contingent inflation target (analyzed in question (d)) different from the state-contingent linear contract?

This difference results from the fact that the state-contingent inflation target appears "squared" in the loss function, whereas a linear state-contingent contract comes *linearly* (as the name shows) in the loss function:

$$L\left(\pi_t, x_t; \bar{\pi}, \bar{x}, \lambda\right) = \frac{1}{2}\left[\left(\pi_t - \bar{\pi}\right)^2 + \lambda \cdot \left(x_t - \bar{x}\right)^2\right] + \left(t_1 + t_x \cdot x_{t-1}\right) \cdot \left(\pi_t - \bar{\pi}\right)$$

In that case, the first order condition becomes

$$\frac{\partial W^B\left(x_{t-1}; \Psi^B\right)}{\partial \pi_t} = \left(\pi_t - \bar{\pi}\right) + \lambda \cdot \left(x_t - \bar{x}\right) + t_1 + t_x \cdot x_{t-1} - \beta \cdot W_x^B\left(x_t; \Psi^B\right) = 0. \quad (17.10)$$

Substituting for the parameters of W^B (remember problem 15.5, where we said that the loss function can be written as $W^B\left(x_t; \Psi^B\right) = \omega_0^B + \omega_1^B \cdot x_t + \frac{\omega_2^B}{2} \cdot x_t^2$), (17.10) becomes:

$$\left(1 - \beta\omega_2^B + \lambda\right)\pi_t + \left(\lambda\rho + t_x - \beta\rho\omega_2^B\right)x_{t-1} + \left(\beta\omega_2^B - \lambda\right)\pi_t^e + ...$$
$$... + \left(\beta\omega_2^B - \lambda\right)\varepsilon_t - \bar{\pi} - \lambda\bar{x} + t_1 - \beta\omega_1^B = 0. \quad (17.11)$$

Taking expectations, we obtain:

$$\mathsf{E}_{t-1}\left[\pi_t\right] + \left(\lambda\rho + t_x - \beta\rho\omega_2^B\right)x_{t-1} - \bar{\pi} - \lambda\bar{x} + t_1 - \beta\omega_1^B = 0.$$

Therefore, setting $\left(\lambda\rho + t_x - \beta\rho\omega_2^B\right) = 0$ implies that inflation becomes insensitive to x_{t-1} (no state-contingent bias). Similarly, setting $t_1 = \lambda\bar{x} + \beta\omega_1^B$ removes the inflation bias. In this case, the inflation policy of the bank will boil down to $\pi_t = \bar{\pi} + \psi_\varepsilon^B \cdot \varepsilon_t$. Substituting for these values of t_1, t_x and π_t into (17.10), we find:

$$\left[\psi_\varepsilon^B + \left(1 - \psi_\varepsilon^B\right)\left(\beta\omega_2^B - \lambda\right)\right] \cdot \varepsilon_t = 0$$

which must hold for any value of ε_t. Therefore,

$$\psi_\varepsilon^B = \frac{\lambda - \beta\omega_2^B}{1 + \lambda - \beta\omega_2^B}$$

which is identical to ψ_ε^C, the coefficient that prevails under commitment (equation (15.19) in problem 15.5, page 193. Following the same steps as in that problem, we find the value of ω_2^B and see that the optimal reaction of the central bank (with a preference parameter $\lambda^B = \lambda$, i.e. the social one) is identical to the optimal reaction under commitment.

Chapter 18

International policy coordination

18.1 Commitment and cooperation

Consider a loss function $L(\pi, \pi^e; \boldsymbol{\vartheta}, \boldsymbol{\omega})$ in which π denotes inflation (controlled directly by the policymaker), π^e denotes expected inflation i.e., $\pi^e = \mathsf{E}[\pi|\boldsymbol{\vartheta}]$, and $\boldsymbol{\vartheta}$ is a vector of random shocks whose realization is observed before expectations are formed. $\boldsymbol{\omega}$ is a vector of shocks whose realization is observed after expectations are formed but before π is chosen. Both $\boldsymbol{\vartheta}$ and $\boldsymbol{\omega}$ are i.i.d. over time (i.e. there is no autocorrelation).

a. Compute the optimal policy under commitment for this general loss function. To this end, minimize the loss function subject to the constraint $\pi^e = \mathsf{E}[\pi|\boldsymbol{\vartheta}]$.

b. Apply this methodology to the loss function used in section 18.2.1 (commitment and cooperation). That is, derive (18.7) in the main book. How would this result change if both countries were subject to a different observable shock, that is $\theta \neq \theta^*$?

c. Compute the coefficients of the optimal policy rule in (18.8) under the assumption that $\theta = \theta^*$.

d. Going back to the general loss function, compute the equilibrium policy under discretion, where π^e is taken as given. How can one evaluate the equilibrium value of π^e?

e. Apply this methodology to the loss function used in section 18.2.3 (discretion and cooperation). That is, derive (18.11) in the text. How would this result change if $\theta \neq \theta^*$?

f. Apply this methodology to the loss function used in section 18.2.2 (discretion and non cooperation). That is, derive (18.9). How would this change if $\theta \neq \theta^*$?

Answer

a. Taking the first order condition with respect to π, we find:

$$L_\pi \left(\pi, \pi^e; \boldsymbol{\vartheta}, \boldsymbol{\omega}\right) + \Omega = 0,$$

where Ω is the multiplier of the rational expectations constraint. Similarly, the first order condition with respect to π^e yields:

$$\mathsf{E} L_{\pi^e} \left(\pi, \pi^e; \boldsymbol{\vartheta}, \boldsymbol{\omega}\right) - \Omega = 0.$$

As π^e responds to $\boldsymbol{\vartheta}$ but not to $\boldsymbol{\omega}$, the optimal policy under commitment should not react to the shocks on $\boldsymbol{\vartheta}$.

b. In section 18.2.1, the loss function is given by

$$\mathsf{E}\left(L + L^*\right) = \frac{1}{2}\left[\pi^2 + \pi^{*2} + \lambda\left(x^2 + x^{*2}\right) + \mu\left((z - \chi)^2 + (-z - \chi^*)^2\right)\right],$$

where we dropped the arguments $(\boldsymbol{\vartheta}, \boldsymbol{\omega})$ for the sake of clarity.

$\boldsymbol{\vartheta} = \{\theta, \chi, \chi^*\}$ are the random variables observed before wage setters make their expectations. Those which realize only after expectations formation are $\boldsymbol{\omega} = \{\varepsilon, \varepsilon^*, v, v^*, \phi\}$. Let us compute the two first order conditions:

$$\pi + \alpha\delta\left(\pi - \pi^*\right) + \lambda x + \mu\delta\left(2z - \chi + \chi^*\right) \quad = \quad -\Omega \qquad (18.1)$$

$$\mathsf{E}\left[\alpha\delta\left(\pi^* - \pi\right) - \lambda x - \mu\delta\left(2z - \chi + \chi^*\right)\right] \quad = \quad \Omega \qquad (18.2)$$

Under rational expectations, and as $\theta = \theta^*$, (18.2) simplifies into:

$$-\lambda\theta + \mu\delta\left(\chi - \chi^*\right) = \Omega.$$

Let us substitute for this value of Ω into (18.1):

$$\pi + \alpha\delta\left(\pi - \pi^*\right) + \lambda x + \mu\delta\left(2z - \chi + \chi^*\right) - \lambda\theta + \mu\delta\left(\chi - \chi^*\right) = 0.$$

Simplifying and ordering these terms as in the textbook, we obtain:

$$\pi + \lambda\left(x - \theta\right) + 2\mu\delta z + \alpha\delta\left(\pi - \pi^*\right) = 0, \qquad (18.3)$$

which is equation (18.7) in the manual.

By contrast, if $\theta \neq \theta^*$, however, (18.2) simplifies down to

$$-\lambda\theta - 2\left((\alpha\delta)^2 + \mu\delta^2\right)\left(\theta - \theta^*\right) + \mu\delta\left(\chi - \chi^*\right) = \Omega.$$

Substituting into (18.1) yields:

$$\pi + \alpha\delta\left(\pi - \pi^*\right) + \lambda\left(x - \theta\right) + 2\mu\delta z - 2\left((\alpha\delta)^2 + \mu\delta^2\right)\left(\theta - \theta^*\right) = 0$$

c. Solving for the values of the parameters ψ in equation (18.8) requires extremely lengthy algebra. For this reason, we only explain the procedure we are following and then present the solution.

The first step is to solve for the problem of the foreign country in the same way as we did for the home country. This gives another first order condition:

$$\pi^* + \lambda \left(x^* - \theta \right) - 2\mu\delta z - \alpha\delta \left(\pi - \pi^* \right) = 0. \tag{18.4}$$

To proceed through the next steps, we would recommend the use of some mathematical package: take (18.4) and expand it completely, substituting for π, π^*, z, and so on, and solve for m^*. This gives you an equation where m^* depends on the parameters, the shocks, and m.

Now take (18.3) and proceed through the same systematic substitution, including the solution for m^* you just derived. Solving for m finally obtains:

$$\psi_\varepsilon = \frac{\lambda}{1+\lambda}$$

$$\psi_{\varepsilon\varepsilon^*} = \frac{1}{1+\lambda} \frac{\alpha\delta \left(1 - \lambda \right) + 2\delta^2 \left(\alpha^2 + \mu \right)}{\left(1 + \lambda \right) + 4\delta \left[\alpha + \delta \left(\alpha^2 + \mu \right) \right]}$$

$$\psi_\phi = \frac{\alpha + 2\delta \left(\alpha^2 + \mu \right)}{\left(1 + \lambda \right) + 4\delta \left[\alpha + \delta \left(\alpha^2 + \mu \right) \right]}$$

d. If the central bank considers π^e as given, the first order condition becomes

$$L_\pi \left(\pi, \pi^e; \boldsymbol{\vartheta}, \boldsymbol{\omega} \right) = 0.$$

To find π^e, one has then to take the expectation of this equation:

$$L_\pi \left(\pi^e, \pi^e; \boldsymbol{\vartheta}, \mathsf{E}\boldsymbol{\omega} \right) = 0,$$

and solve for π^e.

e. Under discretion and cooperation, the loss function is the same as in question (b), but expectations are given. The first order condition with respect to p is then:

$$\pi + \alpha\delta \left(\pi - \pi^* \right) + \lambda x + \mu\delta \left(2z - \chi + \chi^* \right) = 0.$$

Adding $\left(-\lambda\theta + \mu\delta \left(\chi - \chi^* \right) \right)$ on both sides of the equality and reordering the terms yields:

$$\pi + \lambda \left(x - \theta \right) + 2\mu\delta z + \alpha\delta \left(\pi - \pi^* \right) = -\lambda\theta + \mu\delta \left(\chi - \chi^* \right),$$

which is equation (18.11) in the textbook. This last operation is just meant to make this first order condition comparable with (18.7). This condition is not affected by the assumption $\theta = \theta^*$.

f. Under the non cooperative equilibrium, the loss function is:

$$L = \frac{1}{2} \left[\pi^2 + \lambda x^2 + \mu \left(z - \chi \right)^2 \right].$$

Taking the first derivative of this loss with respect to p, we obtain:

$$\pi \left(1 + \alpha\delta \right) + \lambda x + \mu\delta \left(z - \chi \right) = 0.$$

For the same reason as in question (e), add $\left(-\lambda\theta + \mu\delta\chi + \mu\delta z - \alpha\delta\pi^* \right)$ on both sides of this condition. Rearranging the terms, you find the same condition as equation (18.9) in the text.

18.2 Output directly dependent on the real exchange rate

This problem is based on Canzoneri and Gray (1985). Consider a version of the model presented in section 18.1 with symmetric shocks ($\varepsilon = \varepsilon^*$ and $\theta = \theta^*$), but suppose that $\mu = \phi = v = 0$, and replace the output equation (18.4) with

$$x = \theta + (p - p^e) + \rho z - \varepsilon, \text{ with } 0 < \rho < \frac{1}{2} \qquad (18.5)$$

a. Suppose $\varepsilon = 0$ and $\theta < 0$. Show that inflation is zero under commitment and cooperation and positive under discretion and non cooperation (i.e. $\pi^{D,N}(\theta, 0) > \pi^{C,C}(\theta, 0) = 0$). Verify that (1) the inflation bias is more acute the larger is ρ –that is the larger the incentive for a competitive devaluation–, and (2) inflation is lower the higher is α (the share of foreign goods in the consumption basket).

b. Suppose central banks coordinate but cannot commit to a policy. For $\varepsilon = 0$ and $\theta < 0$, show that inflation is higher than under no coordination and discretion (i.e. $\pi^{D,C}(\theta, 0) > \pi^{D,N}(\theta, 0)$) iff $\alpha > \rho$.

c. Suppose $\varepsilon > 0$ and $\theta = 0$. Show that the cooperative solution under commitment leads to the same inflation rate as in a closed economy with commitment, or $\pi^{C,C}(\theta, 0) = \lambda\varepsilon/(1 + \lambda)$. Show that non cooperative and discretionary policies are too contractionary in equilibrium (i.e., $\pi^{D,N}(\theta, 0) < \pi^{C,C}(\theta, 0)$) iff $\alpha > \rho$.

Answer

a. First, we have to derive the relationship between output and inflation. Substituting for z (which is defined in equation (18.4) in the textbook) into (18.5), we find:

$$x = \frac{\theta + (p - p^e) - \rho\delta x^* - \varepsilon}{1 - \rho\delta}, \qquad (18.6)$$

and a similar expression holds for x^*. Substituting for the latter in (18.6) yields

$$x = \theta + a(p - p^e) - b(p^* - p^{e*}) - \varepsilon, \qquad (18.7)$$

where

$$a = \frac{1 - \rho\delta}{1 - 2\rho\delta} > 0 \quad \text{and} \quad b = \frac{\rho\delta}{1 - 2\rho\delta} > 0.$$

This gives us the equilibrium relationship between output and producer price inflation. Let us now compute the equilibrium inflation for the different cases to study.

Commitment and cooperation:
Under commitment, as shown in section 18.2.1 and in chapter 15, inflation is independent of θ and there is no inflation bias. If $\varepsilon = 0$, the realized inflation rate must be equal to the expected one and the resulting level of output is θ. Since,

for a given (expected) level of employment, central banks minimize inflation, this implies they commit to $m = 0$, resulting in zero inflation.

Discretion and non-cooperation:
For a given θ, each central banks minimizes $L = 1/2 \left[\pi^2 + \lambda x^2 \right]$, taking p^* as given. Output is given by (18.7). Substituting for π, z, and x into the loss function, and taking the first order condition with respect to p, we find:

$$\pi (1 + \alpha (a + b)) + \lambda a x = \pi \left(1 + \frac{\alpha \delta}{1 - 2\rho\delta} \right) + \lambda a x = 0.$$

Since in equilibrium $x = \theta$, this yields:

$$\pi^{D,N}(\theta, 0) = -\frac{1 - \rho\delta}{1 - 2\rho\delta + \alpha\delta} \lambda\theta$$

Clearly, with $\theta < 0$, we have $\pi^{D,N}(\theta, 0) > 0$. By taking the derivative of the RHS of this expression, one sees that $\pi^{D,N}(\theta, 0)$ is increasing in ρ and decreasing in α.

b. If central banks coordinate, both countries minimize $L = 1/2 \left[\pi^2 + \pi^{*} + \lambda x^2 + \lambda x^{*2} \right]$. As a result, in equilibrium, $\pi = \pi^*$ and $x = x^*$. The first order condition with respect to p yields:

$$\pi + \lambda x = 0$$

or

$$\pi^{D,C}(\theta, 0) = -\lambda\theta$$

Comparing this result with $\pi^{D,N}(\theta, 0)$, we see that inflation is larger under coordination (i.e. $\pi^{D,N}(\theta, 0) < \pi^{D,C}(\theta, 0)$) iff $\frac{1-\rho\delta}{1-2\rho\delta+\alpha\delta} < 1$, which holds for $\rho < \alpha$.

c. Suppose central banks coordinate and commit to an inflation policy. We know from previous derivations that, in this case, the optimal inflation will take the form $p = \psi\varepsilon$ and $p^* = \psi^*\varepsilon$. Substituting these policies into (18.7) and under rational expectations, we find:

$$x = c\varepsilon \quad \text{and} \quad x^* = c^*\varepsilon,$$

where $c = a\psi - b\psi^* - 1$ and $c^* = a\psi^* - b\psi - 1$. Under coordination, central banks minimize

$$\frac{1}{2}\mathsf{E} \left[\pi^2 + \pi^{*2} + \lambda x^2 + \lambda x^{*2} \right] = \dots$$

$$\dots = \frac{1}{2}\mathsf{E} \left[p^2 + p^{*2} + 2\alpha^2 z^2 + 2\alpha z(p - p^*) + \lambda x^2 + \lambda x^{*2} \right]$$

$$\dots = \frac{1}{2}2 \left[\psi^2\sigma_\varepsilon^2 + 2\alpha^2\mathsf{E}(z^2) + 2\alpha(\psi - \psi^*)\mathsf{E}\left[z\varepsilon\right] + \lambda\left(c^2 + c^{*2}\right)\sigma_\varepsilon^2 \right]$$

Since $\partial\mathsf{E}(z^2)/\partial\psi = 0$, and in equilibrium $\psi = \psi^*$ and $z = 0$, the first order condition with respect to ψ can be written as:

$$\psi + \lambda c = 0.$$

Given $\pi = m = \psi\varepsilon$ in equilibrium, we find:

$$\pi^{C,C}(\theta, 0) = \frac{\lambda}{1+\lambda}\varepsilon. \tag{18.8}$$

Let us now turn to the second part of the question and analyze the non co-operative solution under discretion. In this case, the home country minimizes $\left[\pi^2 + \lambda x^2\right]/2$. The first order condition with respect to p yields:

$$\lambda xa + \pi(1 + \alpha\delta\,[a + b]) = 0$$

From (18.5) and the fact that $p^e = 0$ and $z = 0$ in equilibrium, we have $x = \pi - \varepsilon$. Hence,

$$
\begin{aligned}
\pi^{D,N}(\theta, 0) &= \frac{\lambda a}{1 + \alpha\delta\,[a + b] + \lambda a}\varepsilon \\
&= \frac{\lambda}{\left(\dfrac{1 - 2\rho\delta + \alpha\delta}{1 - 2\rho\delta}\right) + \lambda}\varepsilon
\end{aligned}
$$

It follows that $\pi^{D,N}(\theta, 0) < \pi^{C,C}(\theta, 0)$ if and only if $\rho < \alpha$.

18.3 Exchange rate pegs with symmetric supply shocks

Consider a version of the model in section 18.1 in which the countries are subject only to a symmetric supply shock, that is $\varepsilon^* = \varepsilon$ and $\theta = \theta^* = v = v^* = 0$. Moreover, set $\mu = 0$. Before any other event takes place, the home country (but not the foreign country) imposes a non linear performance contract on its central bank. The contract is defined over the change in the nominal exchange rate, s:

$$T(s) = \begin{cases} B & \text{if } s = 0 \\ B - c & \text{otherwise,} \end{cases}$$

where c is a positive number and B is chosen so as to satisfy the agent's participation constraint. Thus if the home central bank abandons the pegged exchange rate, it faces a prohibitive cost, provided that c is high enough. The timing of events is as follows (1) Society commits to a contract in the home country, (2) Expectations p^e and p^{*e} are formed, (3) The shock ε is realized, (4) The foreign policymaker chooses p^*, (5) The home central bank chooses p, (6) Macroeconomic outcomes are realized.

a. Show that the performance contract will make the home central bank choose the same money growth as the foreign policymaker, to keep the exchange rate fixed, that is $p(\varepsilon) = p^*(\varepsilon)$.

b. Compute the first-best solution (cooperative solution under commitment) $p^C(\varepsilon)$.

c. Show that when the home country commits to the above-mentioned contract $T(s)$, the foreign country implements this first-best cooperative outcome even in the non cooperative Nash equilibrium.

d. Show that the same result holds when employment is also affected by a symmetric observable shock $\theta = \theta^*$ and the foreign central bank can commit ex ante to a policy $p^*(\theta, \varepsilon)$.

Answer

a. In order to have $s \equiv z - (p^* - p) = 0$, we need:

$$\delta[p - p^e - (p^* - p^{*e})] = p^* - p$$

or

$$\delta(p^{e*} - p^e) = (1 + \delta)(p^* - p)$$

Since $\theta = \theta^*$, this equality requires $p^e = p^{*e}$ (same inflation on average), and hence $p = p^*$ (same inflation whatever the value of ε). Moreover, with c sufficiently large, the home central bank always prefers to stick to this rule.

b. Given that $\theta = 0$, we have $p^e = 0$. Since $z = 0$ in equilibrium (due to the symmetric setup), it follows from the Phillips curve that $x = \pi - \varepsilon$. As $\pi = \pi^*$ in equilibrium, the first order condition (18.7) derived in the textbook implies:

$$\pi = \frac{\lambda}{1 + \lambda} \varepsilon$$

This solution is the same as in a closed economy.

c. We showed that an exchange rate peg implies $p = p^*$ and $z = 0$. If the foreign country chooses p in order to minimize its loss function, taking into account that the home country always implements the same policy, it minimizes

$$L^{ERP} = \frac{1}{2}\left[p^{*2} + \lambda(p^* - \varepsilon)^2\right].$$

Taking the first order condition with respect to p^*, we find:

$$p^* + \lambda(p^* - \varepsilon) = 0$$

which in turn implies:

$$\pi = p = \frac{\lambda}{1 + \lambda}\varepsilon.$$

d. Again, from the commitment solution, we know that the foreign country commits to a policy of the form $p^* = \psi^* \varepsilon$. Given the exchange rate peg, $z = 0$. Therefore, the foreign country chooses ψ^* to minimize

$$
\begin{aligned}
L^{ERP} &= \mathsf{E}\left(\frac{1}{2}\left[p^2 + \lambda x^2\right]\right)\\
&= \frac{1}{2}\psi^* \sigma_\varepsilon^2 + \lambda\left[\theta^2 + (\psi^* - 1)^2 \sigma_\varepsilon^2\right].
\end{aligned}
$$

The first order condition with respect to ψ^* yields $\psi^* + \lambda(\psi^* - 1) = 0$. Given that $\pi^* = p^* = \psi^* \varepsilon$, we find

$$\pi^* = \frac{\lambda}{1+\lambda}\varepsilon.$$

18.4 Exchange rate pegs with asymmetric supply shocks

Suppose that the two countries are hit by common shocks of opposite sign (correlation -1), $\varepsilon = -\varepsilon^* > 0$, and that $\mu = \phi = \theta = \theta^* = v = v^* = 0$. The economy is otherwise similar to that in section 18.1.

a. Show that the cooperative equilibrium implements an inflationary policy ($\pi^C > 0$) in the home country and a deflationary policy ($\pi^{*C} < 0$) in the foreign country.

b. Compute the non cooperative equilibrium and show that the policy of the home country is still inflationary but too contractionary ($\pi^C > \pi^N > 0$) whereas that of the foreign country is still deflationary but too expansionary ($\pi^{*C} < \pi^{*N} < 0$).

c. Suppose that the home country imposes an exchange rate peg on its central bank as described in problem 3. Then show, first, that this policy leads to deflation (instead of inflation) in the home country. Next, show that this level of deflation, in absolute terms, is higher than the inflation in both the cooperative and non cooperative equilibrium ($-\pi^{erp} > \pi^C > \pi^N$). Finally, show that (1) the home country performs worse not only than in the cooperative equilibrium, but also than in the non cooperative equilibrium and (2) the foreign country still deflates, but less than in the cooperative equilibrium ($\pi^{*C} < \pi^{*erp} < 0$). Assume $\alpha\delta < 1/2$ throughout.

Answer

a. In the cooperative equilibrium, policies will be mirror images of each other. This is shown in two steps. First, under commitment, we know that $p^* = \psi^* \varepsilon^*$ and $p = \psi\varepsilon$, and as both countries minimize their joint loss, we also have $\psi^* = -\psi$. But we assumed $\varepsilon^* = -\varepsilon$ in this problem. That is, $p^* = -\psi^* \varepsilon$ and $p = \psi\varepsilon$. For the sake of simplicity, we shall use the notation $\psi^* = -\psi$ and refer to the same shock ε in the remainder of the resolution.

In terms of the other variables, this policy implies $x = [\psi - 1]\varepsilon$; $x^* = [1 - \psi]\varepsilon$; $z = \delta[x - x^*] = 2\delta[\psi - 1]\varepsilon$ and thus:

$$\begin{aligned} \pi &= p + \alpha z \\ &= [1 + 2\alpha\delta][\psi - 1]\varepsilon + \varepsilon \\ &= [1 + 2\alpha\delta]x + \varepsilon. \end{aligned}$$

Isolating x, we find:

$$x = \frac{\pi - \varepsilon}{1 + 2\alpha\delta}$$

Next, we know that the first order condition is given by equation (18.7) in the textbook. Setting $\mu = 0$ and $\pi = -\pi^*$ in that equation yields:

$$\pi + \lambda x = 0.$$

Substituting for x, we obtain:

$$\pi^C = -\pi^{*C} = \frac{\lambda\varepsilon}{1 + 2\alpha\delta + \lambda}.$$

b. Again, it is easy to see that non-cooperative equilibria will be mirror images from each other, or $p^* = -p$. To see this, compute the first order condition in each country. This yields the following two equalities:

$$p + \lambda(p - \varepsilon) = -\alpha z \quad \text{and} \quad p^* + \lambda(p^* + \varepsilon) = \alpha z.$$

Solving them together proves the symmetry. It follows that $x^* = -x$, and $z = \delta(x - x^*) = 2\delta x$. In addition, as $x = p - \varepsilon$, we find:

$$\pi = p + \alpha z = [1 + 2\alpha\delta]x + \varepsilon,$$

and therefore $x = \dfrac{\pi - \varepsilon}{1 + 2\alpha\delta}$. We are now ready to derive the first order condition:

$$\pi[1 + 2\alpha\delta] + \lambda x = 0.$$

Substituting for x, we find again that the home country implements an inflationary policy and the foreign country a deflationary policy:

$$\pi^N = -\pi^{*N} = \frac{\lambda\varepsilon}{(1 + 2\alpha\delta)^2 + \lambda} > 0.$$

Comparing this result with the cooperative solution shows that the policy of the home country is too contractionary, i.e. $\pi^N < \pi^C$, whereas that of the foreign country is too expansionary, i.e. $0 > \pi^{*N} > \pi^{*C}$.

c. If the home country enforces an exchange rate peg $s = 0$, then $p = p^*$. This in turn implies $x = p^* - \varepsilon$, $x^* = p^* + \varepsilon$ and $z = \delta(x - x^*) = -2\delta\varepsilon$. Hence:

$$\pi^* = p^* - \alpha z = x^* - (1 - 2\alpha\delta)\varepsilon,$$

and thus $x^* = \pi^* + (1 - 2\alpha\delta)\varepsilon$. The foreign country's central bank minimizes

$$L = \frac{1}{2}\left[\pi^{*2} + \lambda x^{*2}\right],$$

and hence the first order condition is:

$$\pi^* + \lambda x^* = 0 \Leftrightarrow \pi^* + \lambda[\pi^* + (1 - 2\alpha\delta)\varepsilon] = 0.$$

Solving for π^{*ERP}, we find:

$$\pi^{*ERP} = -\frac{(1 - 2\alpha\delta)\lambda}{1 + \lambda}\varepsilon.$$

Inflation in the home country instead satisfies:

$$\pi^{ERP} = p + \alpha z = \pi^{ERP*} + 2\alpha z = -\frac{(1 - 2\alpha\delta)\lambda}{1 + \lambda}\varepsilon - 4\alpha\delta\varepsilon < 0 \tag{18.9}$$

This shows that the home country experiences deflation, instead of inflation. Some straightforward algebra also shows that $|\pi^{erp}| > \pi^C$ for any value of $\alpha\delta > 0$.

We do not even need algebra to understand that the exchange rate peg generates larger losses than under non cooperation. Indeed, the home country is forced to reinforce the shocks, instead of using inflation to countervail their effect on output.

For the last part of the question, we can compare π^{*ERP} with π^{*C} and check the inequality:

$$\frac{-\lambda\varepsilon}{1 + 2\alpha\delta + \lambda} < -\frac{(1 - 2\alpha\delta)\lambda}{1 + \lambda}\varepsilon$$
$$1 + \lambda > (1 - 2\alpha\delta)(1 + \lambda + 2\alpha\delta)$$
$$1 + \lambda > 1 - 2\alpha\delta.$$

18.5 Endogenous exchange rate pegs

Consider the two-country model with symmetric supply shocks of problem 3 and assume $\mu = 0$. Suppose that the home country can now implement any change it wishes in the nominal exchange rate s by writing a contract $T(s; \hat{s})$:

$$T(s; \hat{s}) = \begin{cases} B & \text{if } s = \hat{s} \\ B - c & \text{otherwise,} \end{cases} \tag{18.10}$$

where c is a positive number and B is chosen so as to satisfy the agent's participation constraint. The foreign country, on the other hand, can only implement a discretionary policy.

a. Show that fixing $\hat{s}$ automatically determines the difference in money growth $m - m^*$ and the real exchange rate z.

b. Show that the optimal level of $\hat{s}$ is zero if the home country can only commit to a constant exchange rate peg.

c. Assume that the home country can write a contract with its central bank that makes $\hat{s}$ contingent on ε at stage (1) (the timing is defined in problem 3). Under this assumption, show that $\hat{s} = k\varepsilon$, where $k < 0$, that is the home country depreciates its currency when $\varepsilon < 0$ and appreciates it if $\varepsilon > 0$.

d. Show that by making its exchange rate peg conditional on ε, the home country improves upon the cooperative outcome.

Answer

a. By definition:
$$z = \delta(x - x^*) = \hat{s} + p^* - p.$$

In equilibrium, $p^e = p^{e*}$, and hence

$$p - p^* = \frac{\hat{s}}{1 + \delta} \quad \text{and} \quad z = \frac{\delta \hat{s}}{1 + \delta}.$$

As $m = p - v$ and v is assumed to be zero, fixing $\hat{s}$ also determines $m - m^*$.

b. For a given $\hat{s}$, the foreign country minimizes

$$\frac{1}{2}\left[(p^* - \alpha \hat{z})^2 + \lambda(p^* - \varepsilon)^2\right]$$

where $\hat{z} = \frac{\delta \hat{s}}{1 - \delta}$ and hence is constant. The first order condition yields

$$p^* - \alpha z + \lambda(p^* - \varepsilon) = 0.$$

Solving for p^*, we find:

$$p^* = \frac{\lambda \varepsilon}{1 + \lambda} + \frac{\alpha \hat{z}}{1 + \lambda}$$

and thus

$$p = p^* + \frac{\hat{z}}{\delta} = \frac{\lambda}{1 + \lambda}\varepsilon + \frac{1 + \lambda + \alpha\delta}{\delta(1 + \lambda)}\hat{z} \equiv a\varepsilon + b\hat{z}$$

Now, let us look how $\hat{z}$ can be set optimally. The home country chooses $\hat{z}$ to minimize

$$\frac{1}{2}\mathsf{E}\left[(p + \alpha\hat{z})^2 + \lambda(p - \varepsilon)^2\right] = \frac{1}{2}\mathsf{E}\left[(a\varepsilon + (\alpha + b)\,\hat{z})^2 + \lambda((a - 1)\varepsilon + b\hat{z})^2\right]$$

$$= \frac{1}{2}\left[(a^2 + \lambda(a - 1)^2) \cdot \sigma_\varepsilon^2 + \left[(\alpha + b)^2 + \lambda b^2\right] \cdot \hat{z}^2\right]$$

The first order condition implies $\hat{z} = 0$, and thence $\hat{s} = 0$.

c. The foreign country knows in advance which exchange rate peg the home country will enforce in equilibrium. Given that the foreign country knows how $\hat{s}$ and $\hat{z}$ are fixed by the home country, it chooses $p^* = \frac{\lambda}{1+\lambda}\varepsilon + \frac{\alpha}{1+\lambda}\hat{z}$, as we already showed.

Therefore, in each state of the world (for any value of ε), the home country chooses $\hat{z}$ to minimize:

$$\frac{1}{2}\left[(p + \alpha\hat{z}\,(\varepsilon))^2 + \lambda(p - \varepsilon)^2\right] = \frac{1}{2}\left[(a\varepsilon + (\alpha + b)\,\hat{z}\,(\varepsilon))^2 + \lambda((a - 1)\varepsilon + b\hat{z}\,(\varepsilon))^2\right]$$

Taking the first order condition, we find:

$$\left[(\alpha + b)^2 + \lambda b^2\right]\hat{z}\,(\varepsilon) + [a\,(\alpha + b) + \lambda b\,(a - 1)]\,\varepsilon = 0,$$

and by substituting for a in this condition, we obtain the optimal value of $\hat{z}$:

$$\hat{z}\left(\varepsilon\right) = -\frac{\alpha\alpha}{\left(\alpha+b\right)^{2} + \lambda b^{2}}\varepsilon.$$

As $\hat{z} = \frac{\delta\hat{s}}{1+\delta}$, both $\hat{z}$ and $\hat{s}$ are linearly and inversely related to ε.

d. This stems from revealed preferences: the country could set $k = 0$ but prefers to set it lower than zero. We can thus conclude that the loss is smaller with this value of k.

One may wonder why the country prefers to appreciate its currency when it is hit by an adverse shock. This happens because, with $\alpha > 0$, p has more effect on consumer price inflation (π) than with $\alpha = 0$, whereas its influence on output is constant, independently of α.